Buffy THE VAMPIRE SLAYER™

OUT OF THE WOODWORK

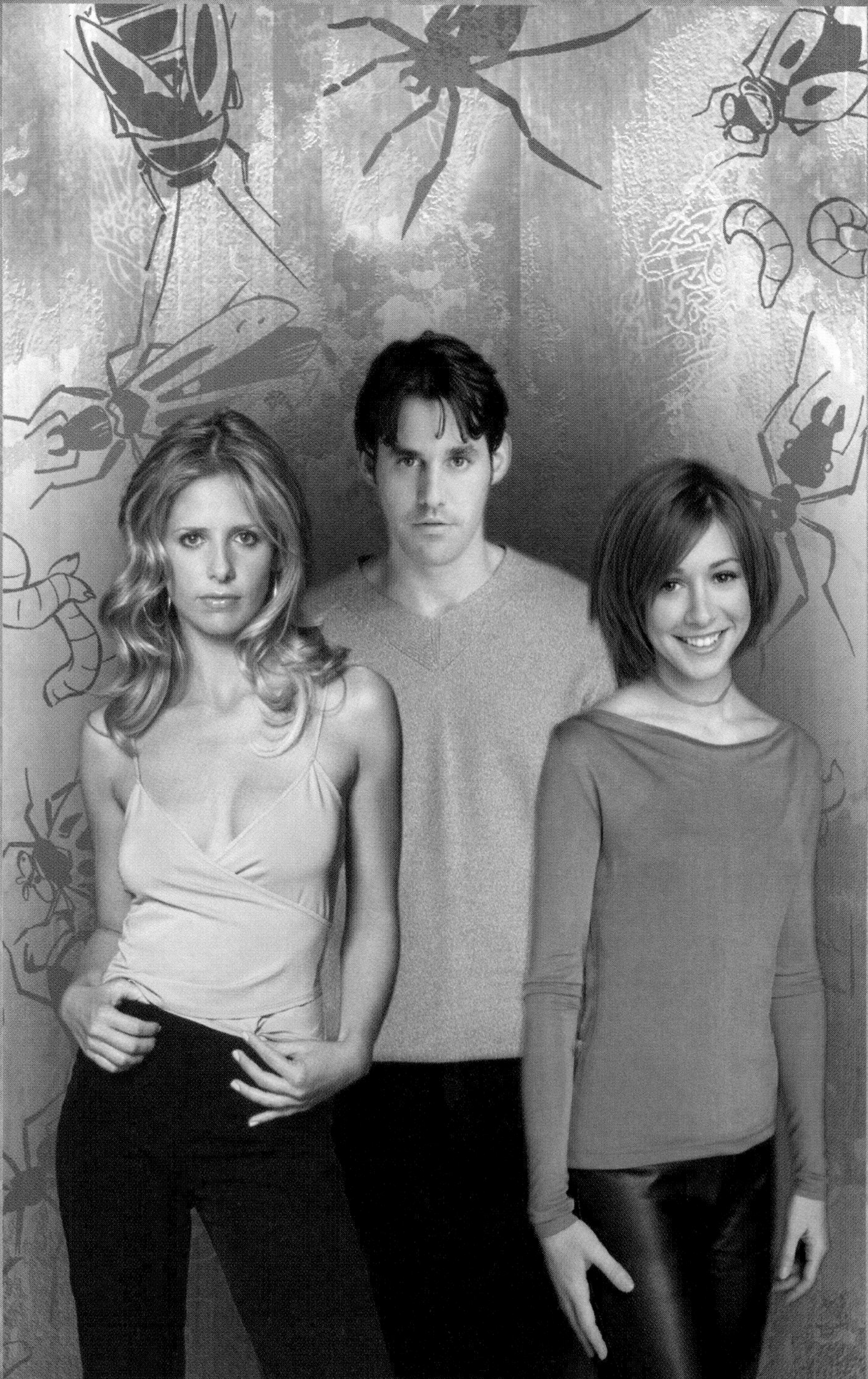

Photo cover by KEITH WOOD

Buffy THE VAMPIRE SLAYER™

OUT OF THE WOODWORK

based on the television series created by
JOSS WHEDON

writers **TOM FASSBENDER & JIM PASCOE**

penciller **CLIFF RICHARDS**

inker **JOE PIMENTEL**

letterer **CLEM ROBINS**

colorist **DAVE McCAIG**

photo covers **KEITH WOOD**

This story takes place after Buffy the Vampire Slayer's fourth season

Dark Horse Comics®

publisher
MIKE RICHARDSON

editor
SCOTT ALLIE
with MICHAEL CARRIGLITTO

collection designer
DEBRA BAILEY

art director
MARK COX

special thanks to
Debbie Olshan at Fox Licensing and
Dave Campiti at Glasshouse Graphics.

PUBLISHED BY
DARK HORSE COMICS, INC.
10956 SE MAIN STREET
MILWAUKIE, OR 97222

FIRST EDITION
JULY 2002
ISBN: 1-56971-738-9

1 3 5 7 9 10 8 6 4 2

printed in china.

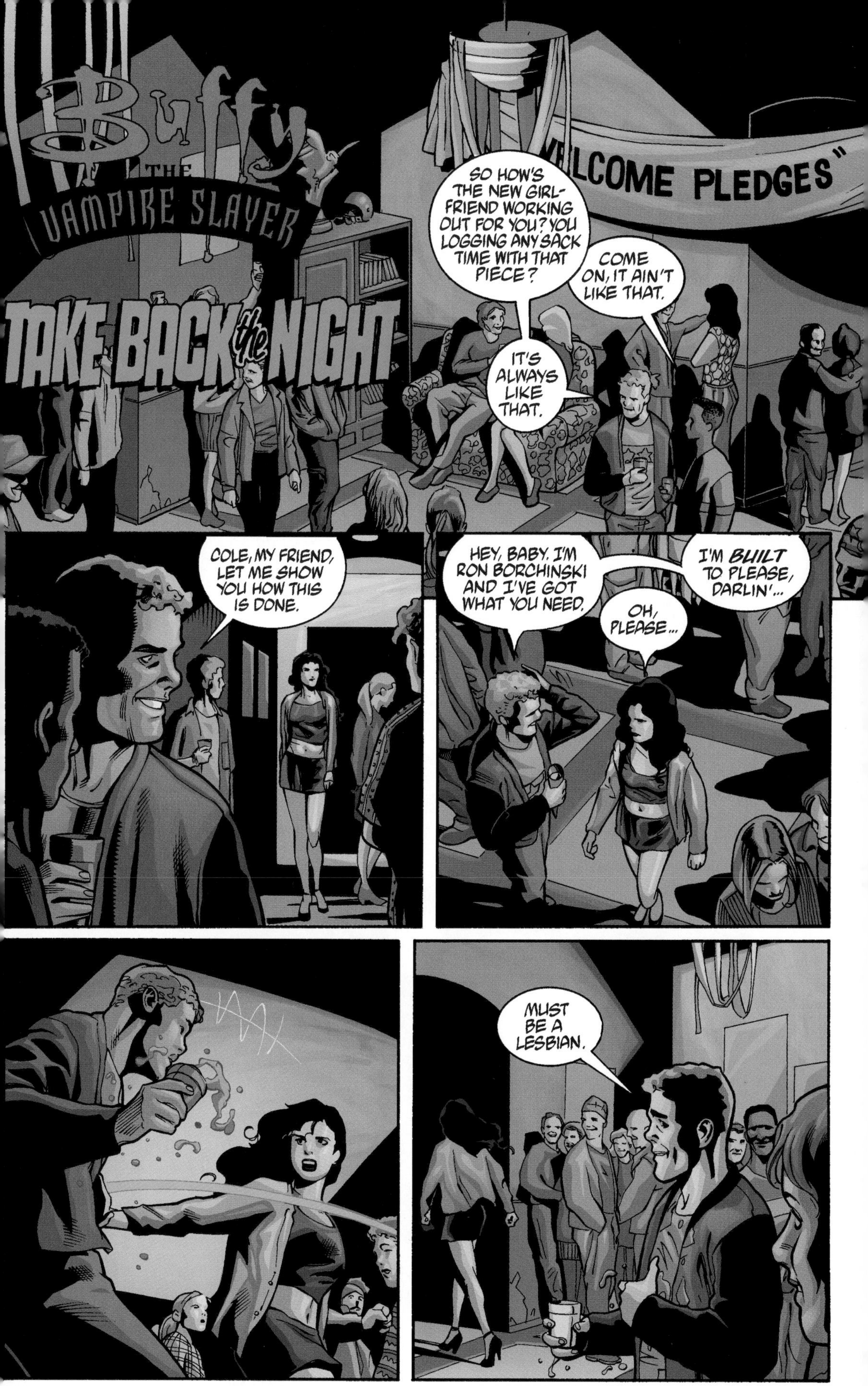
Buffy THE VAMPIRE SLAYER
TAKE BACK the NIGHT
"WELCOME PLEDGES"
SO HOW'S THE NEW GIRL-FRIEND WORKING OUT FOR YOU? YOU LOGGING ANY SACK TIME WITH THAT PIECE?
COME ON, IT AIN'T LIKE THAT.
IT'S ALWAYS LIKE THAT.
COLE, MY FRIEND, LET ME SHOW YOU HOW THIS IS DONE.
HEY, BABY. I'M RON BORCHINSKI AND I'VE GOT WHAT YOU NEED.
I'M BUILT TO PLEASE, DARLIN'...
OH, PLEASE...
MUST BE A LESBIAN.

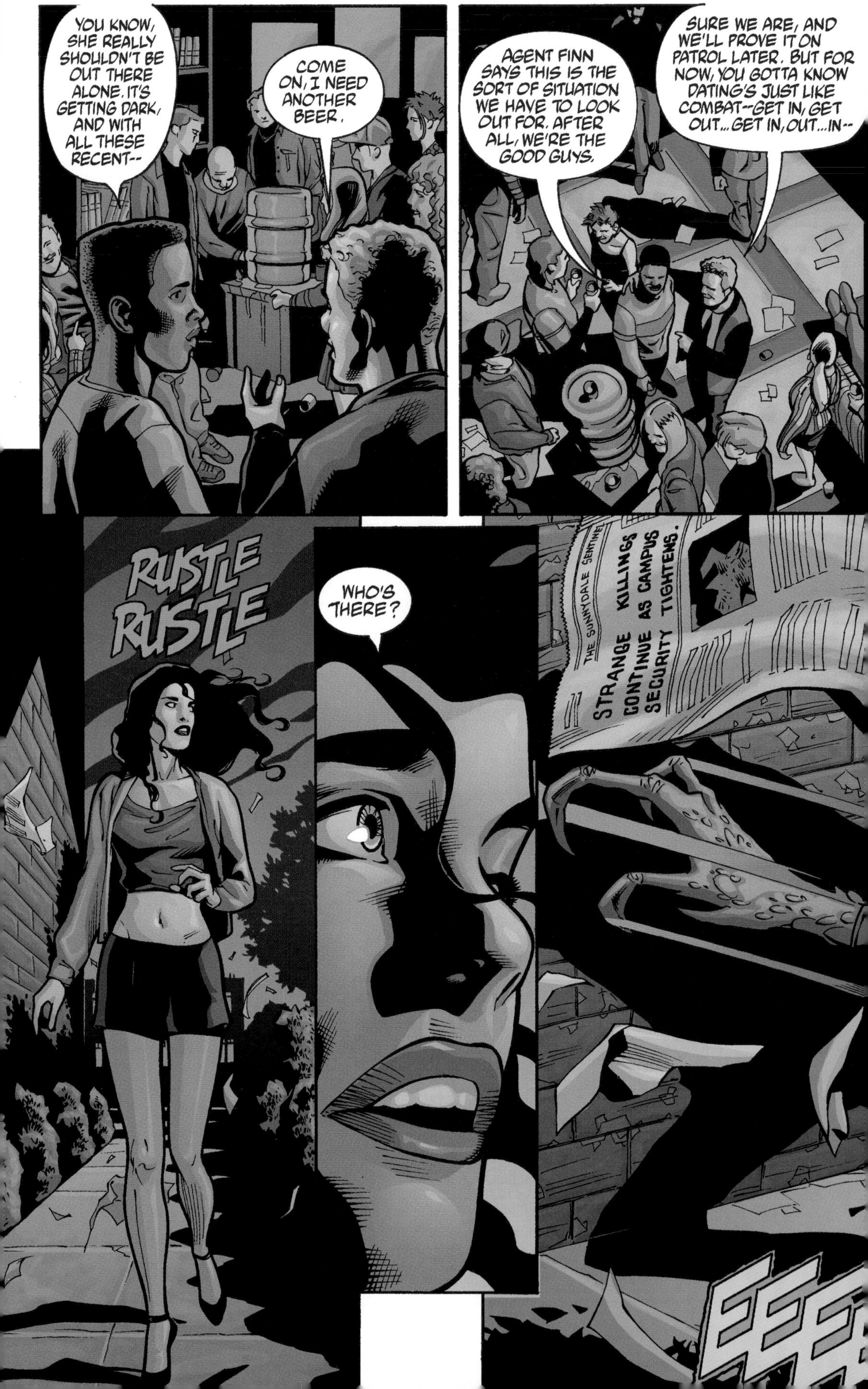
YOU KNOW, SHE REALLY SHOULDN'T BE OUT THERE ALONE. IT'S GETTING DARK, AND WITH ALL THESE RECENT--
COME ON, I NEED ANOTHER BEER.
AGENT FINN SAYS THIS IS THE SORT OF SITUATION WE HAVE TO LOOK OUT FOR. AFTER ALL, WE'RE THE GOOD GUYS.
SURE WE ARE, AND WE'LL PROVE IT ON PATROL LATER. BUT FOR NOW, YOU GOTTA KNOW DATING'S JUST LIKE COMBAT--GET IN, GET OUT... GET IN, OUT... IN--
RUSTLE RUSTLE
WHO'S THERE?
THE SUNNYDALE SENTINEL
STRANGE KILLINGS CONTINUE AS CAMPUS SECURITY TIGHTENS.
EEEE

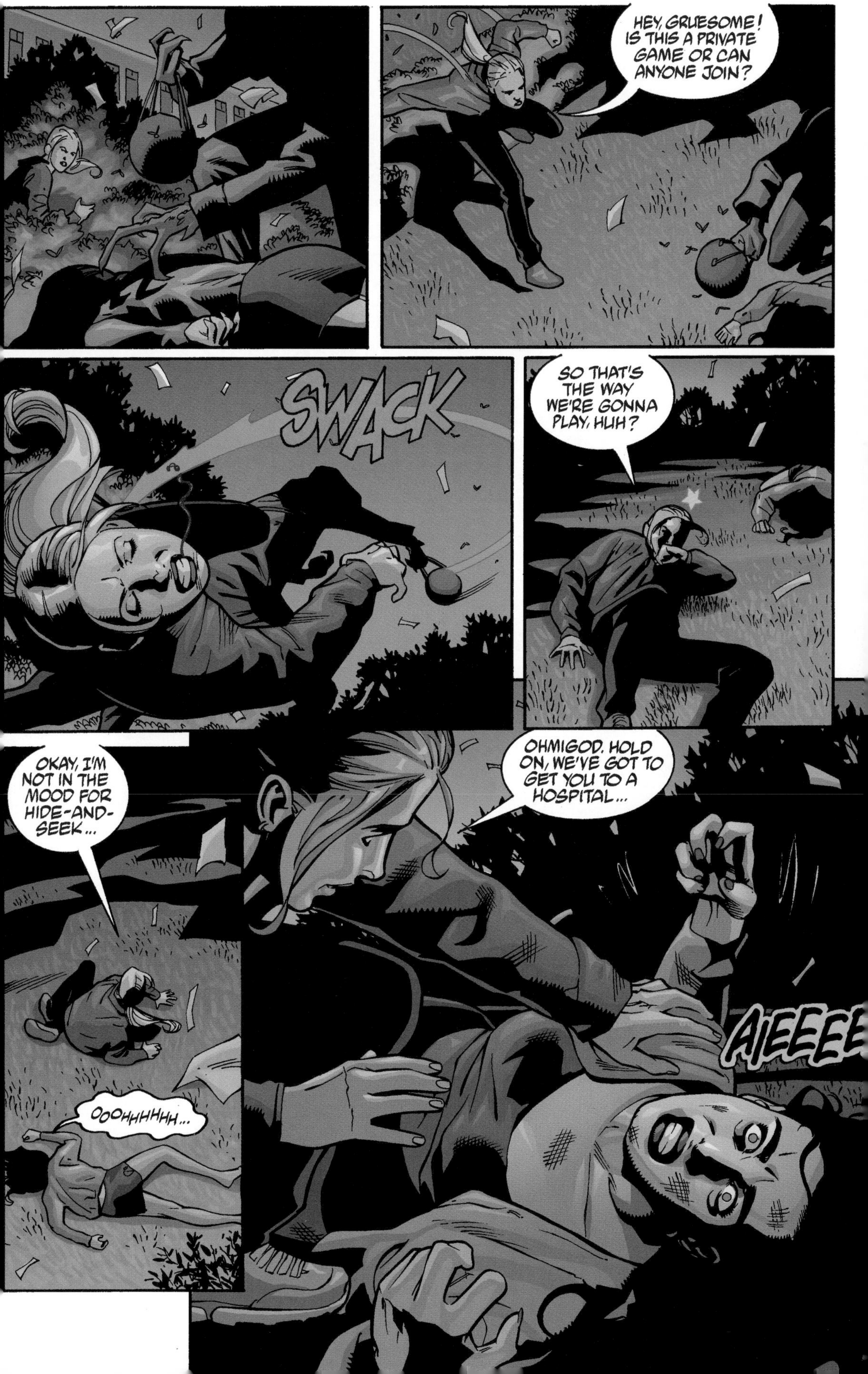
HEY, GRUESOME! IS THIS A PRIVATE GAME OR CAN ANYONE JOIN?
SWACK
SO THAT'S THE WAY WE'RE GONNA PLAY, HUH?
OKAY, I'M NOT IN THE MOOD FOR HIDE-AND-SEEK...
OOOHHHHHH...
OHMIGOD. HOLD ON, WE'VE GOT TO GET YOU TO A HOSPITAL...
AIEEEE

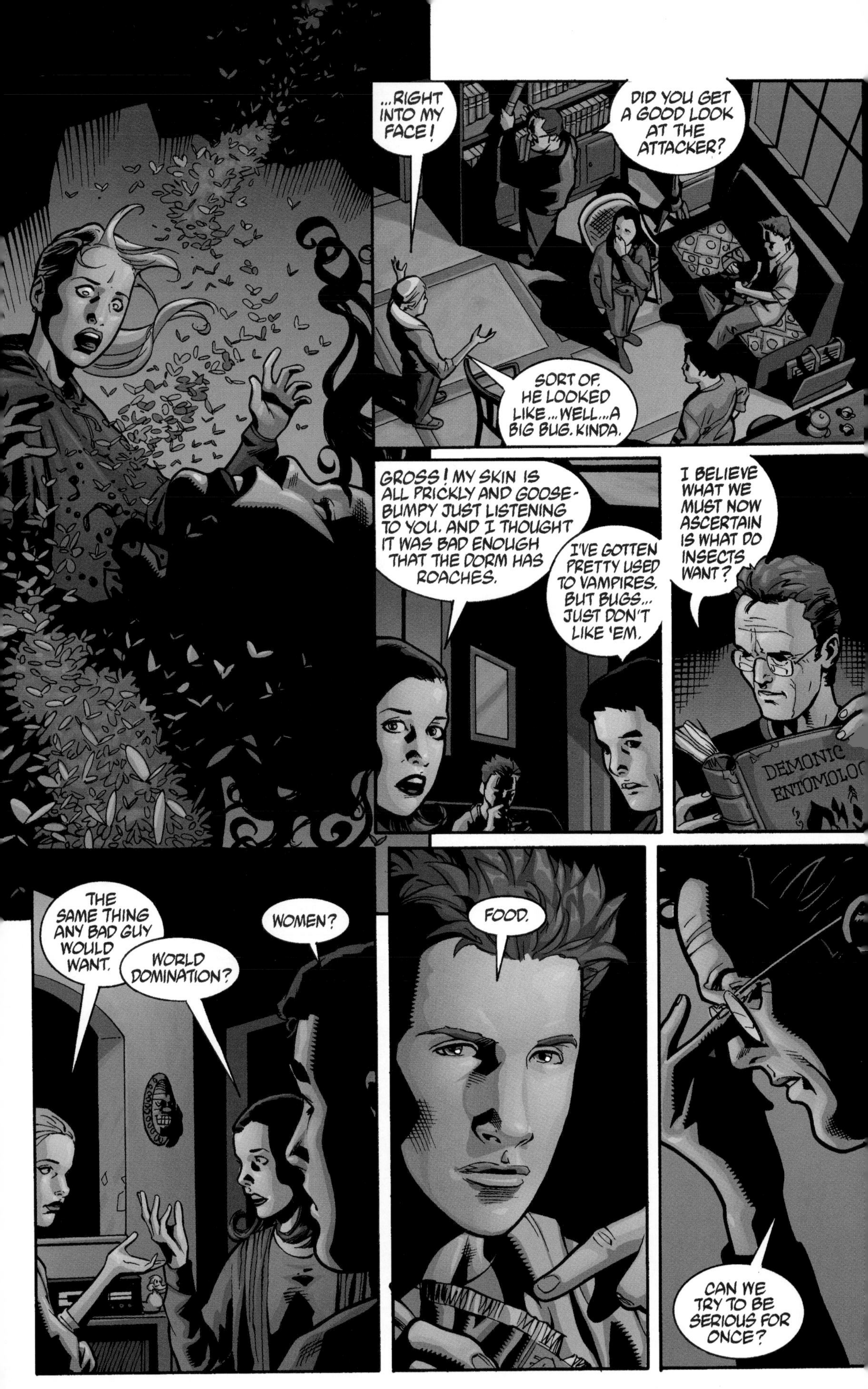
...RIGHT INTO MY FACE!
DID YOU GET A GOOD LOOK AT THE ATTACKER?
SORT OF. HE LOOKED LIKE...WELL...A BIG BUG. KINDA.
GROSS! MY SKIN IS ALL PRICKLY AND GOOSE-BUMPY JUST LISTENING TO YOU. AND I THOUGHT IT WAS BAD ENOUGH THAT THE DORM HAS ROACHES.
I'VE GOTTEN PRETTY USED TO VAMPIRES. BUT BUGS... JUST DON'T LIKE 'EM.
I BELIEVE WHAT WE MUST NOW ASCERTAIN IS WHAT DO INSECTS WANT?
DEMONIC ENTOMOLOG
THE SAME THING ANY BAD GUY WOULD WANT.
WORLD DOMINATION?
WOMEN?
FOOD.
CAN WE TRY TO BE SERIOUS FOR ONCE?

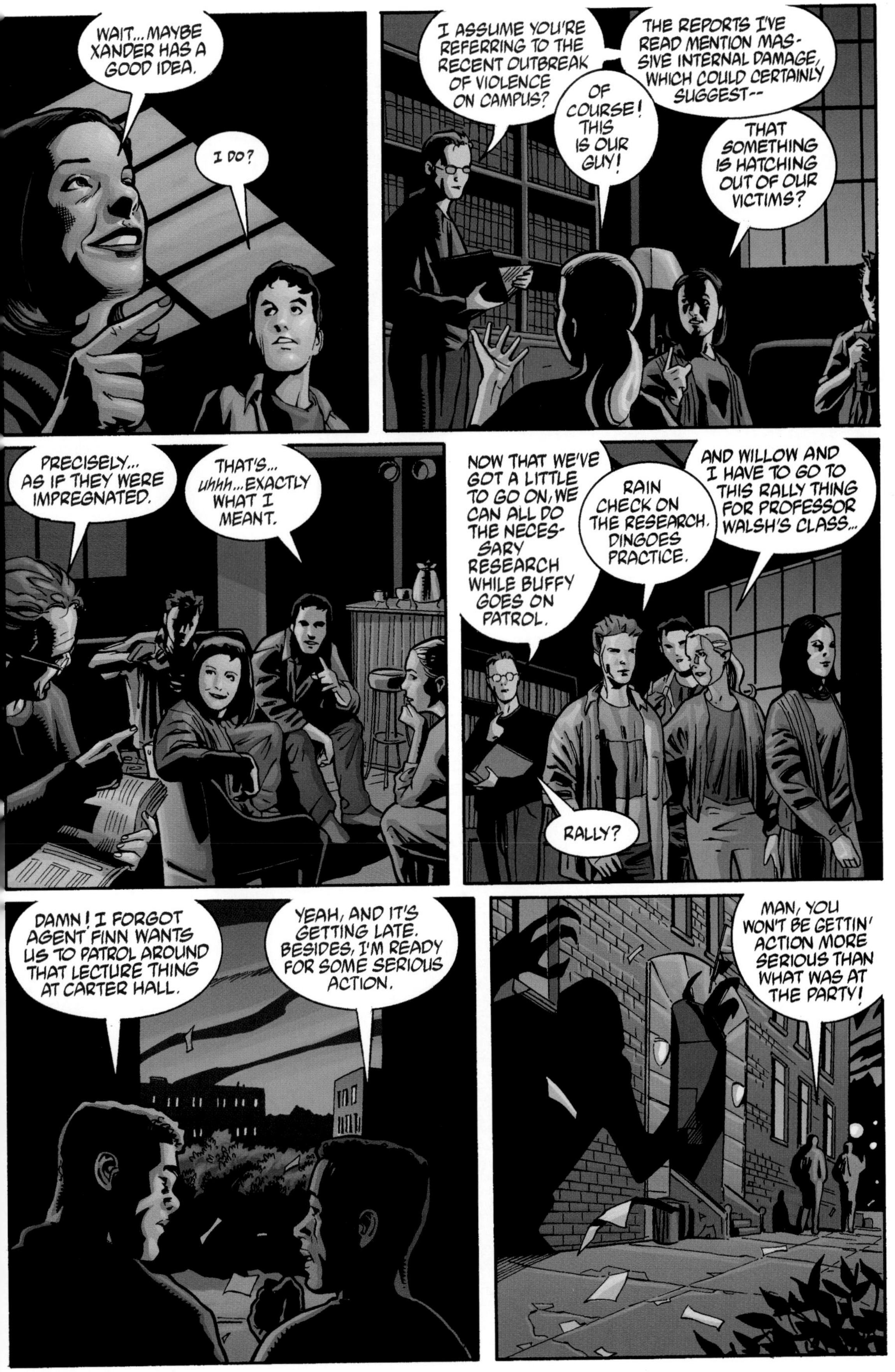

WAIT... MAYBE XANDER HAS A GOOD IDEA.
I DO?
I ASSUME YOU'RE REFERRING TO THE RECENT OUTBREAK OF VIOLENCE ON CAMPUS?
OF COURSE! THIS IS OUR GUY!
THE REPORTS I'VE READ MENTION MASSIVE INTERNAL DAMAGE, WHICH COULD CERTAINLY SUGGEST--
THAT SOMETHING IS HATCHING OUT OF OUR VICTIMS?
PRECISELY... AS IF THEY WERE IMPREGNATED.
THAT'S... *uhhh*... EXACTLY WHAT I MEANT.
NOW THAT WE'VE GOT A LITTLE TO GO ON, WE CAN ALL DO THE NECESSARY RESEARCH WHILE BUFFY GOES ON PATROL.
RAIN CHECK ON THE RESEARCH. DINGOES PRACTICE.
AND WILLOW AND I HAVE TO GO TO THIS RALLY THING FOR PROFESSOR WALSH'S CLASS...
RALLY?
DAMN! I FORGOT AGENT FINN WANTS US TO PATROL AROUND THAT LECTURE THING AT CARTER HALL.
YEAH, AND IT'S GETTING LATE. BESIDES, I'M READY FOR SOME SERIOUS ACTION.
MAN, YOU WON'T BE GETTIN' ACTION MORE SERIOUS THAN WHAT WAS AT THE PARTY!

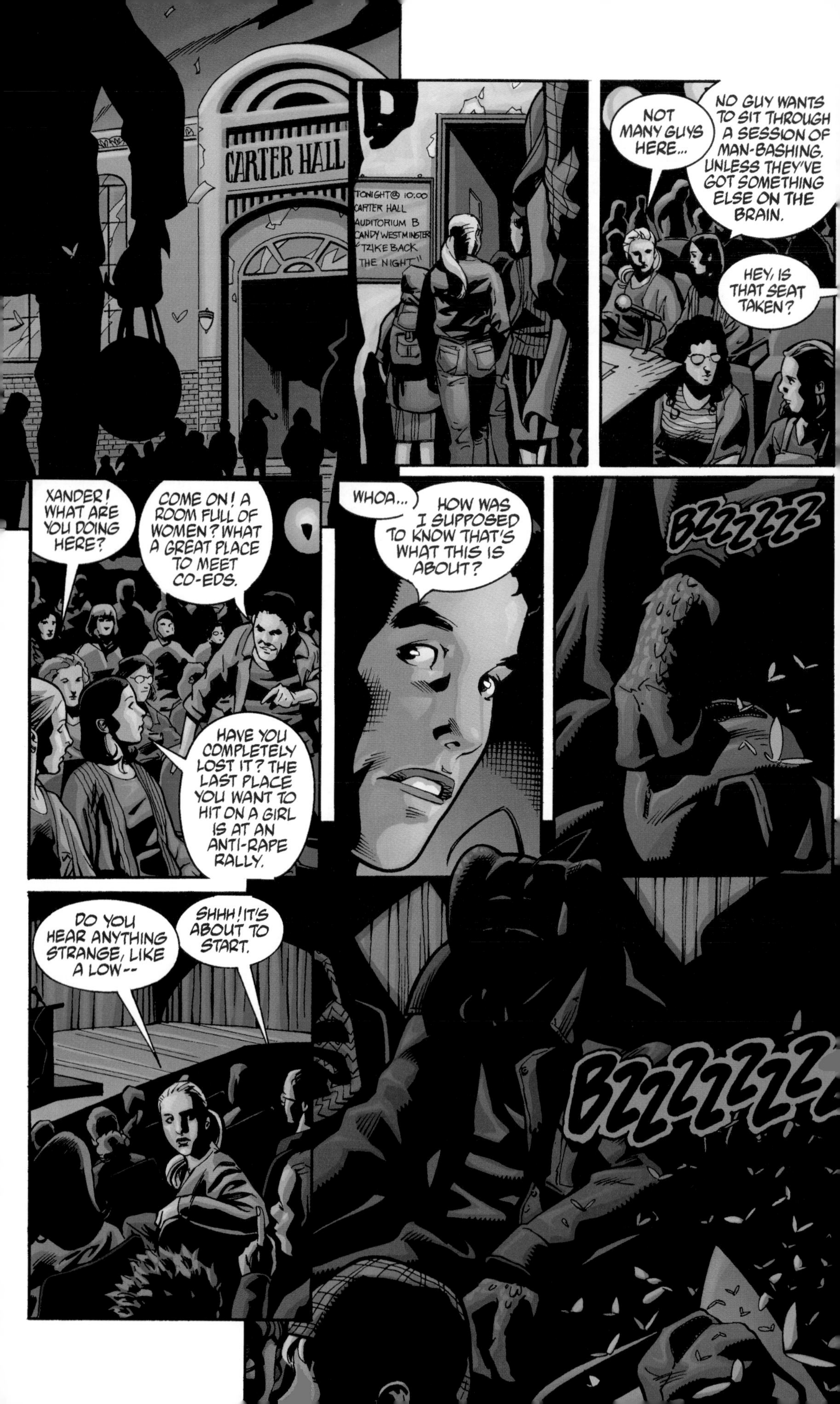
CARTER HALL
TONIGHT@ 10:00 CARTER HALL AUDITORIUM B CANDY WESTMINSTER "TAKE BACK THE NIGHT"
NOT MANY GUYS HERE...
NO GUY WANTS TO SIT THROUGH A SESSION OF MAN-BASHING, UNLESS THEY'VE GOT SOMETHING ELSE ON THE BRAIN.
HEY, IS THAT SEAT TAKEN?
XANDER! WHAT ARE YOU DOING HERE?
COME ON! A ROOM FULL OF WOMEN? WHAT A GREAT PLACE TO MEET CO-EDS.
HAVE YOU COMPLETELY LOST IT? THE LAST PLACE YOU WANT TO HIT ON A GIRL IS AT AN ANTI-RAPE RALLY.
WHOA...
HOW WAS I SUPPOSED TO KNOW THAT'S WHAT THIS IS ABOUT?
BZZZZZZ
DO YOU HEAR ANYTHING STRANGE, LIKE A LOW--
SHHH! IT'S ABOUT TO START.
BZZZZZZ

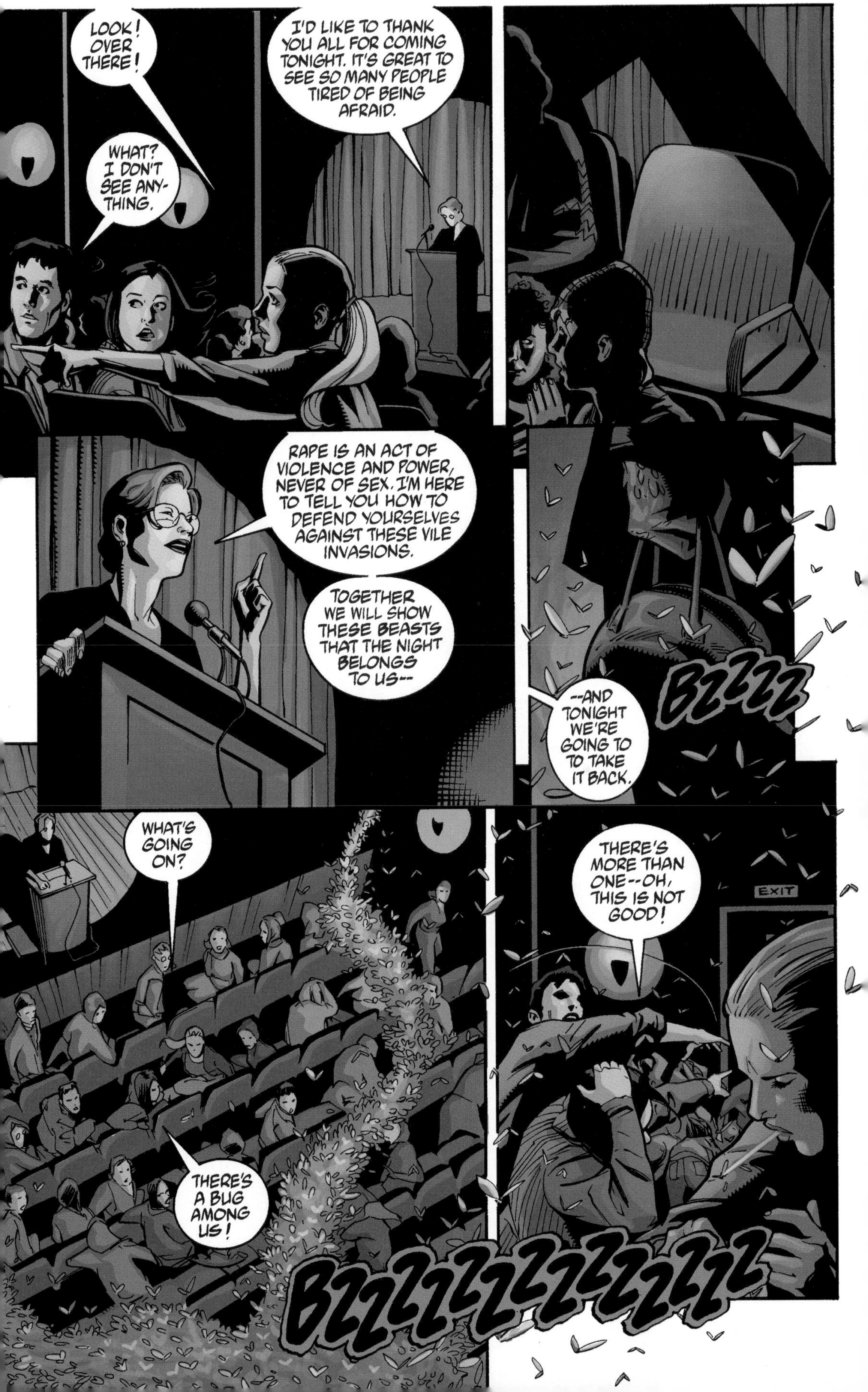
LOOK! OVER THERE!
WHAT? I DON'T SEE ANYTHING.
I'D LIKE TO THANK YOU ALL FOR COMING TONIGHT. IT'S GREAT TO SEE SO MANY PEOPLE TIRED OF BEING AFRAID.
RAPE IS AN ACT OF VIOLENCE AND POWER, NEVER OF SEX. I'M HERE TO TELL YOU HOW TO DEFEND YOURSELVES AGAINST THESE VILE INVASIONS.
TOGETHER WE WILL SHOW THESE BEASTS THAT THE NIGHT BELONGS TO US--
--AND TONIGHT WE'RE GOING TO TO TAKE IT BACK.
BZZZZ
WHAT'S GOING ON?
THERE'S A BUG AMONG US!
THERE'S MORE THAN ONE--OH, THIS IS NOT GOOD!
EXIT
BZZZZZZZZZZZZZ

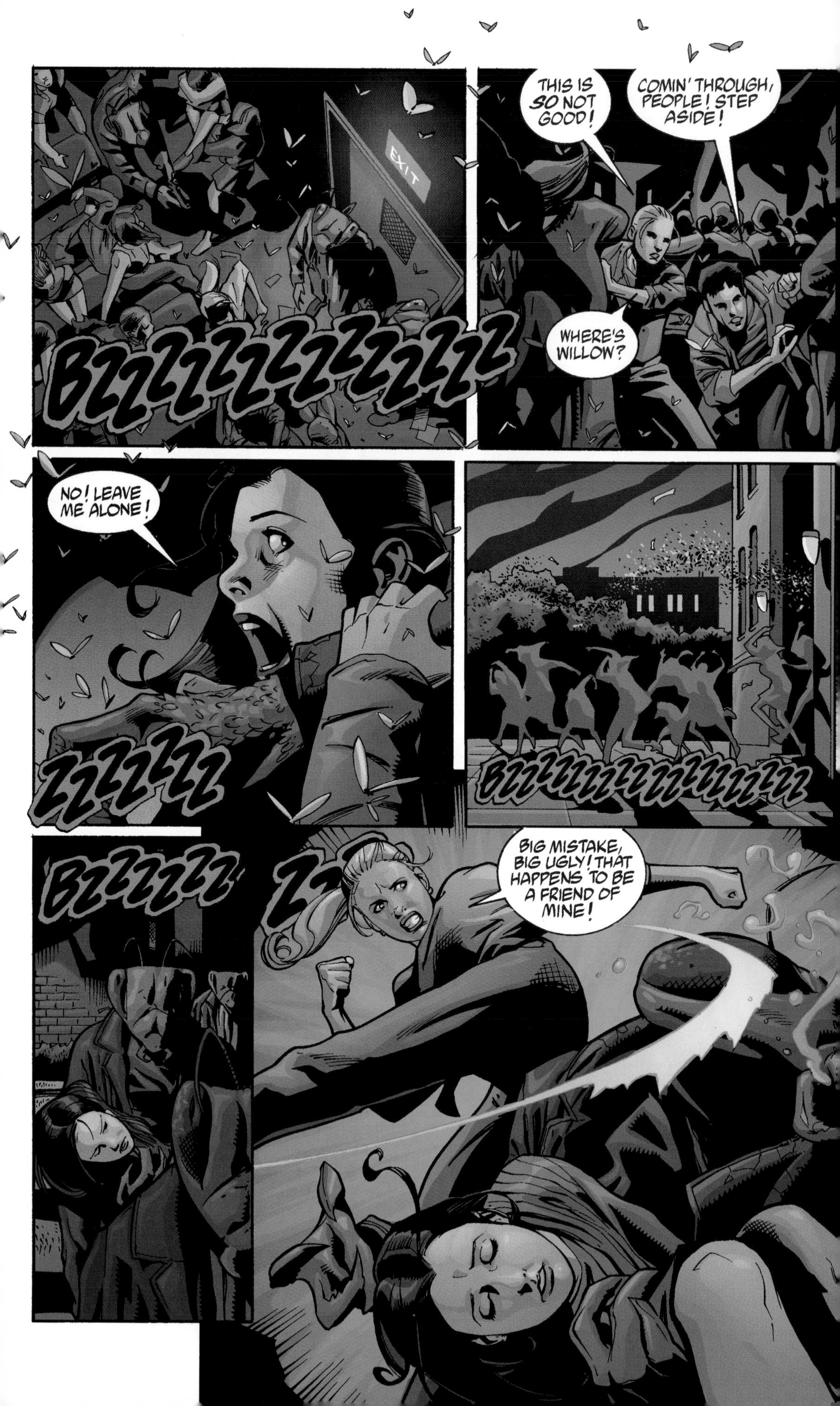
BZZZZZZZZZZZZZZZZ
THIS IS SO NOT GOOD!
COMIN' THROUGH, PEOPLE! STEP ASIDE!
WHERE'S WILLOW?
NO! LEAVE ME ALONE!
ZZZZZZZ
BZZZZZZZZZZZZZZZZZZZZZZ
BZZZZZZZ
BIG MISTAKE, BIG UGLY! THAT HAPPENS TO BE A FRIEND OF MINE!

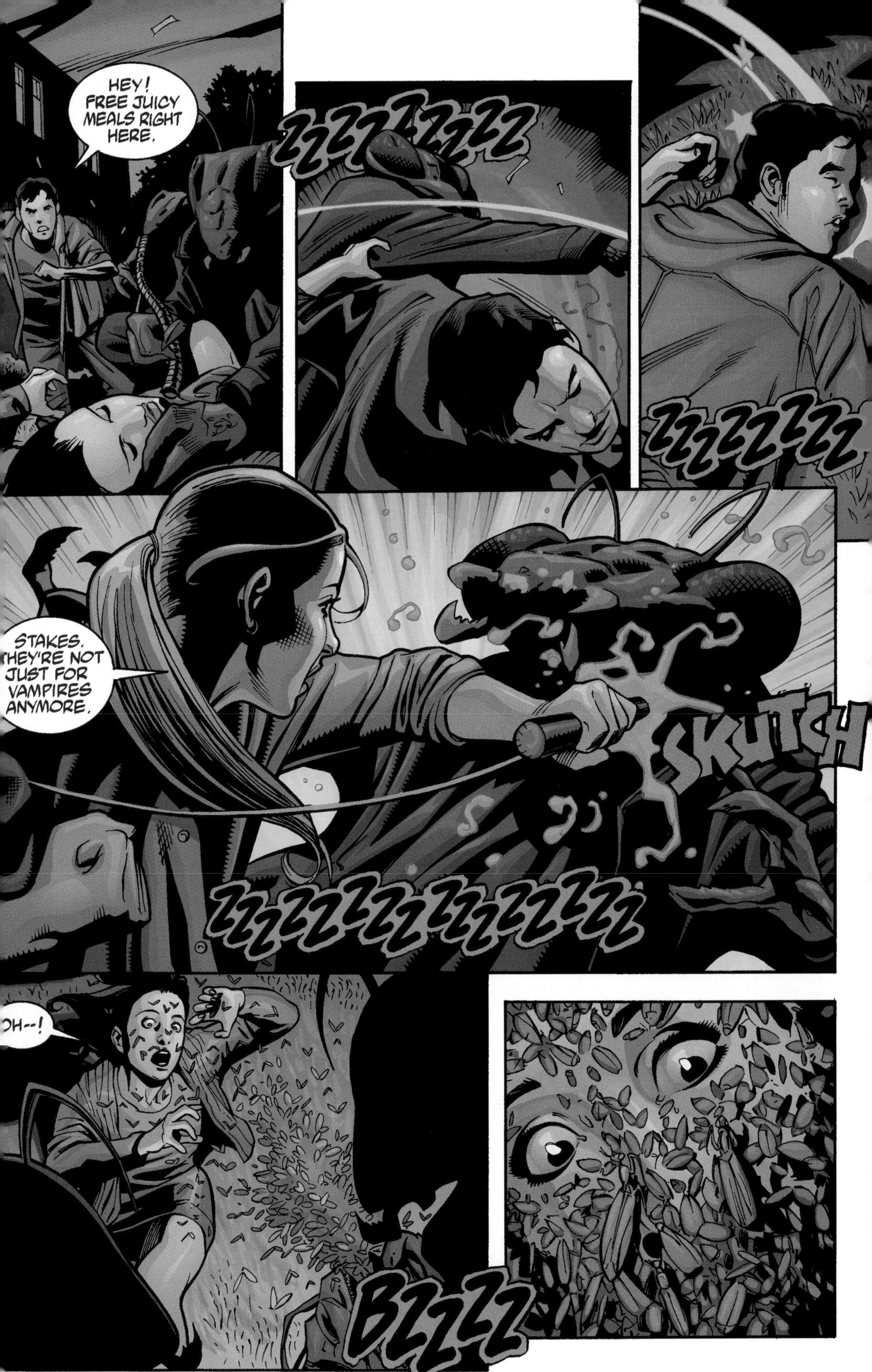

HEY! FREE JUICY MEALS RIGHT HERE.
ZZZZZZZZZZ
ZZZZZZZZZ
STAKES. THEY'RE NOT JUST FOR VAMPIRES ANYMORE.
SKUTCH
ZZZZZZZZZZZZZZZZZ
OH--!
BZZZZ

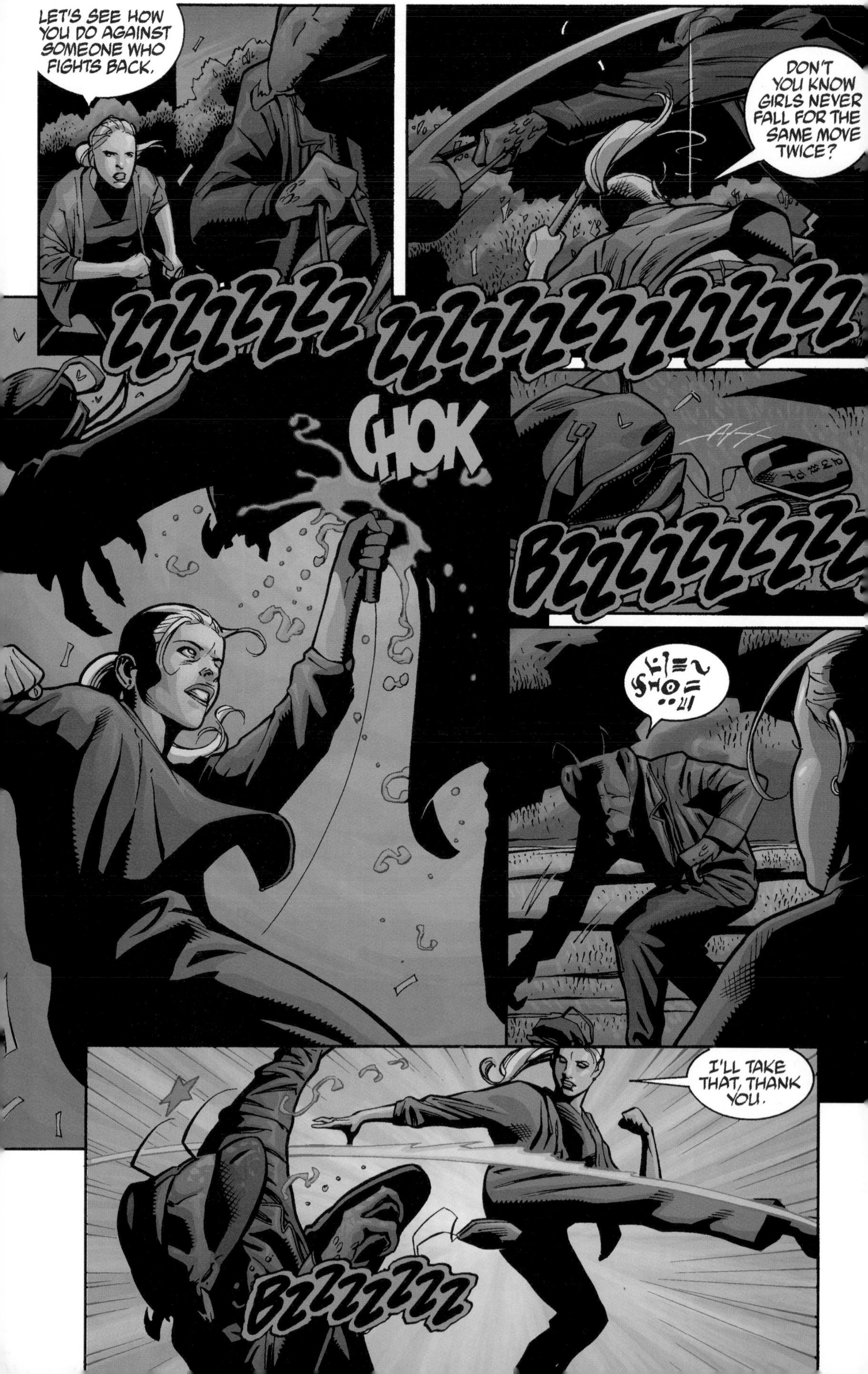
LET'S SEE HOW YOU DO AGAINST SOMEONE WHO FIGHTS BACK.
DON'T YOU KNOW GIRLS NEVER FALL FOR THE SAME MOVE TWICE?
ZZZZZZZZ ZZZZZZZZZZZZZZZZ
CHOK
BZZZZZZZZZ
I'LL TAKE THAT, THANK YOU.
BZZZZZZZ

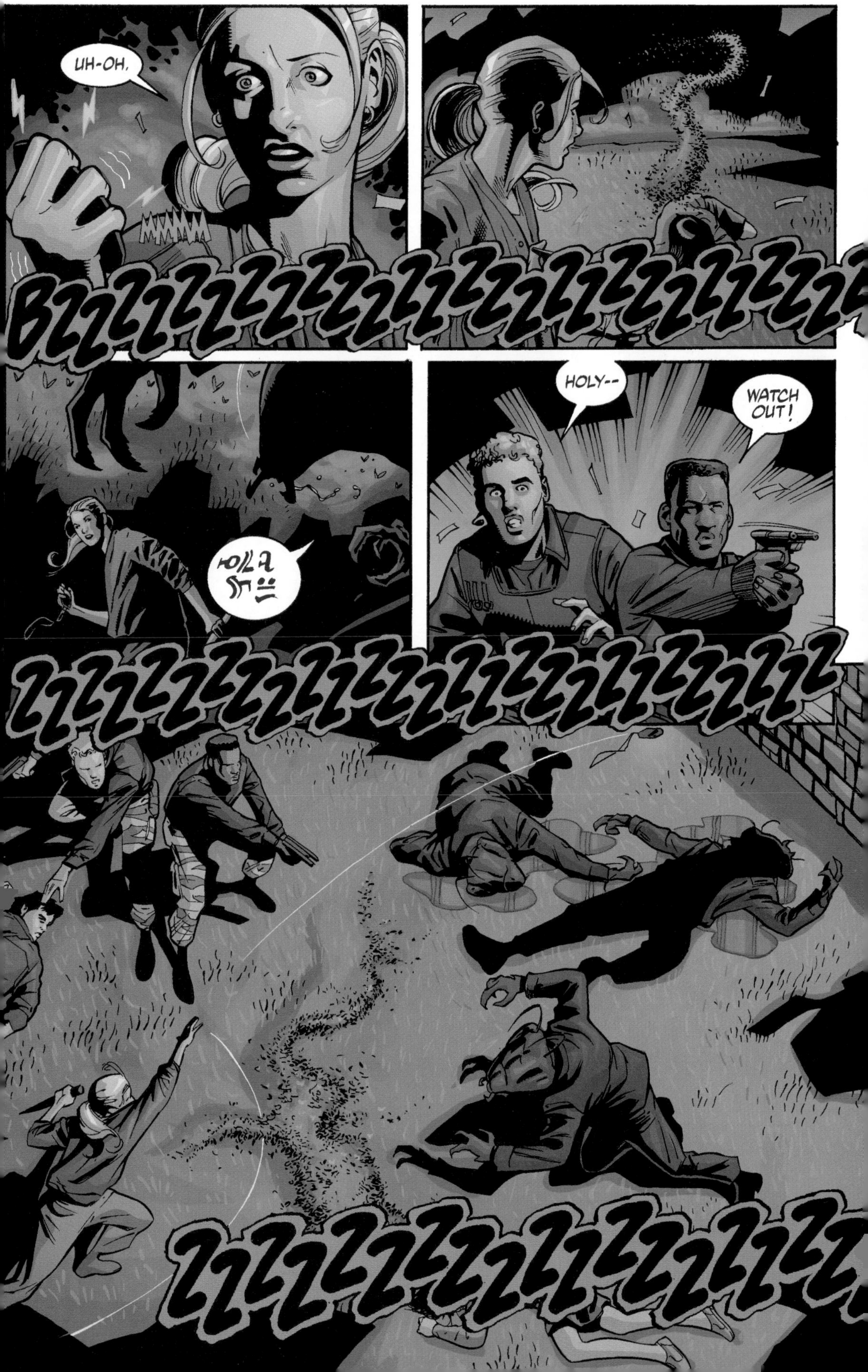
UH-OH,
BZZZZZZZZZZZZZZZZZZZ
HOLY--
WATCH OUT!
ZZZZZZZZZZZZZZZZZZZZ
ZZZZZZZZZZZZZZZZZ

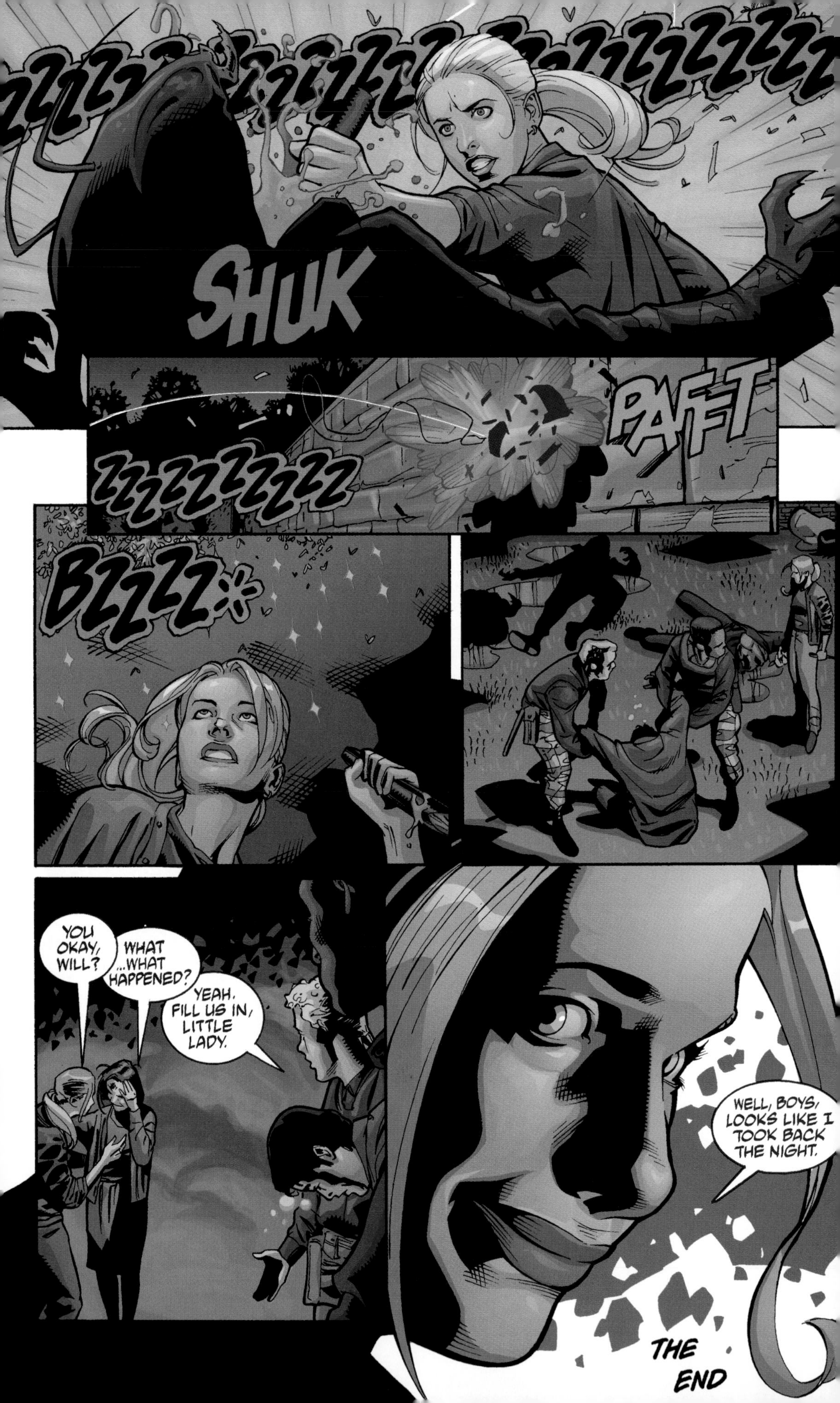

ZZZZZZZZZZZZZZZZZZZZZ
SHUK
PAFT
ZZZZZZZZZZZ
BZZZZ
YOU OKAY, WILL?
WHAT ...WHAT HAPPENED?
YEAH. FILL US IN, LITTLE LADY.
WELL, BOYS, LOOKS LIKE I TOOK BACK THE NIGHT.
THE END

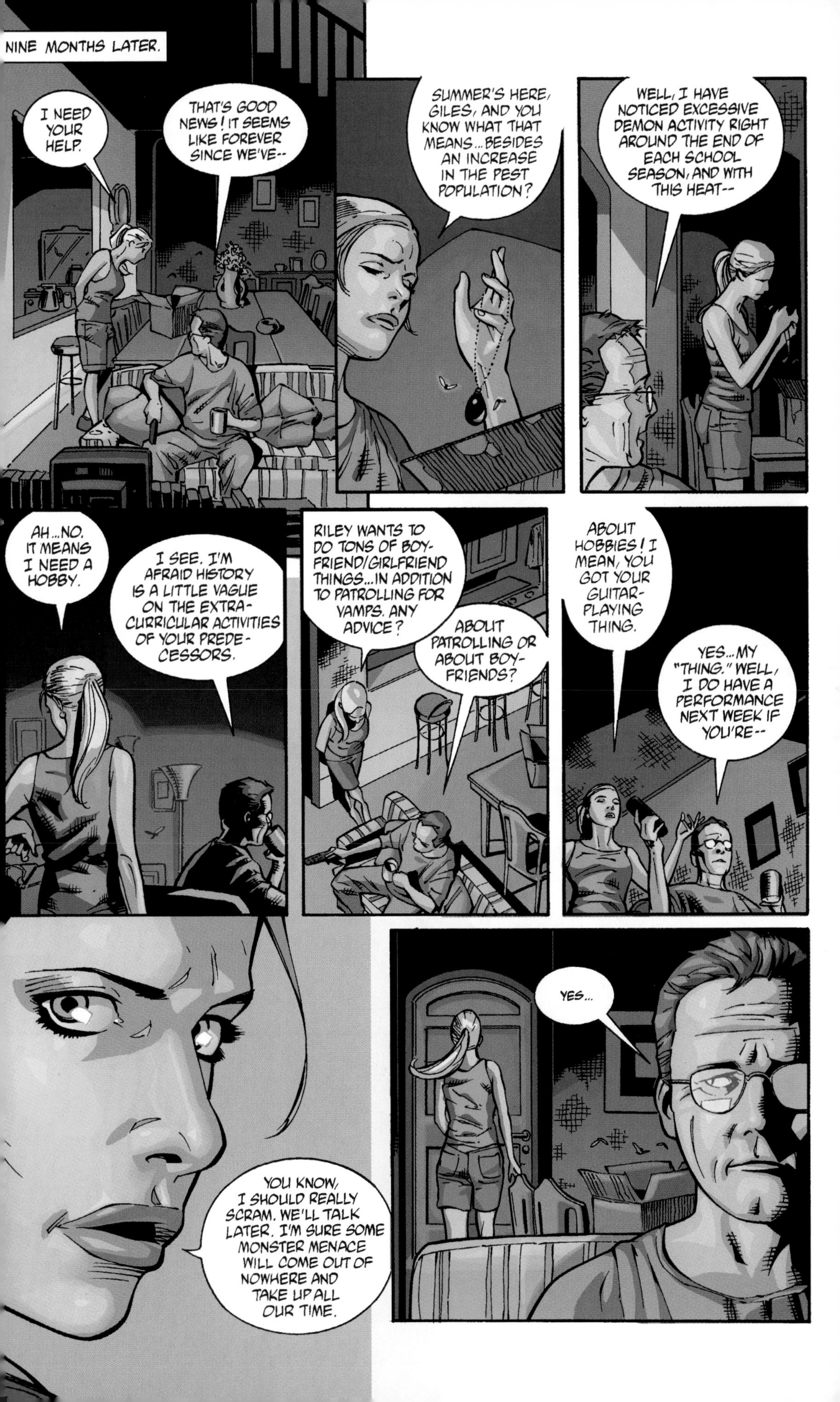
NINE MONTHS LATER.
I NEED YOUR HELP.
THAT'S GOOD NEWS! IT SEEMS LIKE FOREVER SINCE WE'VE--
SUMMER'S HERE, GILES, AND YOU KNOW WHAT THAT MEANS... BESIDES AN INCREASE IN THE PEST POPULATION?
WELL, I HAVE NOTICED EXCESSIVE DEMON ACTIVITY RIGHT AROUND THE END OF EACH SCHOOL SEASON, AND WITH THIS HEAT--
AH... NO. IT MEANS I NEED A HOBBY.
I SEE. I'M AFRAID HISTORY IS A LITTLE VAGUE ON THE EXTRA-CURRICULAR ACTIVITIES OF YOUR PREDE-CESSORS.
RILEY WANTS TO DO TONS OF BOY-FRIEND/GIRLFRIEND THINGS... IN ADDITION TO PATROLLING FOR VAMPS. ANY ADVICE?
ABOUT PATROLLING OR ABOUT BOY-FRIENDS?
ABOUT HOBBIES! I MEAN, YOU GOT YOUR GUITAR-PLAYING THING.
YES... MY "THING." WELL, I DO HAVE A PERFORMANCE NEXT WEEK IF YOU'RE--
YOU KNOW, I SHOULD REALLY SCRAM. WE'LL TALK LATER. I'M SURE SOME MONSTER MENACE WILL COME OUT OF NOWHERE AND TAKE UP ALL OUR TIME.
YES...

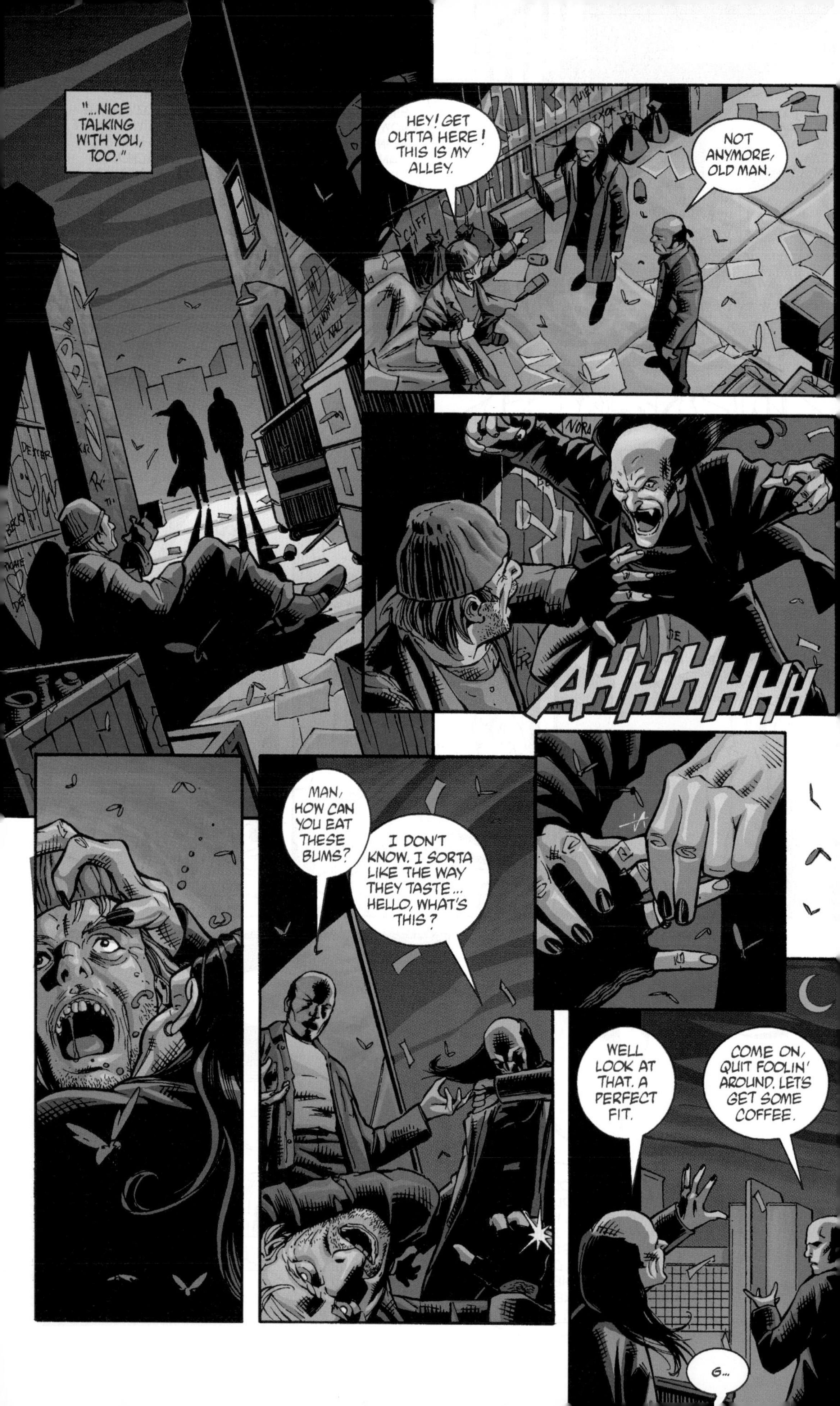

"...NICE TALKING WITH YOU, TOO."
HEY! GET OUTTA HERE! THIS IS MY ALLEY.
NOT ANYMORE, OLD MAN.
AHHHHHH
MAN, HOW CAN YOU EAT THESE BUMS?
I DON'T KNOW. I SORTA LIKE THE WAY THEY TASTE... HELLO, WHAT'S THIS?
WELL LOOK AT THAT. A PERFECT FIT.
COME ON, QUIT FOOLIN' AROUND. LET'S GET SOME COFFEE.
6...

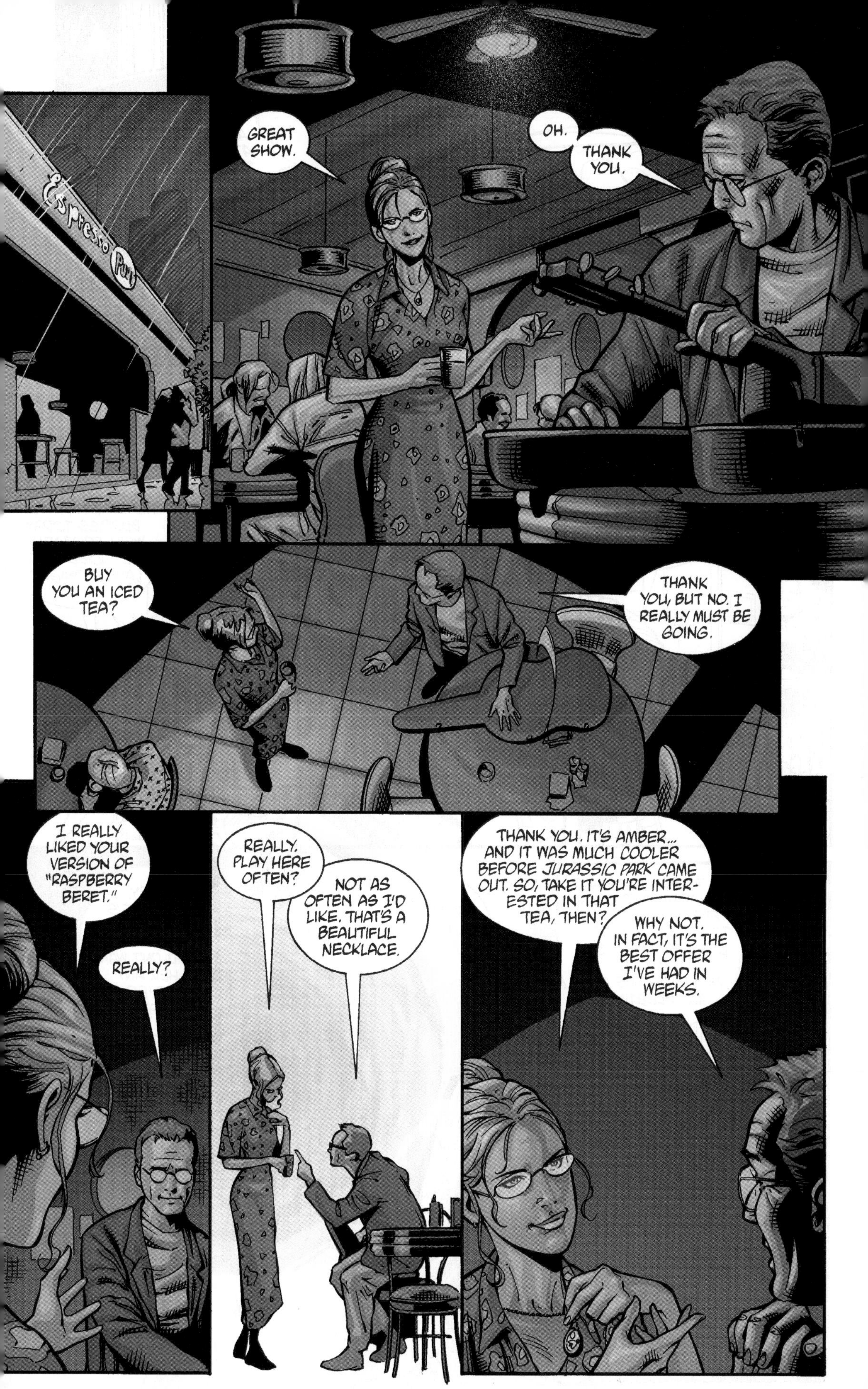
Espresso Pump
GREAT SHOW.
OH.
THANK YOU.
BUY YOU AN ICED TEA?
THANK YOU, BUT NO. I REALLY MUST BE GOING.
I REALLY LIKED YOUR VERSION OF "RASPBERRY BERET."
REALLY?
REALLY. PLAY HERE OFTEN?
NOT AS OFTEN AS I'D LIKE. THAT'S A BEAUTIFUL NECKLACE.
THANK YOU. IT'S AMBER... AND IT WAS MUCH COOLER BEFORE *JURASSIC PARK* CAME OUT. SO, TAKE IT YOU'RE INTERESTED IN THAT TEA, THEN?
WHY NOT. IN FACT, IT'S THE BEST OFFER I'VE HAD IN WEEKS.

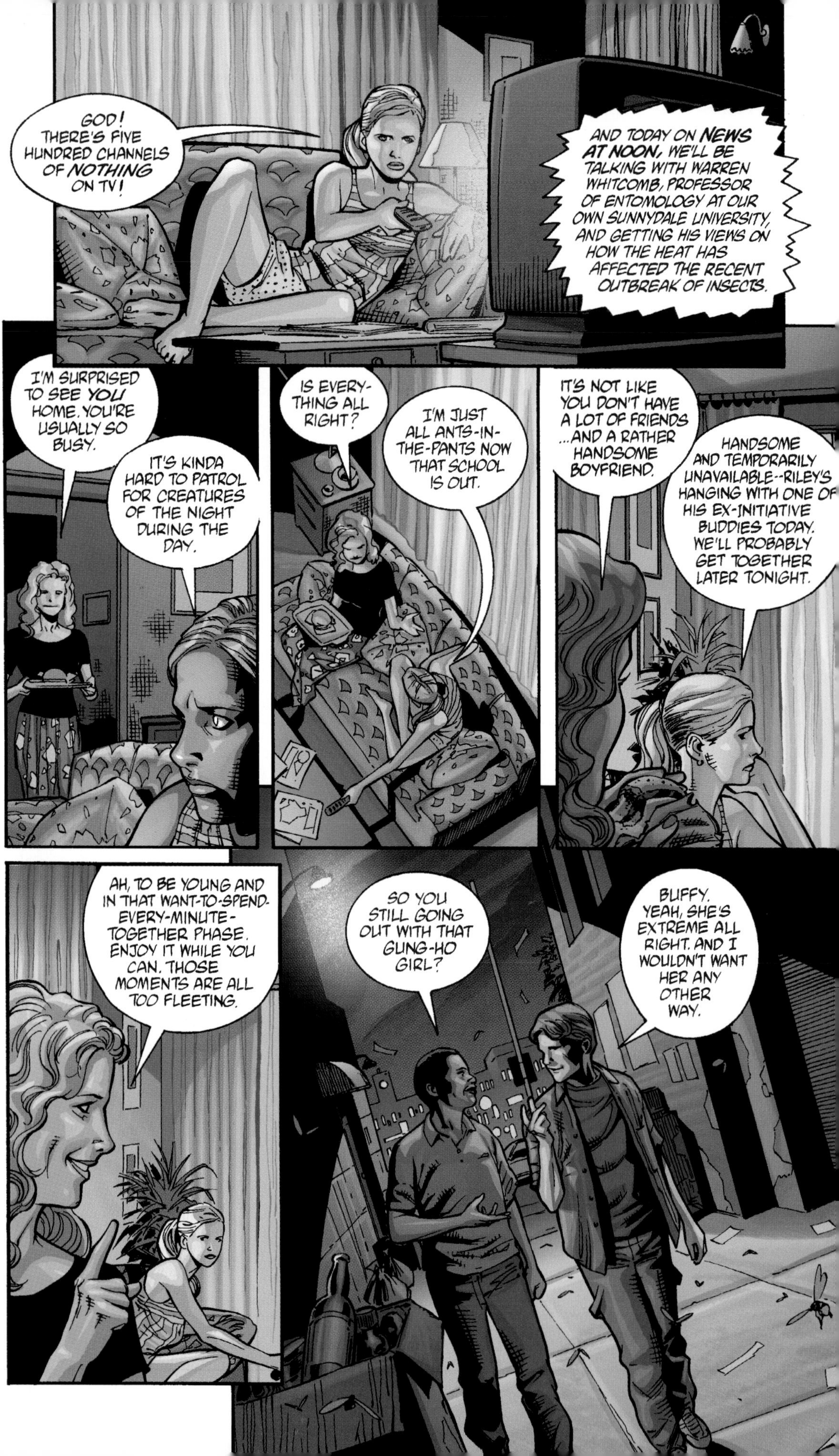
GOD! THERE'S FIVE HUNDRED CHANNELS OF NOTHING ON TV!
AND TODAY ON NEWS AT NOON, WE'LL BE TALKING WITH WARREN WHITCOMB, PROFESSOR OF ENTOMOLOGY AT OUR OWN SUNNYDALE UNIVERSITY, AND GETTING HIS VIEWS ON HOW THE HEAT HAS AFFECTED THE RECENT OUTBREAK OF INSECTS.
I'M SURPRISED TO SEE YOU HOME. YOU'RE USUALLY SO BUSY.
IT'S KINDA HARD TO PATROL FOR CREATURES OF THE NIGHT DURING THE DAY.
IS EVERYTHING ALL RIGHT?
I'M JUST ALL ANTS-IN-THE-PANTS NOW THAT SCHOOL IS OUT.
IT'S NOT LIKE YOU DON'T HAVE A LOT OF FRIENDS ...AND A RATHER HANDSOME BOYFRIEND.
HANDSOME AND TEMPORARILY UNAVAILABLE--RILEY'S HANGING WITH ONE OF HIS EX-INITIATIVE BUDDIES TODAY. WE'LL PROBABLY GET TOGETHER LATER TONIGHT.
AH, TO BE YOUNG AND IN THAT WANT-TO-SPEND-EVERY-MINUTE-TOGETHER PHASE. ENJOY IT WHILE YOU CAN. THOSE MOMENTS ARE ALL TOO FLEETING.
SO YOU STILL GOING OUT WITH THAT GUNG-HO GIRL?
BUFFY. YEAH, SHE'S EXTREME ALL RIGHT. AND I WOULDN'T WANT HER ANY OTHER WAY.

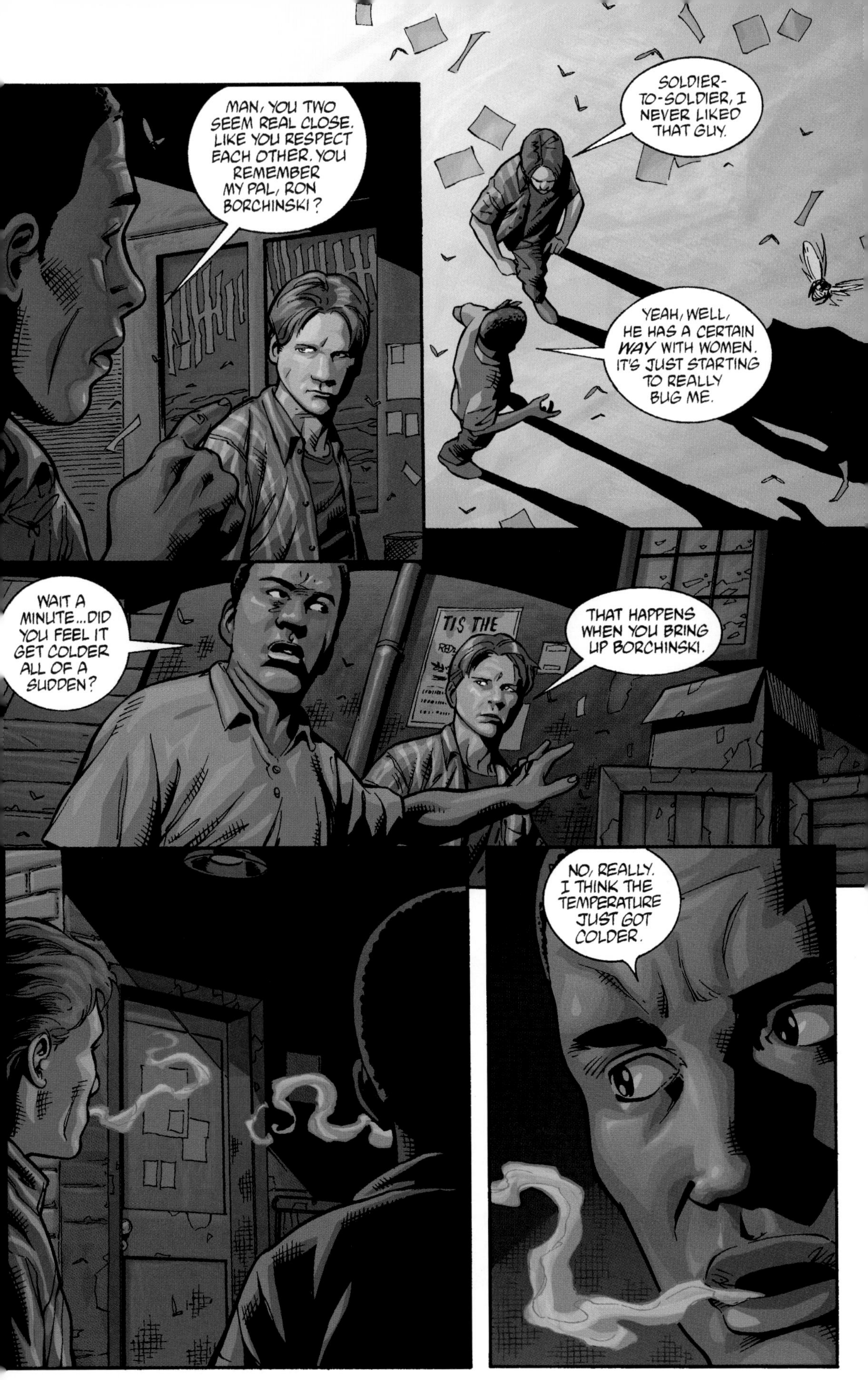
MAN, YOU TWO SEEM REAL CLOSE. LIKE YOU RESPECT EACH OTHER. YOU REMEMBER MY PAL, RON BORCHINSKI?
SOLDIER-TO-SOLDIER, I NEVER LIKED THAT GUY.
YEAH, WELL, HE HAS A CERTAIN *WAY* WITH WOMEN. IT'S JUST STARTING TO REALLY BUG ME.
WAIT A MINUTE...DID YOU FEEL IT GET COLDER ALL OF A SUDDEN?
TIS THE
THAT HAPPENS WHEN YOU BRING UP BORCHINSKI.
NO, REALLY. I THINK THE TEMPERATURE JUST GOT COLDER.

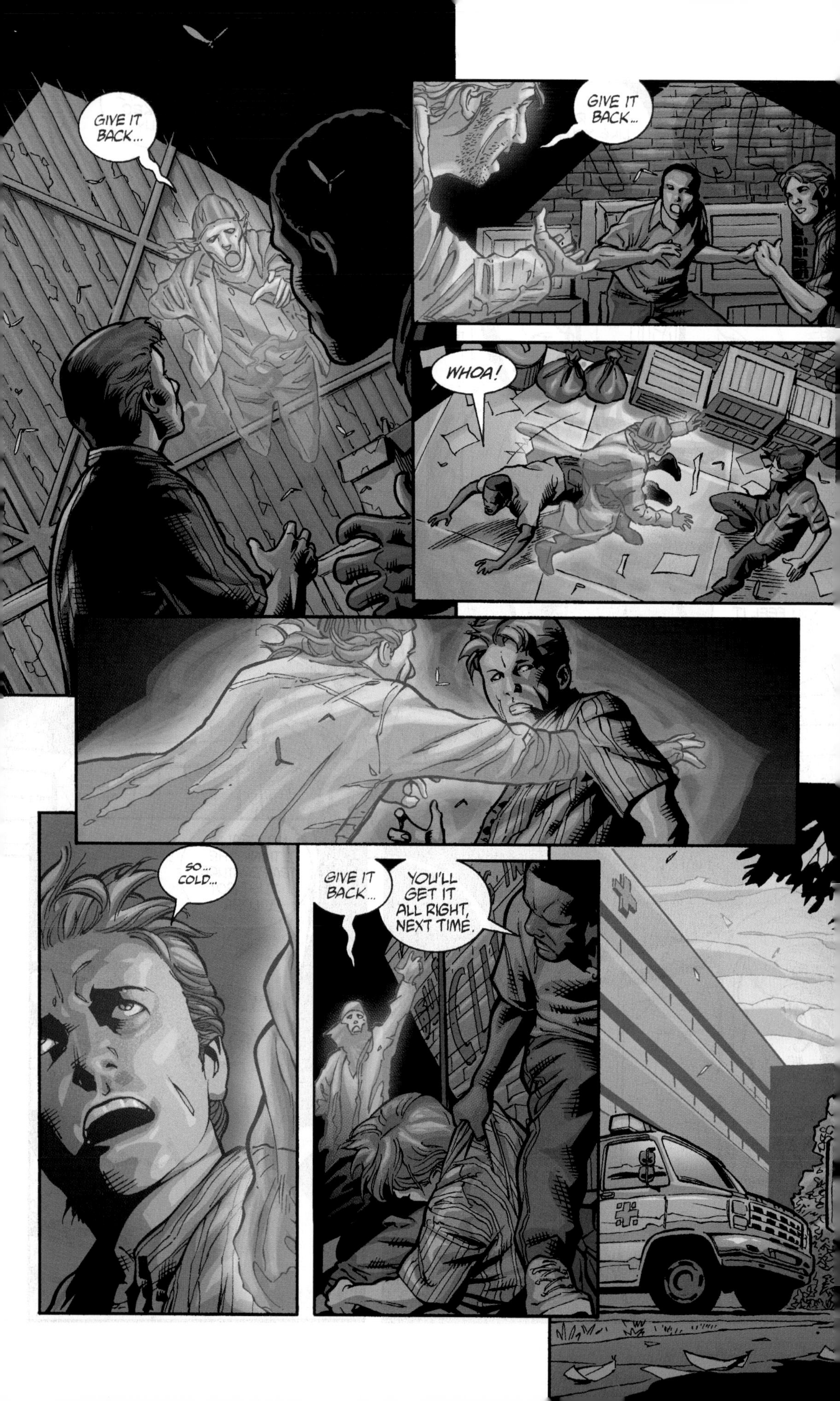
GIVE IT BACK...
GIVE IT BACK...
WHOA!
SO... COLD...
GIVE IT BACK...
YOU'LL GET IT ALL RIGHT, NEXT TIME.

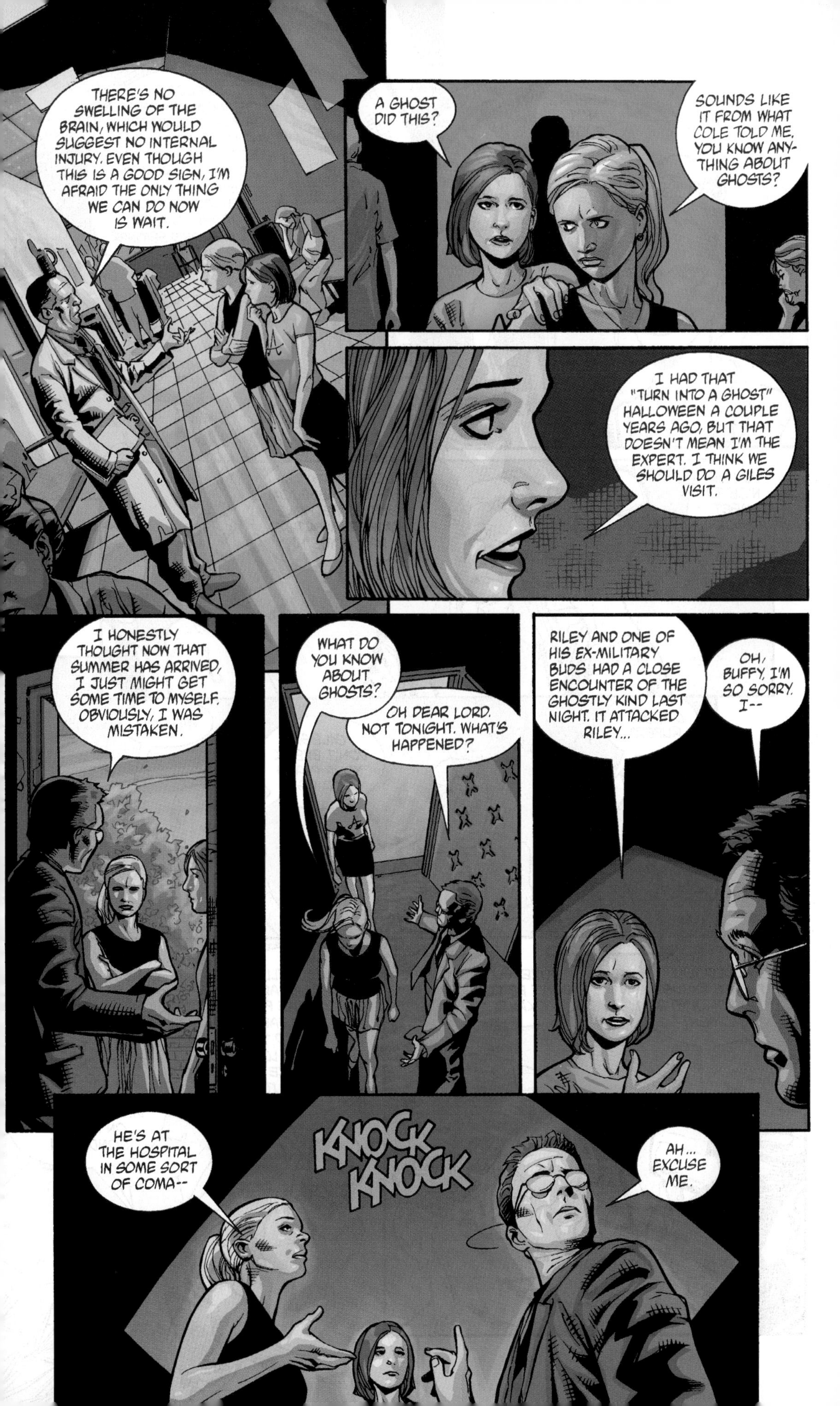
THERE'S NO SWELLING OF THE BRAIN, WHICH WOULD SUGGEST NO INTERNAL INJURY. EVEN THOUGH THIS IS A GOOD SIGN, I'M AFRAID THE ONLY THING WE CAN DO NOW IS WAIT.
A GHOST DID THIS?
SOUNDS LIKE IT FROM WHAT COLE TOLD ME. YOU KNOW ANYTHING ABOUT GHOSTS?
I HAD THAT "TURN INTO A GHOST" HALLOWEEN A COUPLE YEARS AGO, BUT THAT DOESN'T MEAN I'M THE EXPERT. I THINK WE SHOULD DO A GILES VISIT.
I HONESTLY THOUGHT NOW THAT SUMMER HAS ARRIVED, I JUST MIGHT GET SOME TIME TO MYSELF. OBVIOUSLY, I WAS MISTAKEN.
WHAT DO YOU KNOW ABOUT GHOSTS?
OH DEAR LORD. NOT TONIGHT. WHAT'S HAPPENED?
RILEY AND ONE OF HIS EX-MILITARY BUDS HAD A CLOSE ENCOUNTER OF THE GHOSTLY KIND LAST NIGHT. IT ATTACKED RILEY...
OH, BUFFY, I'M SO SORRY. I--
HE'S AT THE HOSPITAL IN SOME SORT OF COMA--
KNOCK KNOCK
AH... EXCUSE ME.

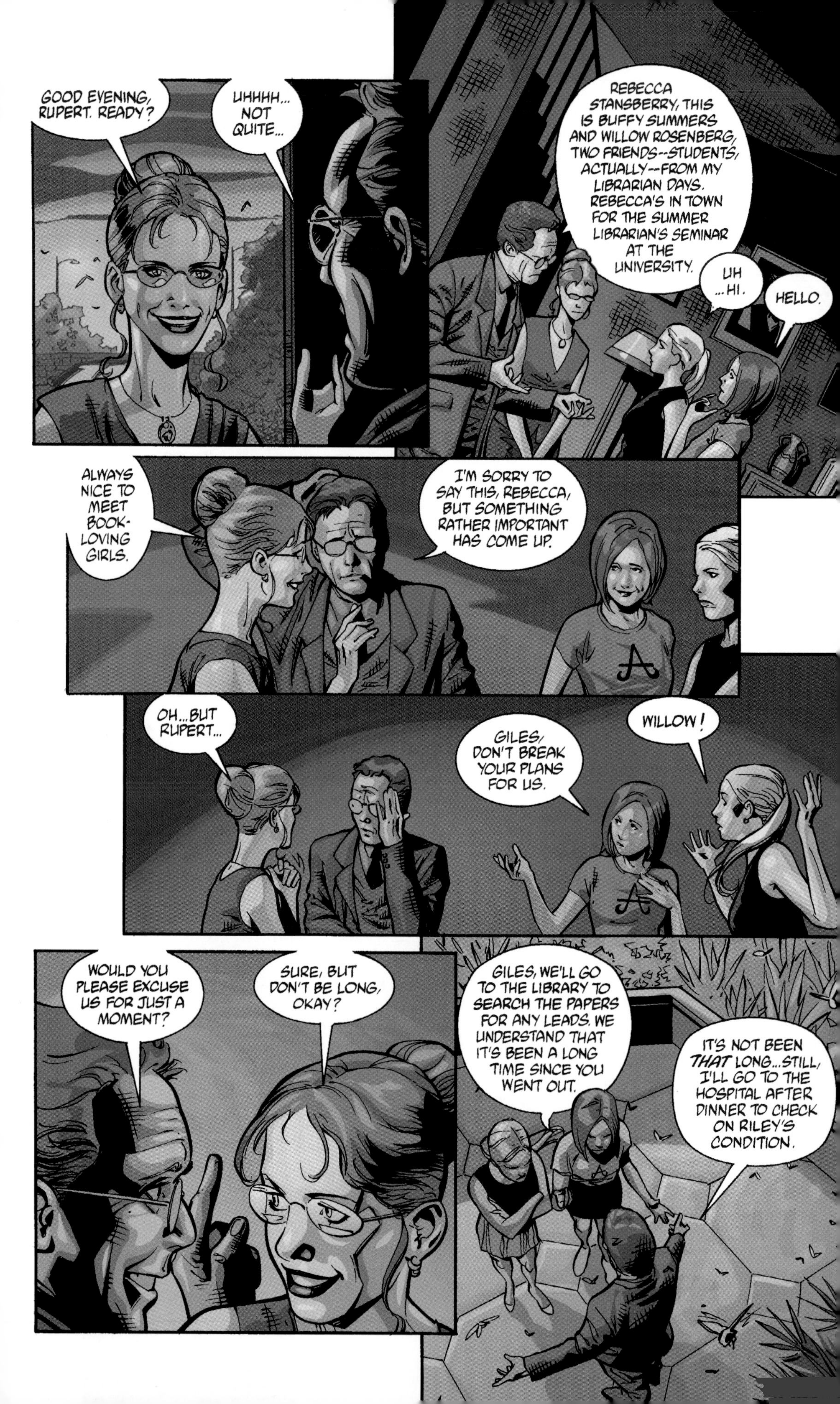
GOOD EVENING, RUPERT. READY?
UHHHH... NOT QUITE...
REBECCA STANSBERRY, THIS IS BUFFY SUMMERS AND WILLOW ROSENBERG, TWO FRIENDS--STUDENTS, ACTUALLY--FROM MY LIBRARIAN DAYS. REBECCA'S IN TOWN FOR THE SUMMER LIBRARIAN'S SEMINAR AT THE UNIVERSITY.
UH ...HI.
HELLO.
ALWAYS NICE TO MEET BOOK-LOVING GIRLS.
I'M SORRY TO SAY THIS, REBECCA, BUT SOMETHING RATHER IMPORTANT HAS COME UP.
OH...BUT RUPERT...
GILES, DON'T BREAK YOUR PLANS FOR US.
WILLOW!
WOULD YOU PLEASE EXCUSE US FOR JUST A MOMENT?
SURE, BUT DON'T BE LONG, OKAY?
GILES, WE'LL GO TO THE LIBRARY TO SEARCH THE PAPERS FOR ANY LEADS. WE UNDERSTAND THAT IT'S BEEN A LONG TIME SINCE YOU WENT OUT.
IT'S NOT BEEN THAT LONG...STILL, I'LL GO TO THE HOSPITAL AFTER DINNER TO CHECK ON RILEY'S CONDITION.

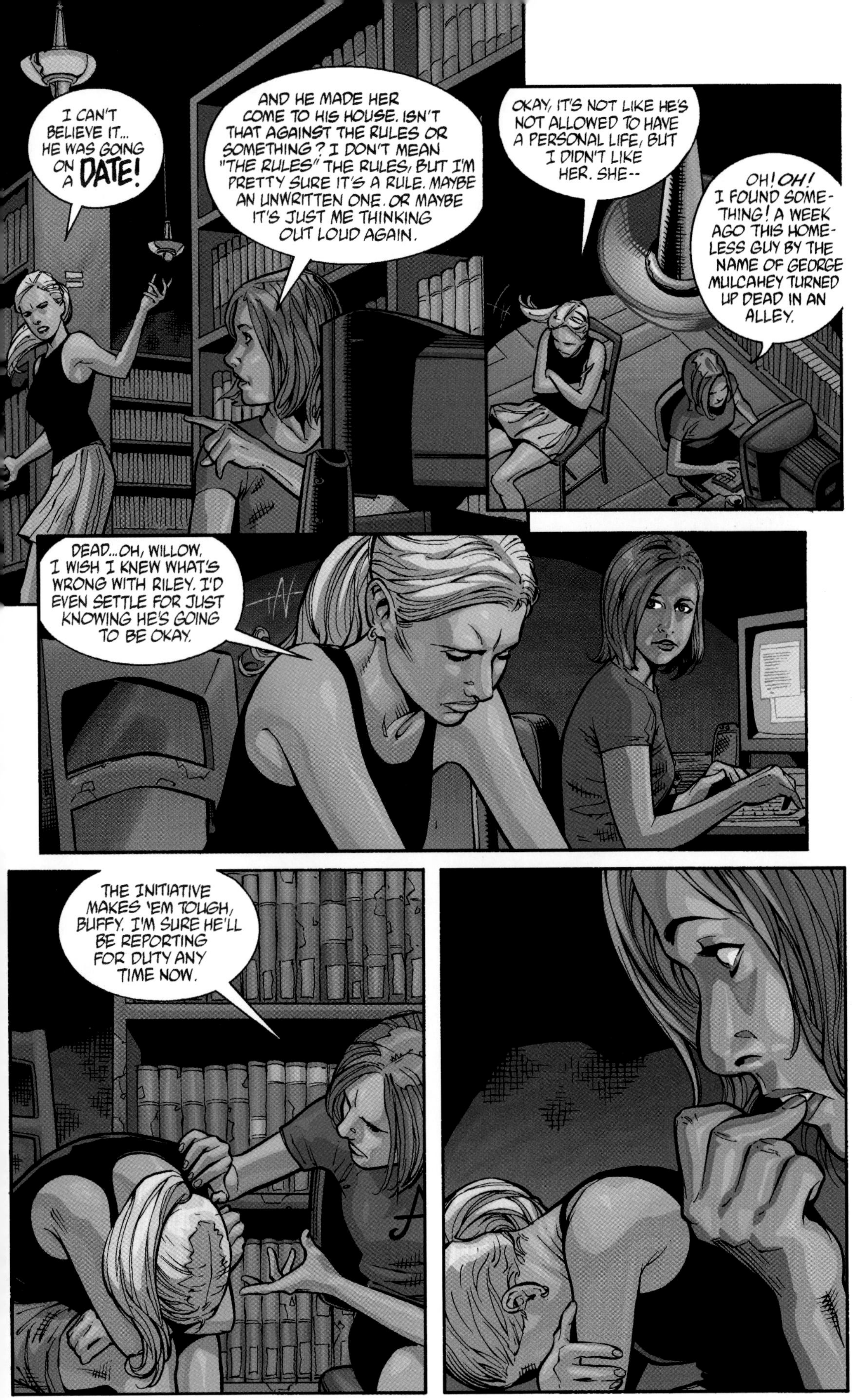
I CAN'T BELIEVE IT... HE WAS GOING ON A DATE!
AND HE MADE HER COME TO HIS HOUSE. ISN'T THAT AGAINST THE RULES OR SOMETHING? I DON'T MEAN "THE RULES" THE RULES, BUT I'M PRETTY SURE IT'S A RULE. MAYBE AN UNWRITTEN ONE. OR MAYBE IT'S JUST ME THINKING OUT LOUD AGAIN.
OKAY, IT'S NOT LIKE HE'S NOT ALLOWED TO HAVE A PERSONAL LIFE, BUT I DIDN'T LIKE HER. SHE--
OH! OH! I FOUND SOMETHING! A WEEK AGO THIS HOMELESS GUY BY THE NAME OF GEORGE MULCAHEY TURNED UP DEAD IN AN ALLEY.
DEAD...OH, WILLOW, I WISH I KNEW WHAT'S WRONG WITH RILEY. I'D EVEN SETTLE FOR JUST KNOWING HE'S GOING TO BE OKAY.
THE INITIATIVE MAKES 'EM TOUGH, BUFFY. I'M SURE HE'LL BE REPORTING FOR DUTY ANY TIME NOW.

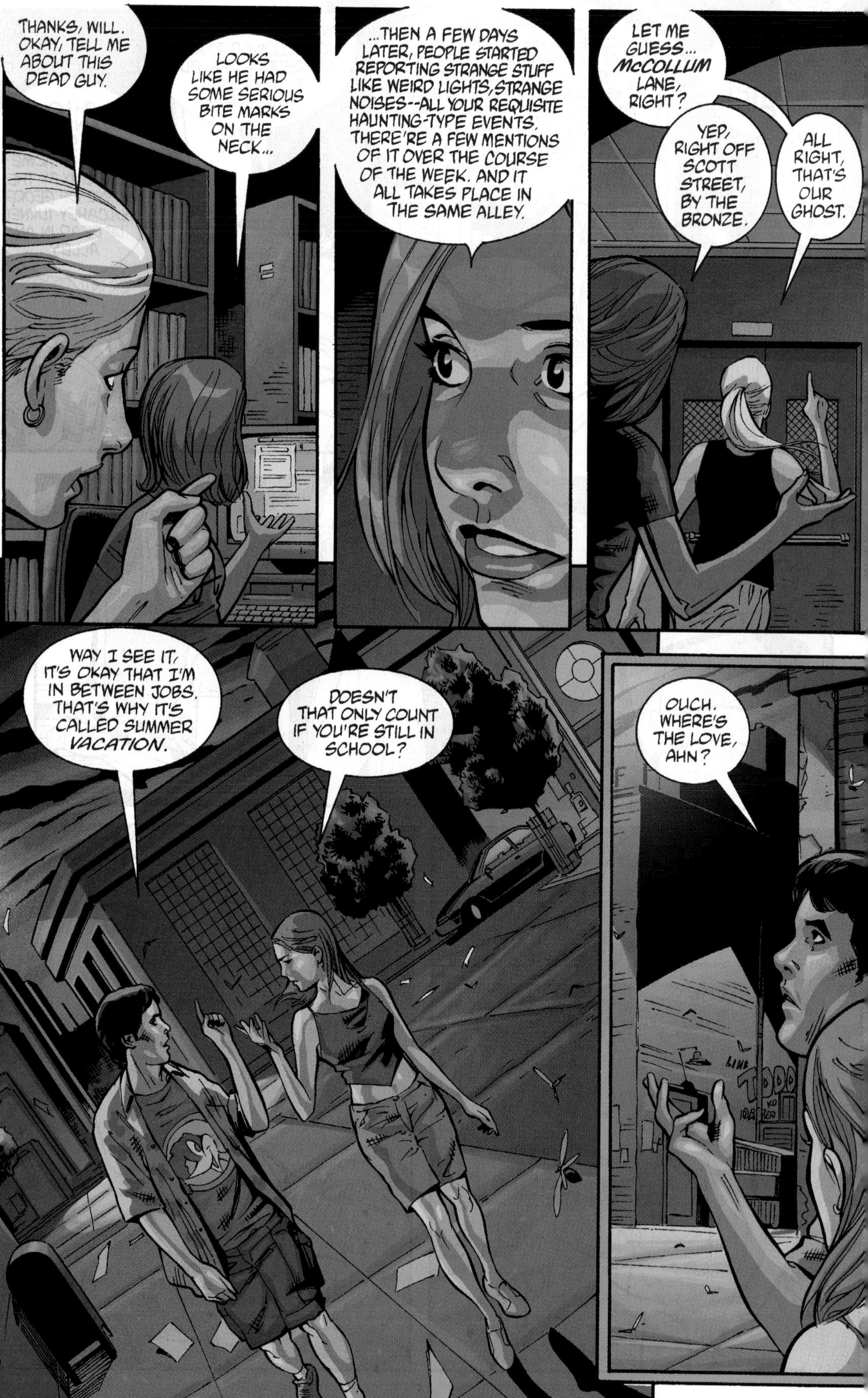
THANKS, WILL. OKAY, TELL ME ABOUT THIS DEAD GUY.
LOOKS LIKE HE HAD SOME SERIOUS BITE MARKS ON THE NECK...
...THEN A FEW DAYS LATER, PEOPLE STARTED REPORTING STRANGE STUFF LIKE WEIRD LIGHTS, STRANGE NOISES--ALL YOUR REQUISITE HAUNTING-TYPE EVENTS. THERE'RE A FEW MENTIONS OF IT OVER THE COURSE OF THE WEEK. AND IT ALL TAKES PLACE IN THE SAME ALLEY.
LET ME GUESS... McCOLLUM LANE, RIGHT?
YEP, RIGHT OFF SCOTT STREET, BY THE BRONZE.
ALL RIGHT, THAT'S OUR GHOST.
WAY I SEE IT, IT'S OKAY THAT I'M IN BETWEEN JOBS. THAT'S WHY IT'S CALLED SUMMER *VACATION*.
DOESN'T THAT ONLY COUNT IF YOU'RE STILL IN SCHOOL?
OUCH. WHERE'S THE LOVE, AHN?

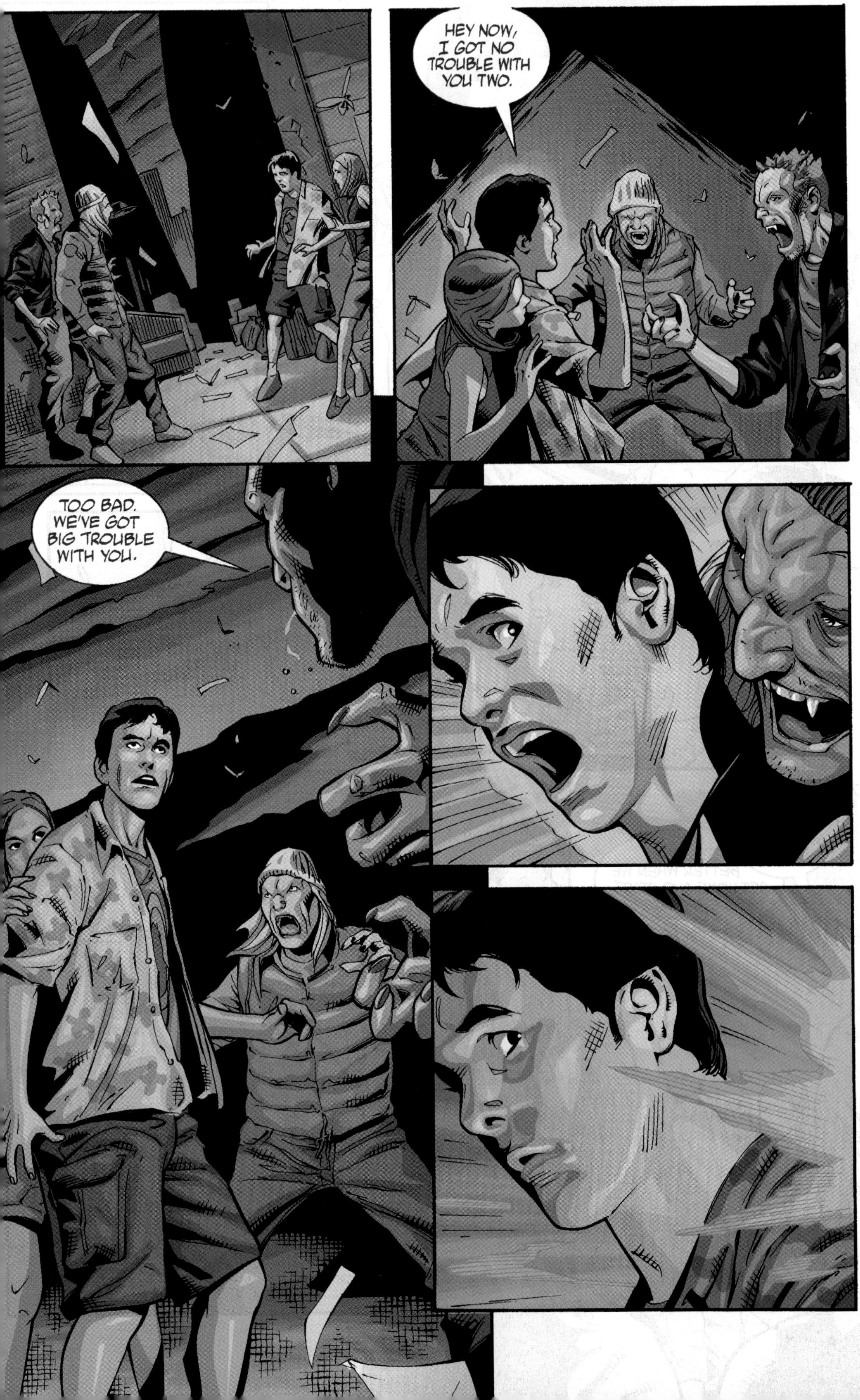
HEY NOW, I GOT NO TROUBLE WITH YOU TWO.
TOO BAD. WE'VE GOT BIG TROUBLE WITH YOU.

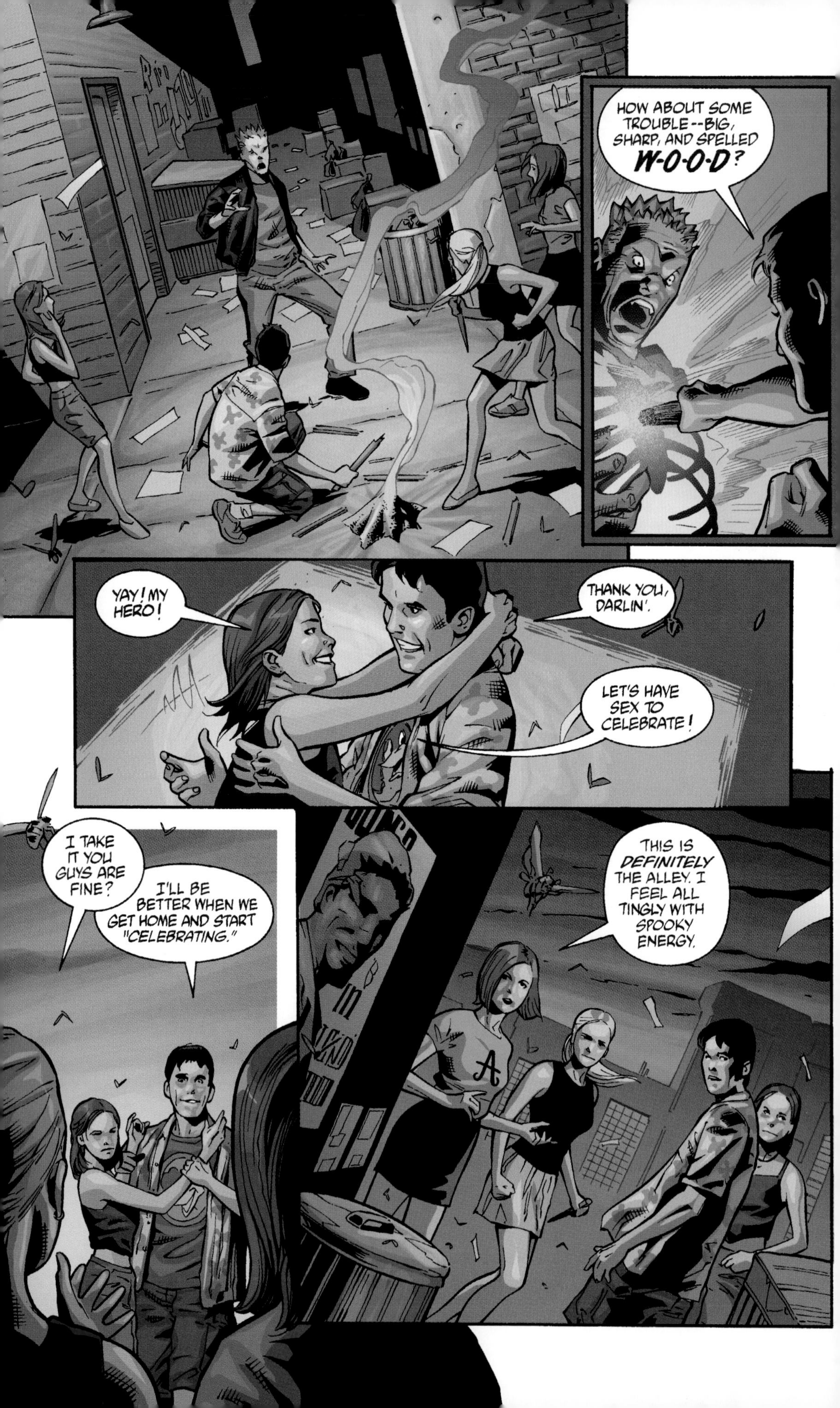
HOW ABOUT SOME TROUBLE--BIG, SHARP, AND SPELLED W-O-O-D?
YAY! MY HERO!
THANK YOU, DARLIN'.
LET'S HAVE SEX TO CELEBRATE!
I TAKE IT YOU GUYS ARE FINE?
I'LL BE BETTER WHEN WE GET HOME AND START "CELEBRATING."
THIS IS DEFINITELY THE ALLEY. I FEEL ALL TINGLY WITH SPOOKY ENERGY.

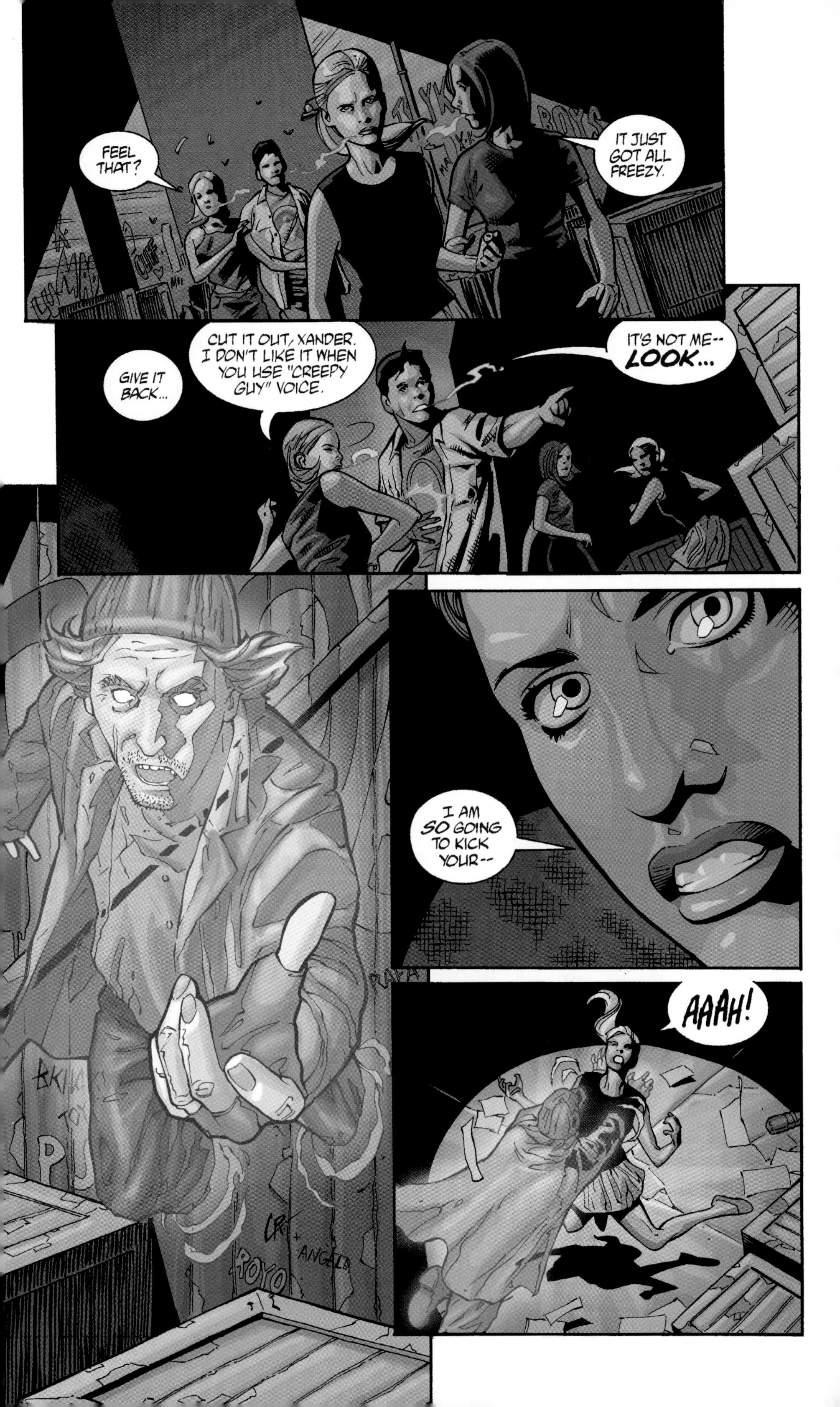

FEEL THAT?
IT JUST GOT ALL FREEZY.
GIVE IT BACK...
CUT IT OUT, XANDER. I DON'T LIKE IT WHEN YOU USE "CREEPY GUY" VOICE.
IT'S NOT ME-- LOOK...
I AM SO GOING TO KICK YOUR--
AAAH!

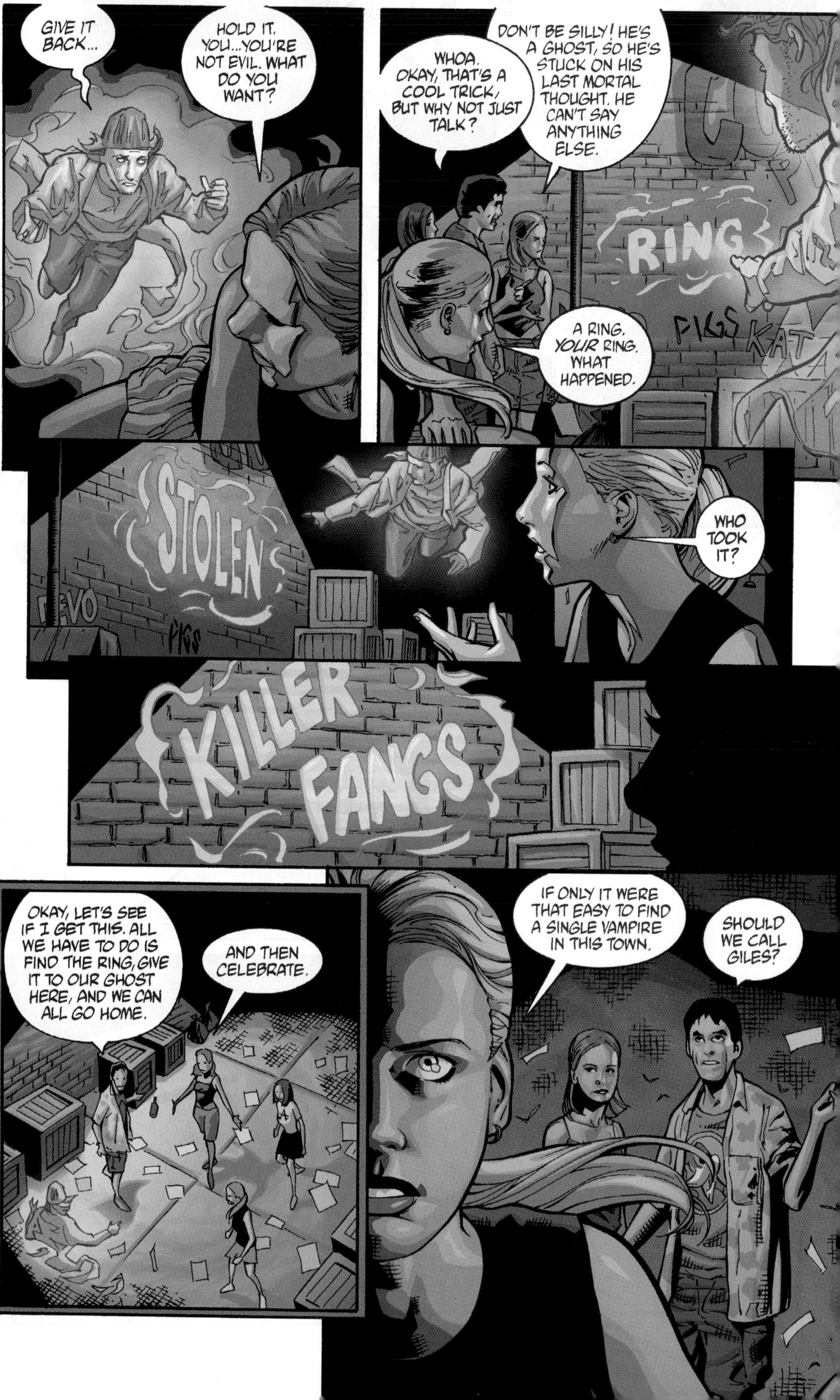
GIVE IT BACK...
HOLD IT. YOU...YOU'RE NOT EVIL. WHAT DO YOU WANT?
WHOA. OKAY, THAT'S A COOL TRICK, BUT WHY NOT JUST TALK?
DON'T BE SILLY! HE'S A GHOST, SO HE'S STUCK ON HIS LAST MORTAL THOUGHT. HE CAN'T SAY ANYTHING ELSE.
RING
PIGS KAT
A RING. *YOUR* RING. WHAT HAPPENED.
STOLEN
DEVO
PIGS
WHO TOOK IT?
KILLER FANGS
OKAY, LET'S SEE IF I GET THIS. ALL WE HAVE TO DO IS FIND THE RING, GIVE IT TO OUR GHOST HERE, AND WE CAN ALL GO HOME.
AND THEN CELEBRATE.
IF ONLY IT WERE THAT EASY TO FIND A SINGLE VAMPIRE IN THIS TOWN.
SHOULD WE CALL GILES?

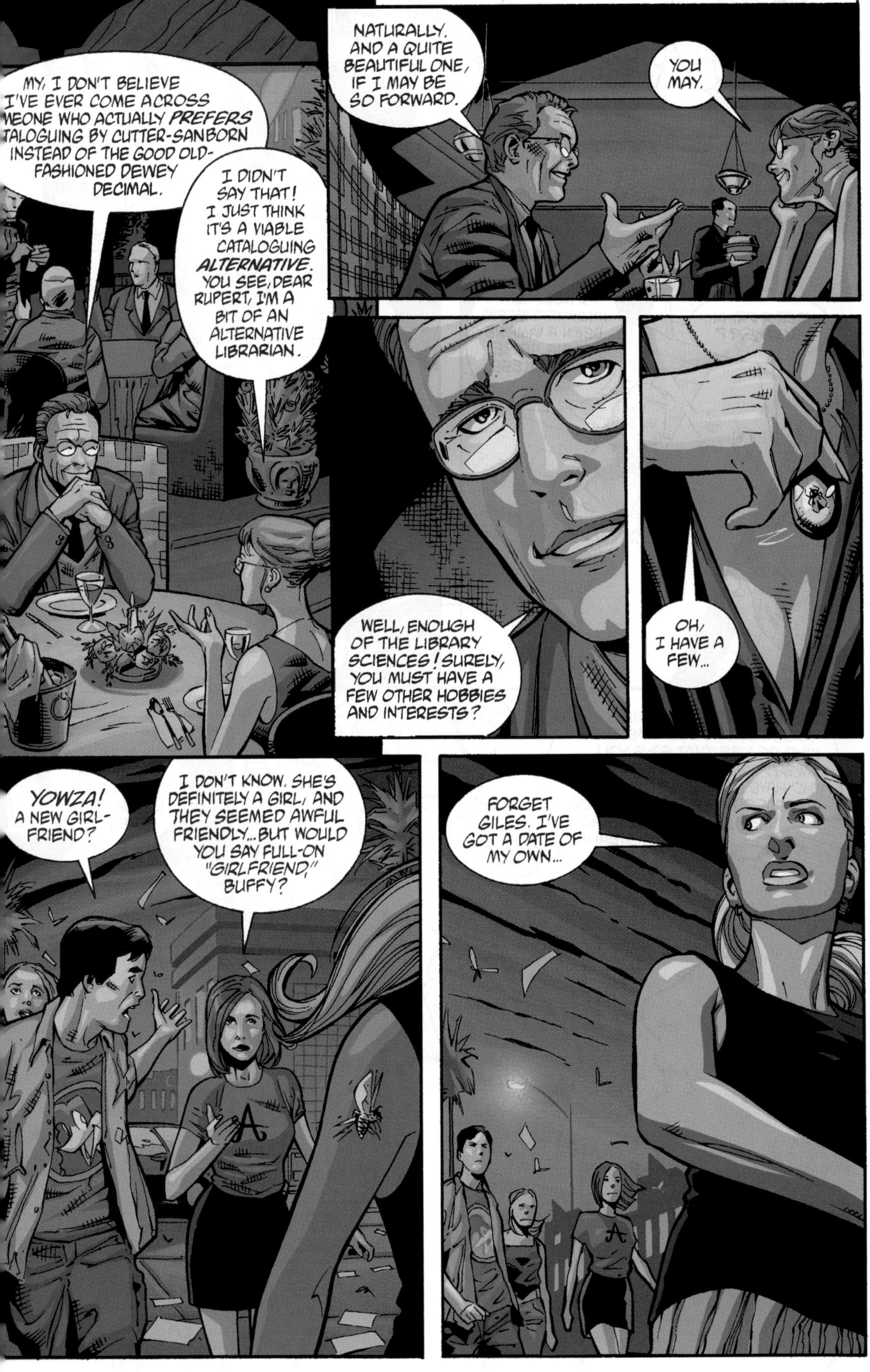
MY, I DON'T BELIEVE I'VE EVER COME ACROSS MEONE WHO ACTUALLY *PREFERS* TALOGUING BY CUTTER-SANBORN INSTEAD OF THE GOOD OLD-FASHIONED DEWEY DECIMAL.
I DIDN'T SAY THAT! I JUST THINK IT'S A VIABLE CATALOGUING ***ALTERNATIVE***. YOU SEE, DEAR RUPERT, I'M A BIT OF AN ALTERNATIVE LIBRARIAN.
NATURALLY. AND A QUITE BEAUTIFUL ONE, IF I MAY BE SO FORWARD.
YOU MAY.
WELL, ENOUGH OF THE LIBRARY SCIENCES! SURELY, YOU MUST HAVE A FEW OTHER HOBBIES AND INTERESTS?
OH, I HAVE A FEW...
YOWZA! A NEW GIRL-FRIEND?
I DON'T KNOW. SHE'S DEFINITELY A GIRL, AND THEY SEEMED AWFUL FRIENDLY...BUT WOULD YOU SAY FULL-ON "GIRLFRIEND," BUFFY?
FORGET GILES. I'VE GOT A DATE OF MY OWN...

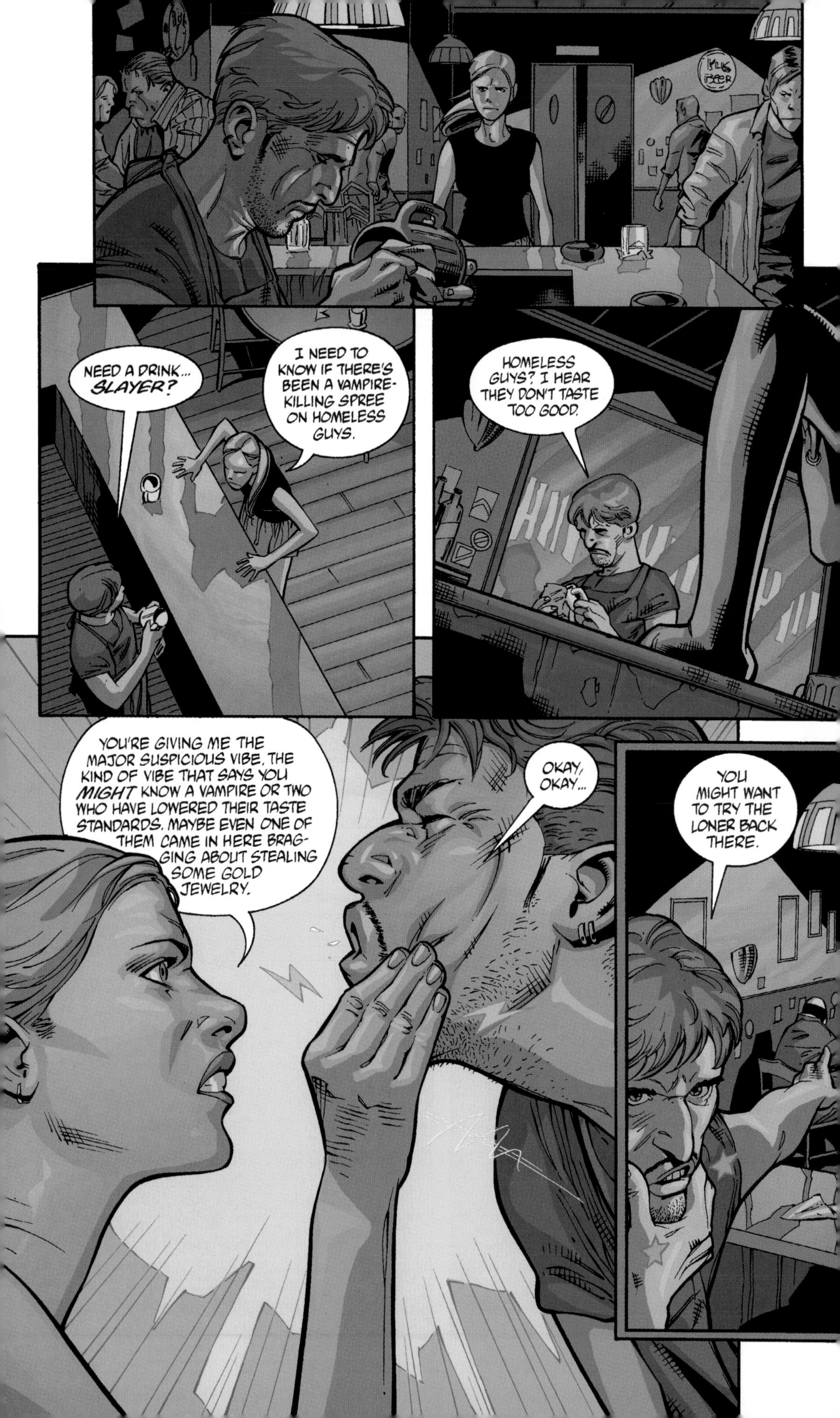
NEED A DRINK... *SLAYER?*
I NEED TO KNOW IF THERE'S BEEN A VAMPIRE-KILLING SPREE ON HOMELESS GUYS.
HOMELESS GUYS? I HEAR THEY DON'T TASTE TOO GOOD.
YOU'RE GIVING ME THE MAJOR SUSPICIOUS VIBE, THE KIND OF VIBE THAT SAYS YOU *MIGHT* KNOW A VAMPIRE OR TWO WHO HAVE LOWERED THEIR TASTE STANDARDS. MAYBE EVEN ONE OF THEM CAME IN HERE BRAGGING ABOUT STEALING SOME GOLD JEWELRY.
OKAY, OKAY...
YOU MIGHT WANT TO TRY THE LONER BACK THERE.

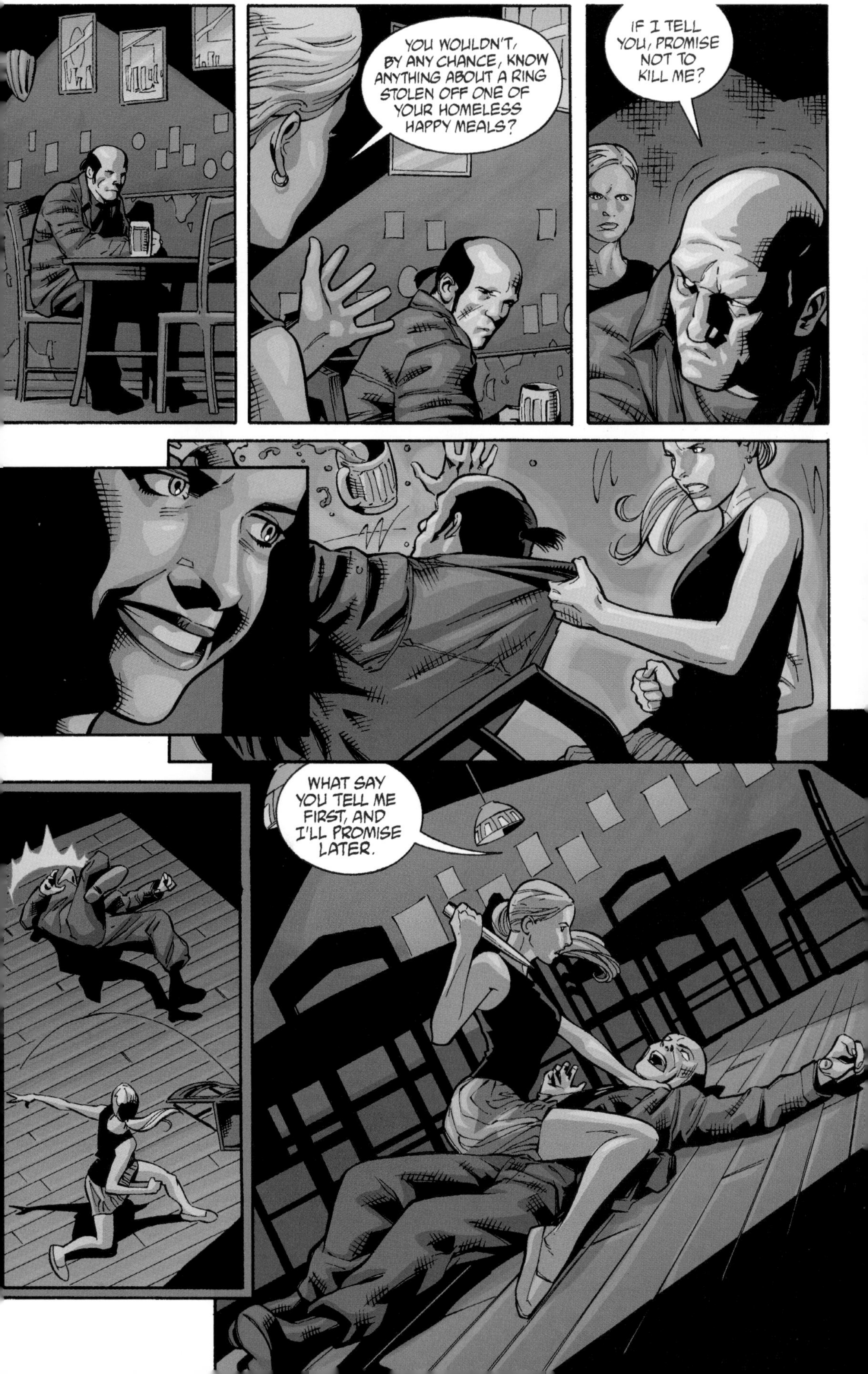
YOU WOULDN'T, BY ANY CHANCE, KNOW ANYTHING ABOUT A RING STOLEN OFF ONE OF YOUR HOMELESS HAPPY MEALS?
IF I TELL YOU, PROMISE NOT TO KILL ME?
WHAT SAY YOU TELL ME FIRST, AND I'LL PROMISE LATER.

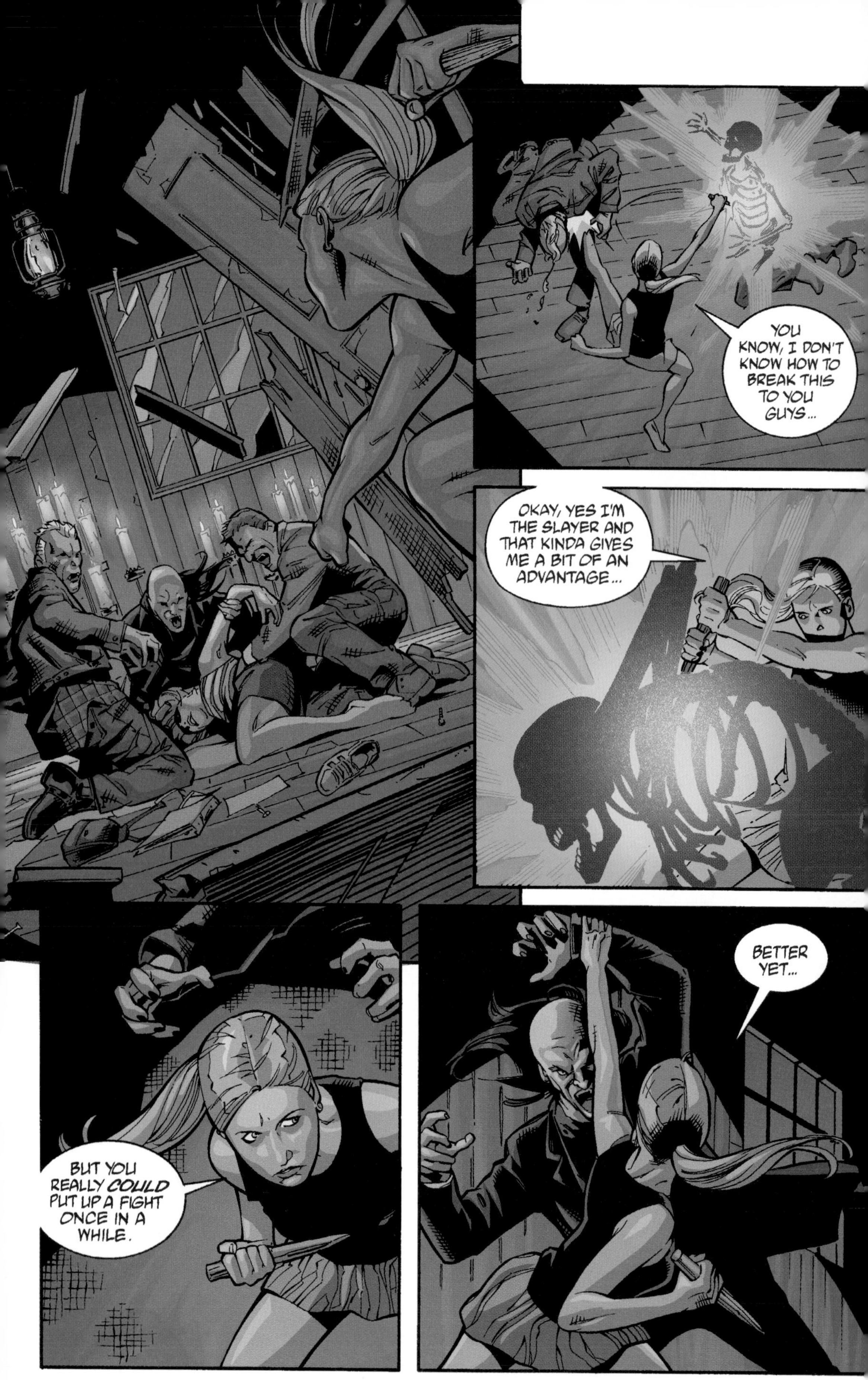
YOU KNOW, I DON'T KNOW HOW TO BREAK THIS TO YOU GUYS...
OKAY, YES I'M THE SLAYER AND THAT KINDA GIVES ME A BIT OF AN ADVANTAGE...
BUT YOU REALLY COULD PUT UP A FIGHT ONCE IN A WHILE.
BETTER YET...

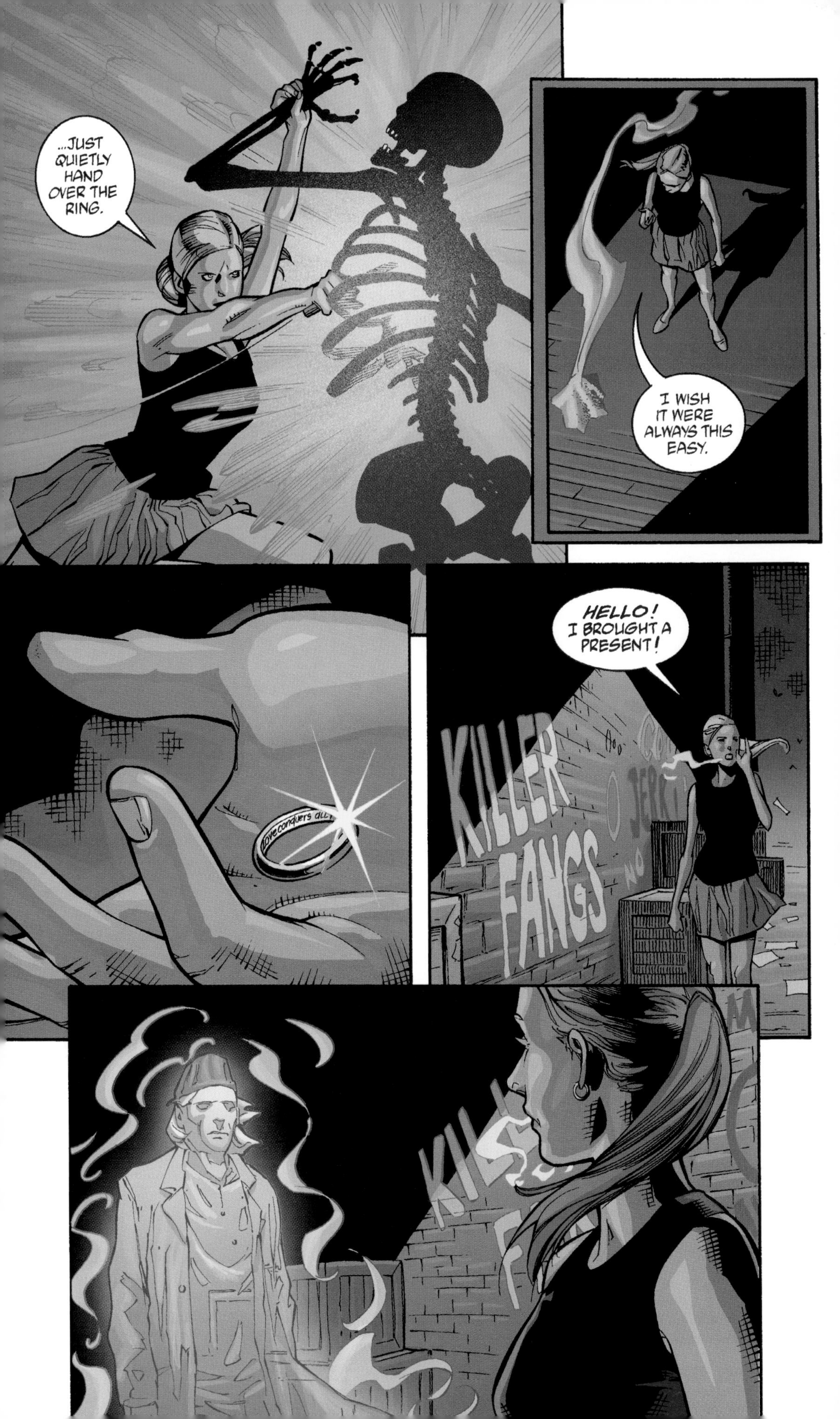
...JUST QUIETLY HAND OVER THE RING.
I WISH IT WERE ALWAYS THIS EASY.
love conquers all
HELLO! I BROUGHT A PRESENT!
KILLER FANGS

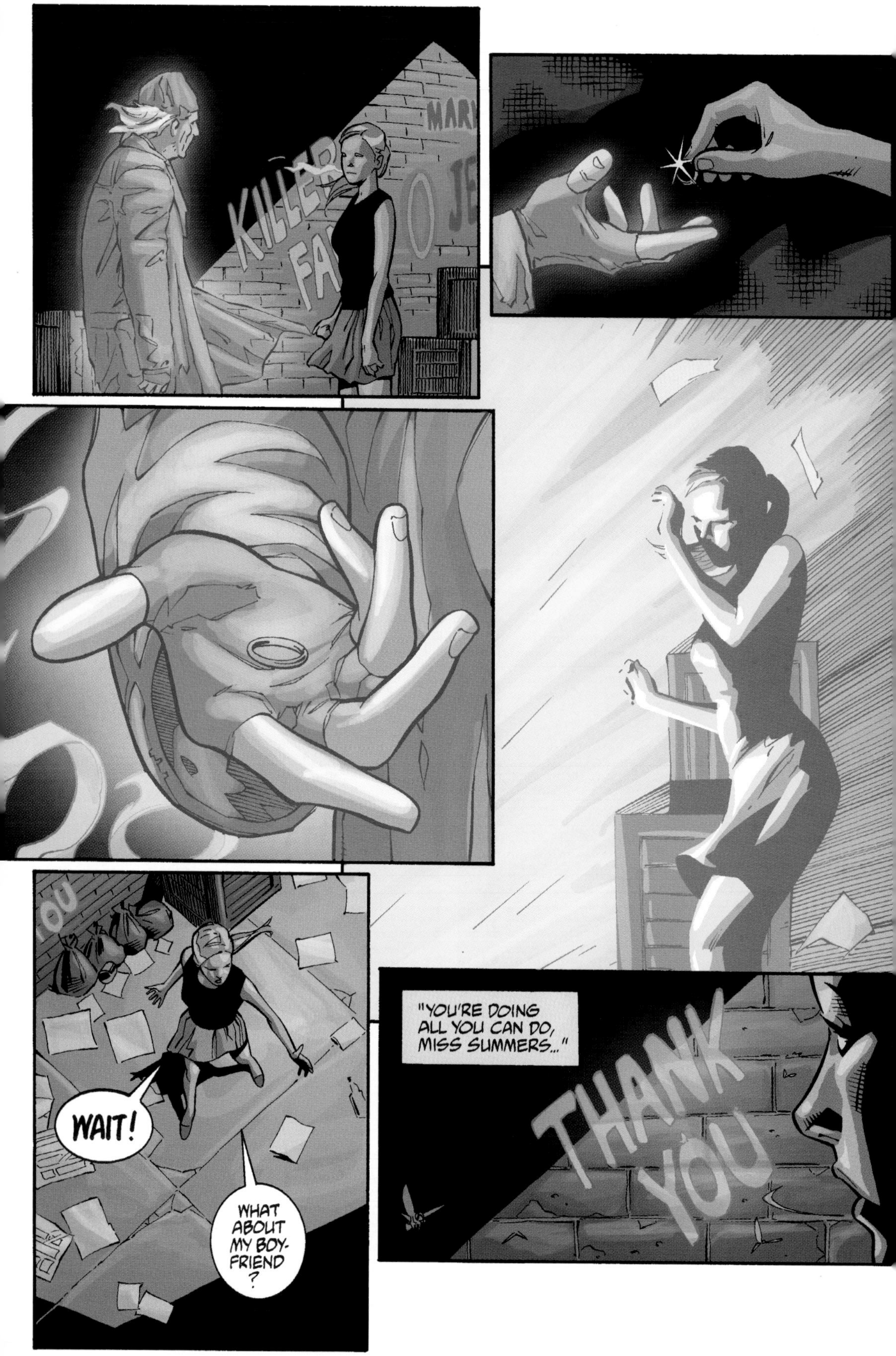
KILLER
MARK
"YOU'RE DOING ALL YOU CAN DO, MISS SUMMERS..."
THANK YOU
WAIT!
WHAT ABOUT MY BOY-FRIEND?

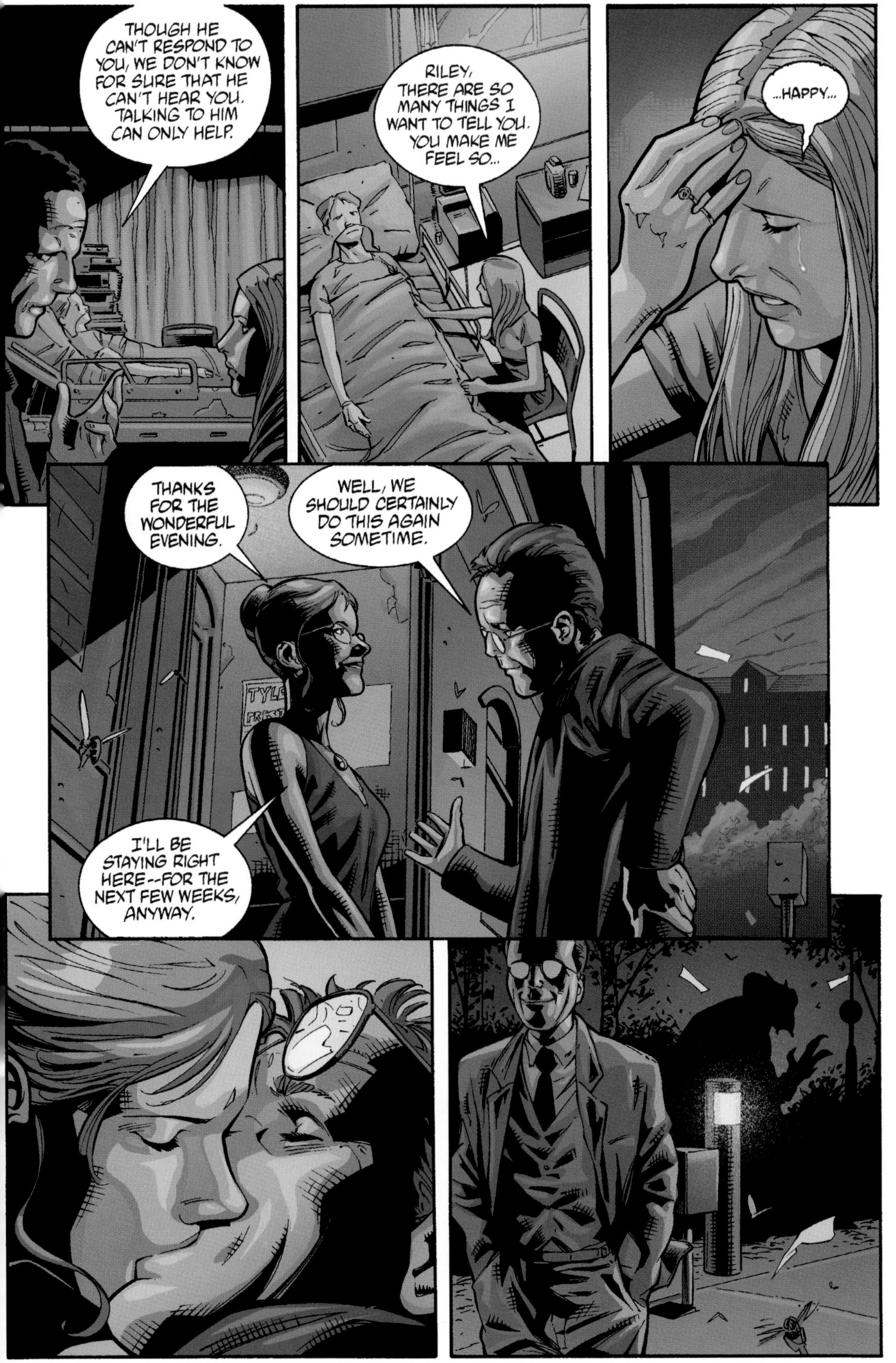
THOUGH HE CAN'T RESPOND TO YOU, WE DON'T KNOW FOR SURE THAT HE CAN'T HEAR YOU. TALKING TO HIM CAN ONLY HELP.
RILEY, THERE ARE SO MANY THINGS I WANT TO TELL YOU. YOU MAKE ME FEEL SO...
...HAPPY...
THANKS FOR THE WONDERFUL EVENING.
WELL, WE SHOULD CERTAINLY DO THIS AGAIN SOMETIME.
I'LL BE STAYING RIGHT HERE--FOR THE NEXT FEW WEEKS, ANYWAY.

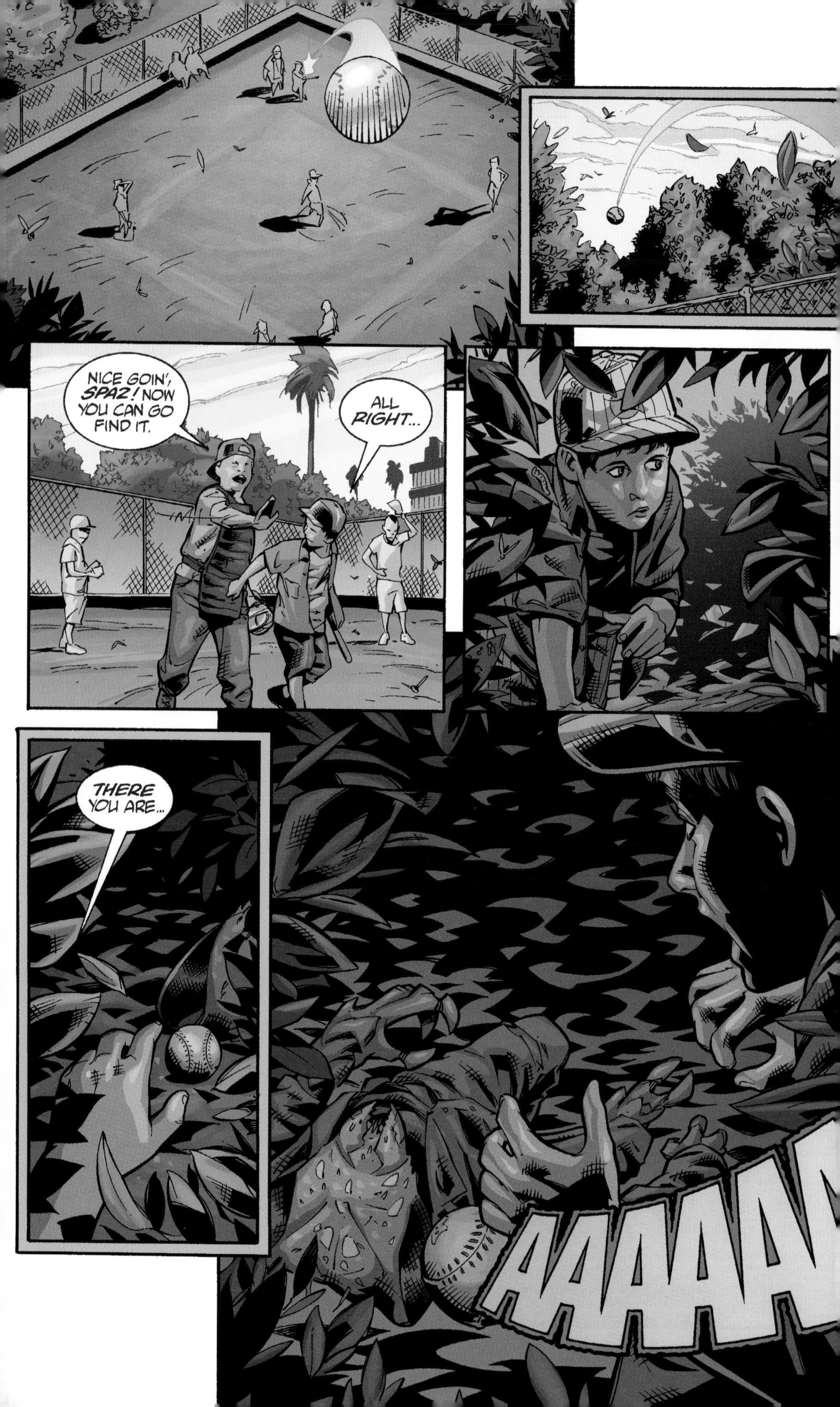
NICE GOIN', SPAZ! NOW YOU CAN GO FIND IT.
ALL RIGHT...
THERE YOU ARE...
AAAAA

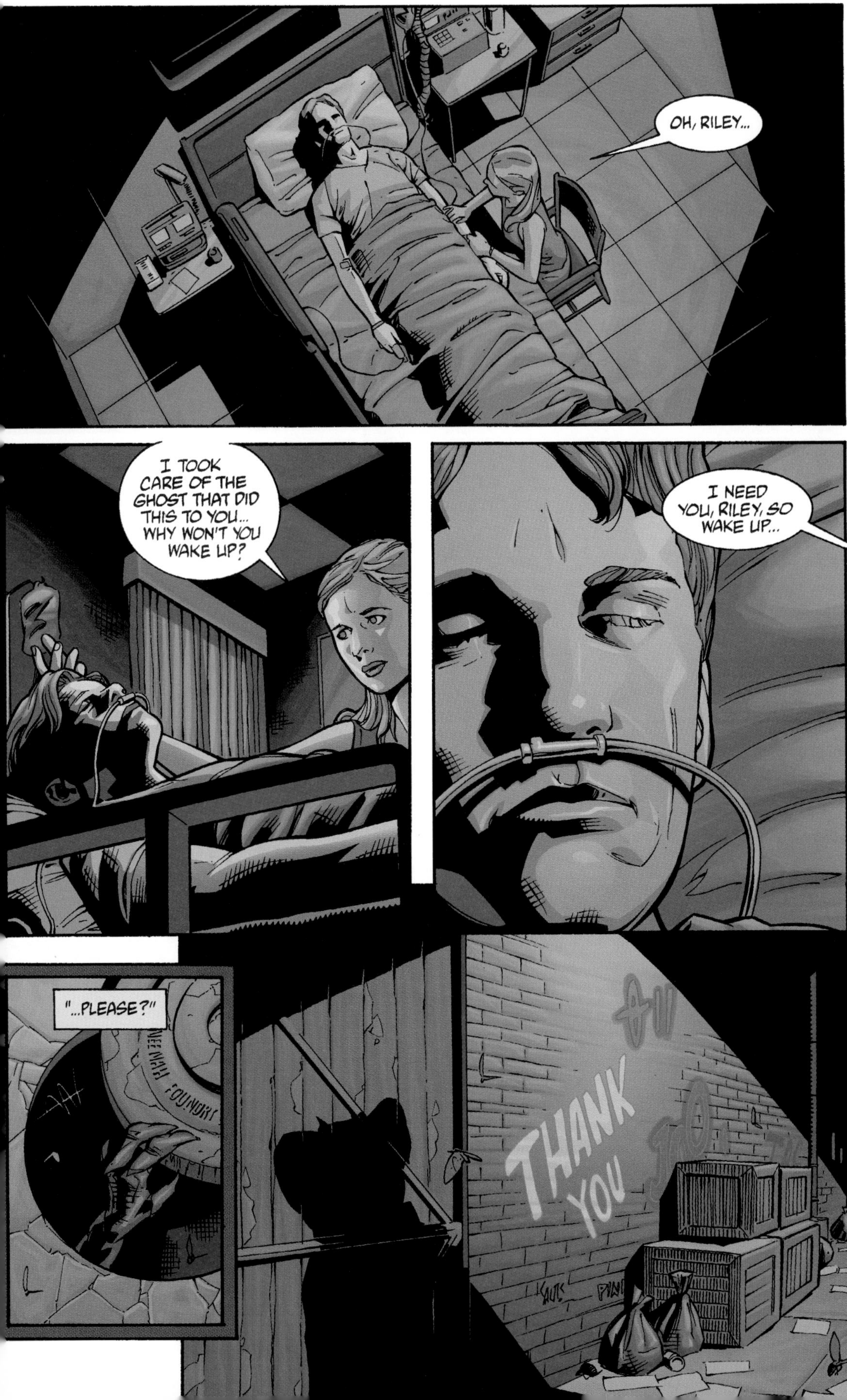
OH, RILEY...
I TOOK CARE OF THE GHOST THAT DID THIS TO YOU... WHY WON'T YOU WAKE UP?
I NEED YOU, RILEY, SO WAKE UP...
"...PLEASE?"
THANK YOU

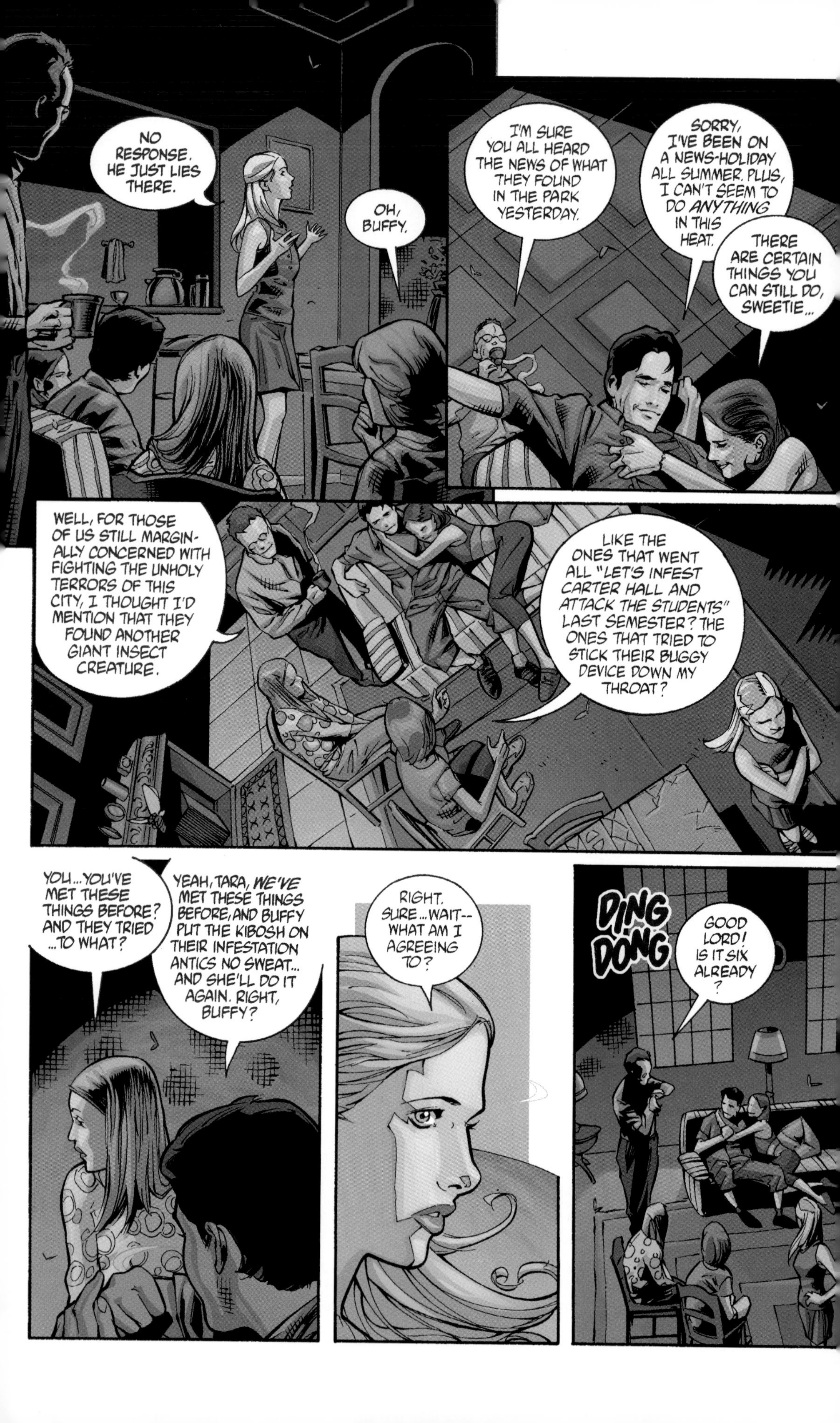

NO RESPONSE. HE JUST LIES THERE.
OH, BUFFY.
I'M SURE YOU ALL HEARD THE NEWS OF WHAT THEY FOUND IN THE PARK YESTERDAY.
SORRY, I'VE BEEN ON A NEWS-HOLIDAY ALL SUMMER. PLUS, I CAN'T SEEM TO DO *ANYTHING* IN THIS HEAT.
THERE ARE CERTAIN THINGS YOU CAN STILL DO, SWEETIE...
WELL, FOR THOSE OF US STILL MARGIN-ALLY CONCERNED WITH FIGHTING THE UNHOLY TERRORS OF THIS CITY, I THOUGHT I'D MENTION THAT THEY FOUND ANOTHER GIANT INSECT CREATURE.
LIKE THE ONES THAT WENT ALL "LET'S INFEST CARTER HALL AND ATTACK THE STUDENTS" LAST SEMESTER? THE ONES THAT TRIED TO STICK THEIR BUGGY DEVICE DOWN MY THROAT?
YOU...YOU'VE MET THESE THINGS BEFORE? AND THEY TRIED ...TO WHAT?
YEAH, TARA, *WE'VE* MET THESE THINGS BEFORE, AND BUFFY PUT THE KIBOSH ON THEIR INFESTATION ANTICS NO SWEAT... AND SHE'LL DO IT AGAIN. RIGHT, BUFFY?
RIGHT. SURE...WAIT-- WHAT AM I AGREEING TO?
DING DONG
GOOD LORD! IS IT SIX ALREADY?

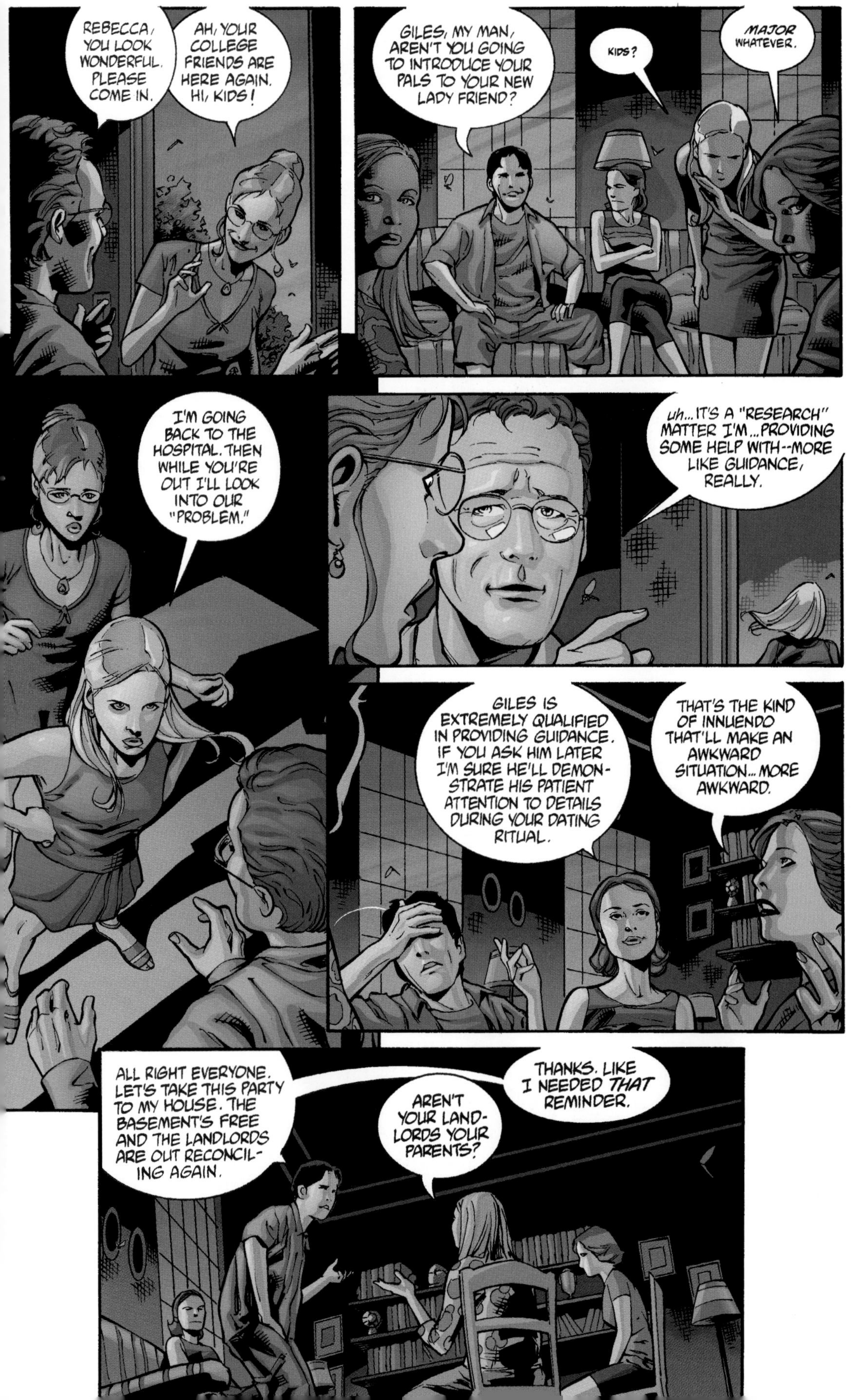
REBECCA, YOU LOOK WONDERFUL. PLEASE COME IN.
AH, YOUR COLLEGE FRIENDS ARE HERE AGAIN. HI, KIDS!
GILES, MY MAN, AREN'T YOU GOING TO INTRODUCE YOUR PALS TO YOUR NEW LADY FRIEND?
KIDS?
MAJOR WHATEVER.
I'M GOING BACK TO THE HOSPITAL. THEN WHILE YOU'RE OUT I'LL LOOK INTO OUR "PROBLEM."
uh... IT'S A "RESEARCH" MATTER I'M... PROVIDING SOME HELP WITH--MORE LIKE GUIDANCE, REALLY.
GILES IS EXTREMELY QUALIFIED IN PROVIDING GUIDANCE. IF YOU ASK HIM LATER I'M SURE HE'LL DEMON-STRATE HIS PATIENT ATTENTION TO DETAILS DURING YOUR DATING RITUAL.
THAT'S THE KIND OF INNUENDO THAT'LL MAKE AN AWKWARD SITUATION... MORE AWKWARD.
ALL RIGHT EVERYONE. LET'S TAKE THIS PARTY TO MY HOUSE. THE BASEMENT'S FREE AND THE LANDLORDS ARE OUT RECONCIL-ING AGAIN.
AREN'T YOUR LAND-LORDS YOUR PARENTS?
THANKS. LIKE I NEEDED THAT REMINDER.

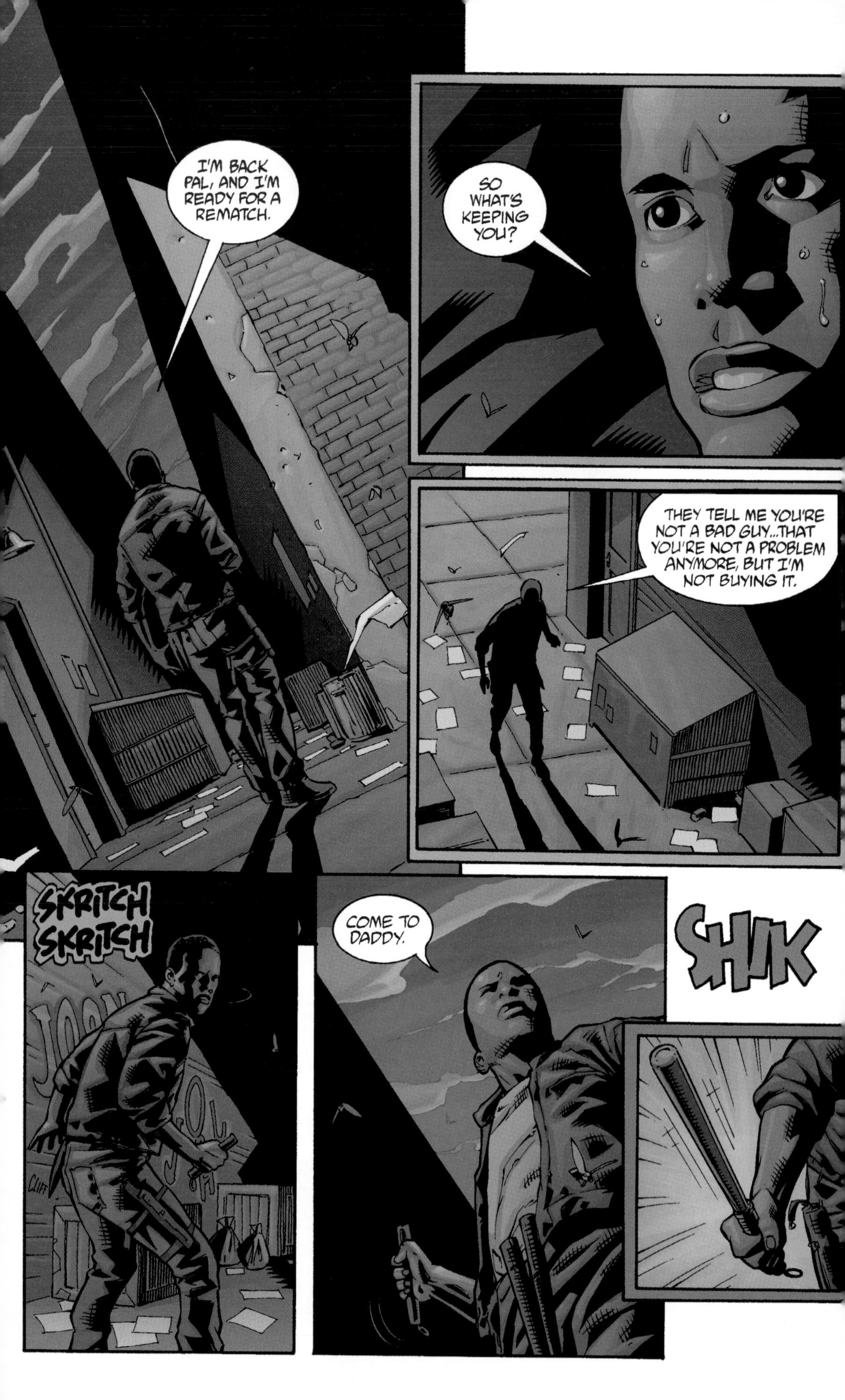
I'M BACK PAL, AND I'M READY FOR A REMATCH.
SO WHAT'S KEEPING YOU?
THEY TELL ME YOU'RE NOT A BAD GUY...THAT YOU'RE NOT A PROBLEM ANYMORE, BUT I'M NOT BUYING IT.
SKRITCH SKRITCH
COME TO DADDY.
SHUK

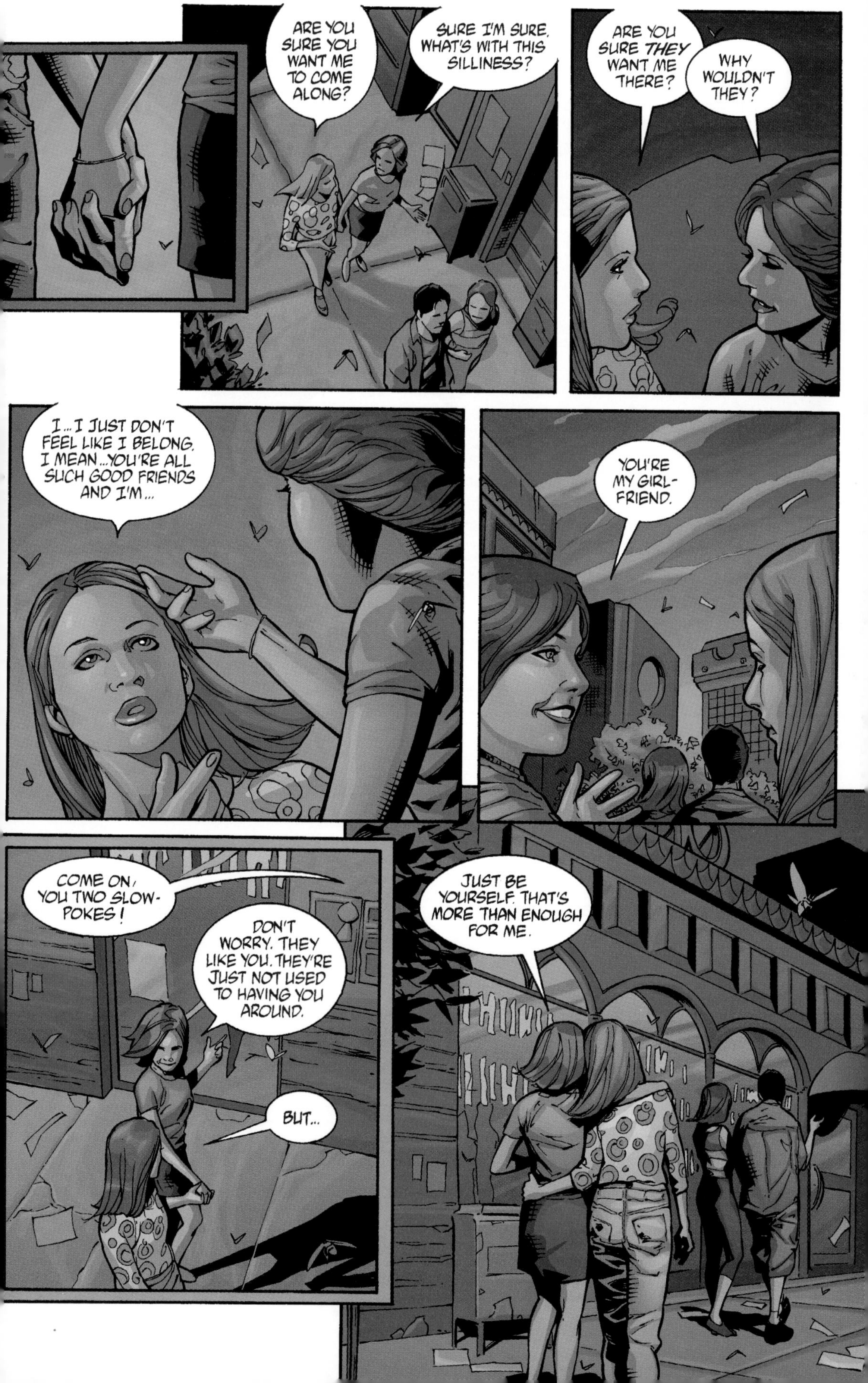
ARE YOU SURE YOU WANT ME TO COME ALONG?
SURE I'M SURE. WHAT'S WITH THIS SILLINESS?
ARE YOU SURE *THEY* WANT ME THERE?
WHY WOULDN'T THEY?
I... I JUST DON'T FEEL LIKE I BELONG. I MEAN... YOU'RE ALL SUCH GOOD FRIENDS AND I'M...
YOU'RE MY GIRL-FRIEND.
COME ON, YOU TWO SLOW-POKES!
DON'T WORRY. THEY LIKE YOU. THEY'RE JUST NOT USED TO HAVING YOU AROUND.
BUT...
JUST BE YOURSELF. THAT'S MORE THAN ENOUGH FOR ME.

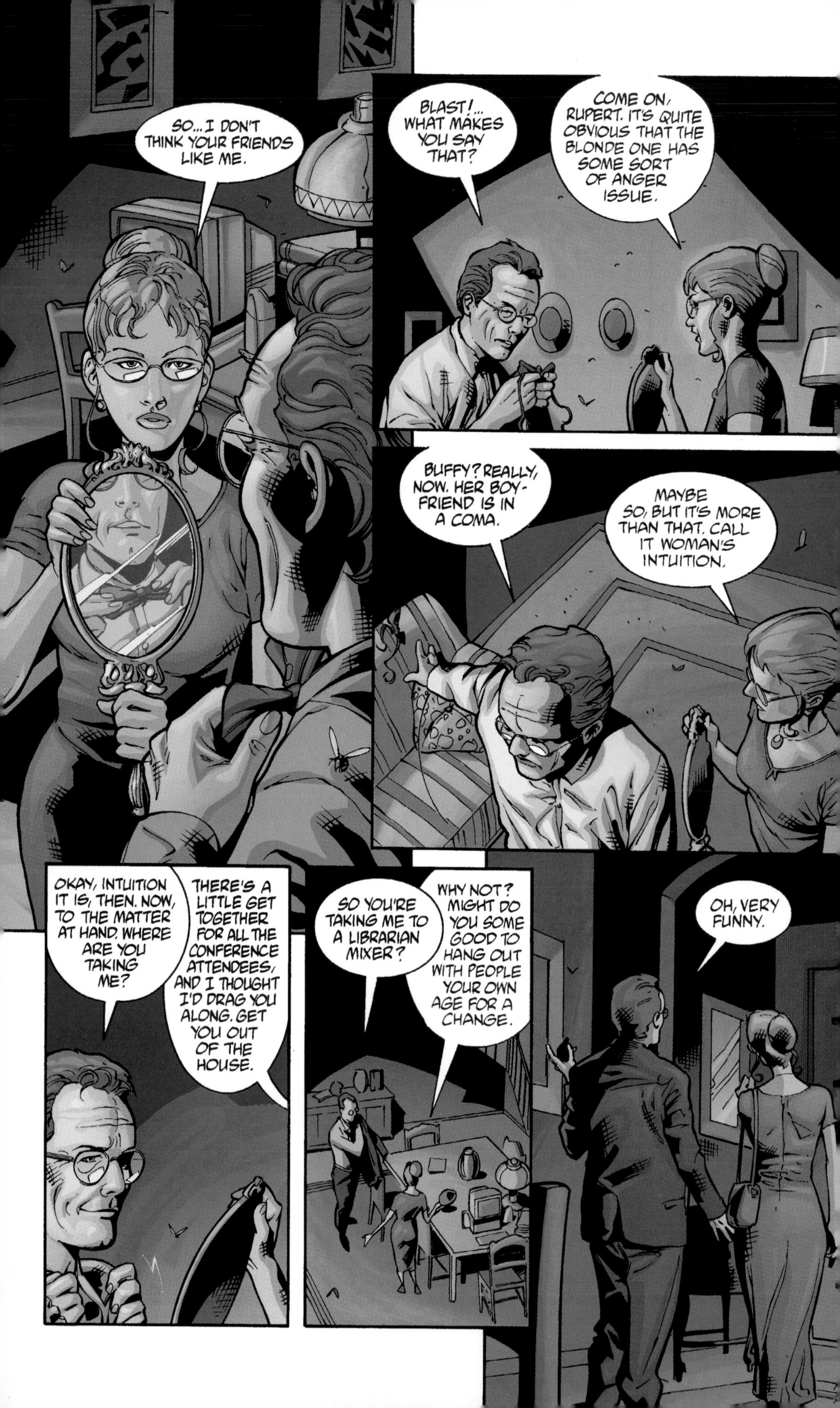
SO... I DON'T THINK YOUR FRIENDS LIKE ME.
BLAST!... WHAT MAKES YOU SAY THAT?
COME ON, RUPERT. IT'S QUITE OBVIOUS THAT THE BLONDE ONE HAS SOME SORT OF ANGER ISSUE.
BUFFY? REALLY, NOW. HER BOY-FRIEND IS IN A COMA.
MAYBE SO, BUT IT'S MORE THAN THAT. CALL IT WOMAN'S INTUITION.
OKAY, INTUITION IT IS, THEN. NOW, TO THE MATTER AT HAND. WHERE ARE YOU TAKING ME?
THERE'S A LITTLE GET TOGETHER FOR ALL THE CONFERENCE ATTENDEES, AND I THOUGHT I'D DRAG YOU ALONG. GET YOU OUT OF THE HOUSE.
SO YOU'RE TAKING ME TO A LIBRARIAN MIXER?
WHY NOT? MIGHT DO YOU SOME GOOD TO HANG OUT WITH PEOPLE YOUR OWN AGE FOR A CHANGE.
OH, VERY FUNNY.

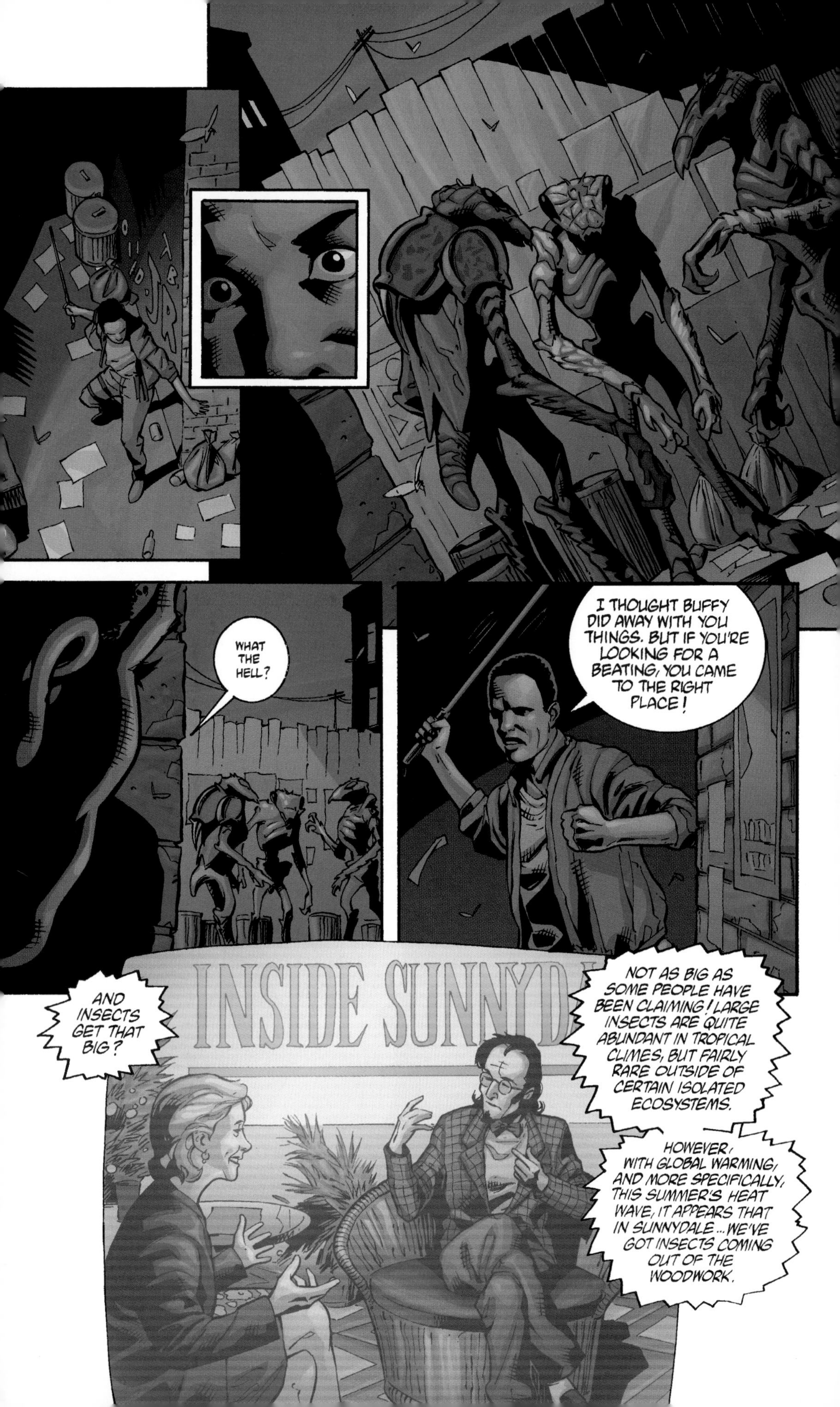
T B
JR
WHAT THE HELL?
I THOUGHT BUFFY DID AWAY WITH YOU THINGS. BUT IF YOU'RE LOOKING FOR A BEATING, YOU CAME TO THE RIGHT PLACE!
INSIDE SUNNYD
AND INSECTS GET THAT BIG?
NOT AS BIG AS SOME PEOPLE HAVE BEEN CLAIMING! LARGE INSECTS ARE QUITE ABUNDANT IN TROPICAL CLIMES, BUT FAIRLY RARE OUTSIDE OF CERTAIN ISOLATED ECOSYSTEMS.
HOWEVER, WITH GLOBAL WARMING, AND MORE SPECIFICALLY, THIS SUMMER'S HEAT WAVE, IT APPEARS THAT IN SUNNYDALE ... WE'VE GOT INSECTS COMING OUT OF THE WOODWORK.

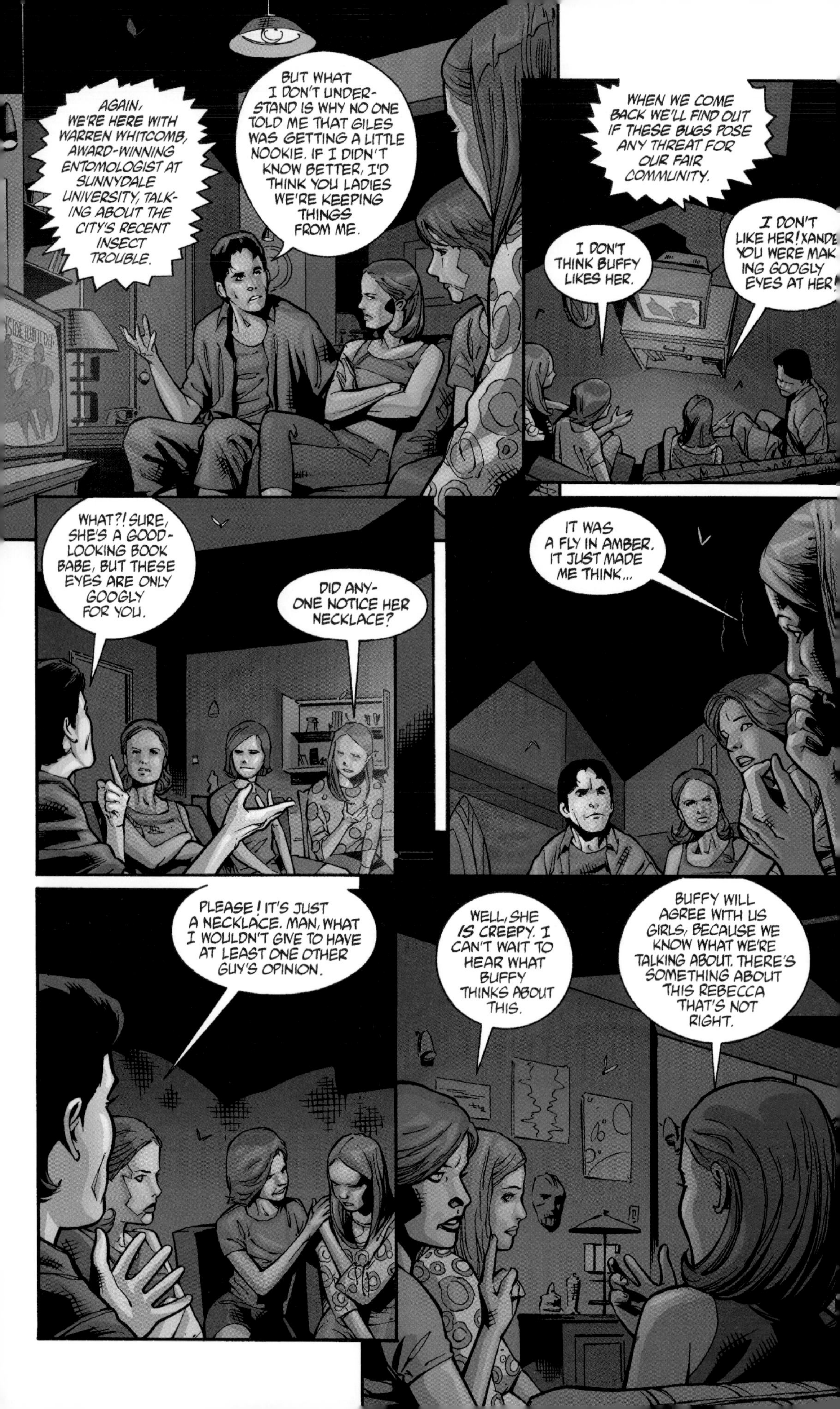
AGAIN, WE'RE HERE WITH WARREN WHITCOMB, AWARD-WINNING ENTOMOLOGIST AT SUNNYDALE UNIVERSITY, TALKING ABOUT THE CITY'S RECENT INSECT TROUBLE.
BUT WHAT I DON'T UNDERSTAND IS WHY NO ONE TOLD ME THAT GILES WAS GETTING A LITTLE NOOKIE. IF I DIDN'T KNOW BETTER, I'D THINK YOU LADIES WE'RE KEEPING THINGS FROM ME.
WHEN WE COME BACK WE'LL FIND OUT IF THESE BUGS POSE ANY THREAT FOR OUR FAIR COMMUNITY.
I DON'T THINK BUFFY LIKES HER.
I DON'T LIKE HER! XANDE YOU WERE MAKING GOOGLY EYES AT HER!
WHAT?! SURE, SHE'S A GOOD-LOOKING BOOK BABE, BUT THESE EYES ARE ONLY GOOGLY FOR YOU.
DID ANYONE NOTICE HER NECKLACE?
IT WAS A FLY IN AMBER. IT JUST MADE ME THINK...
PLEASE! IT'S JUST A NECKLACE. MAN, WHAT I WOULDN'T GIVE TO HAVE AT LEAST ONE OTHER GUY'S OPINION.
WELL, SHE *IS* CREEPY. I CAN'T WAIT TO HEAR WHAT BUFFY THINKS ABOUT THIS.
BUFFY WILL AGREE WITH US GIRLS, BECAUSE WE KNOW WHAT WE'RE TALKING ABOUT. THERE'S SOMETHING ABOUT THIS REBECCA THAT'S NOT RIGHT.

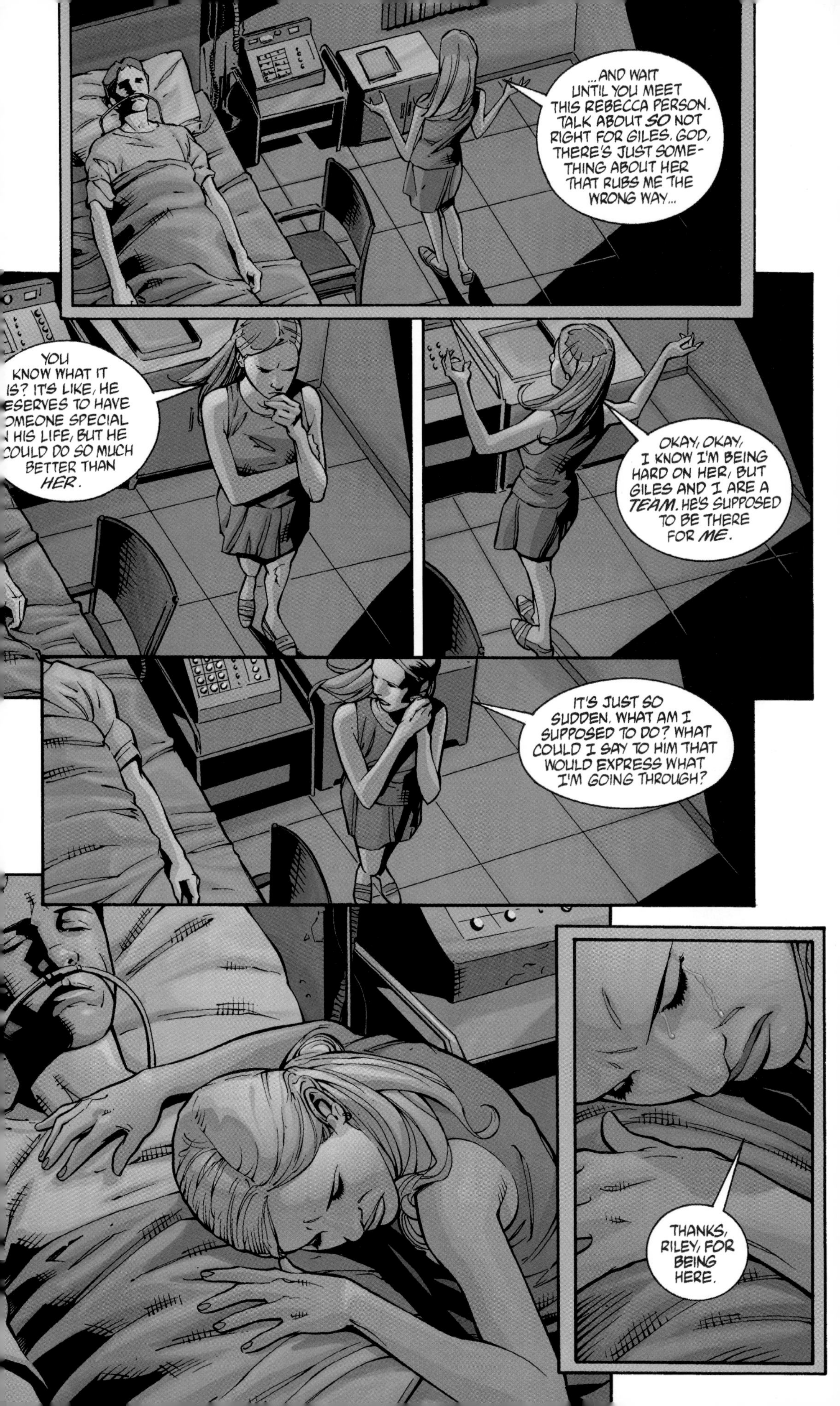
...AND WAIT UNTIL YOU MEET THIS REBECCA PERSON. TALK ABOUT SO NOT RIGHT FOR GILES. GOD, THERE'S JUST SOMETHING ABOUT HER THAT RUBS ME THE WRONG WAY...
YOU KNOW WHAT IT IS? IT'S LIKE, HE DESERVES TO HAVE SOMEONE SPECIAL IN HIS LIFE, BUT HE COULD DO SO MUCH BETTER THAN HER.
OKAY, OKAY, I KNOW I'M BEING HARD ON HER, BUT GILES AND I ARE A TEAM. HE'S SUPPOSED TO BE THERE FOR ME.
IT'S JUST SO SUDDEN. WHAT AM I SUPPOSED TO DO? WHAT COULD I SAY TO HIM THAT WOULD EXPRESS WHAT I'M GOING THROUGH?
THANKS, RILEY, FOR BEING HERE.

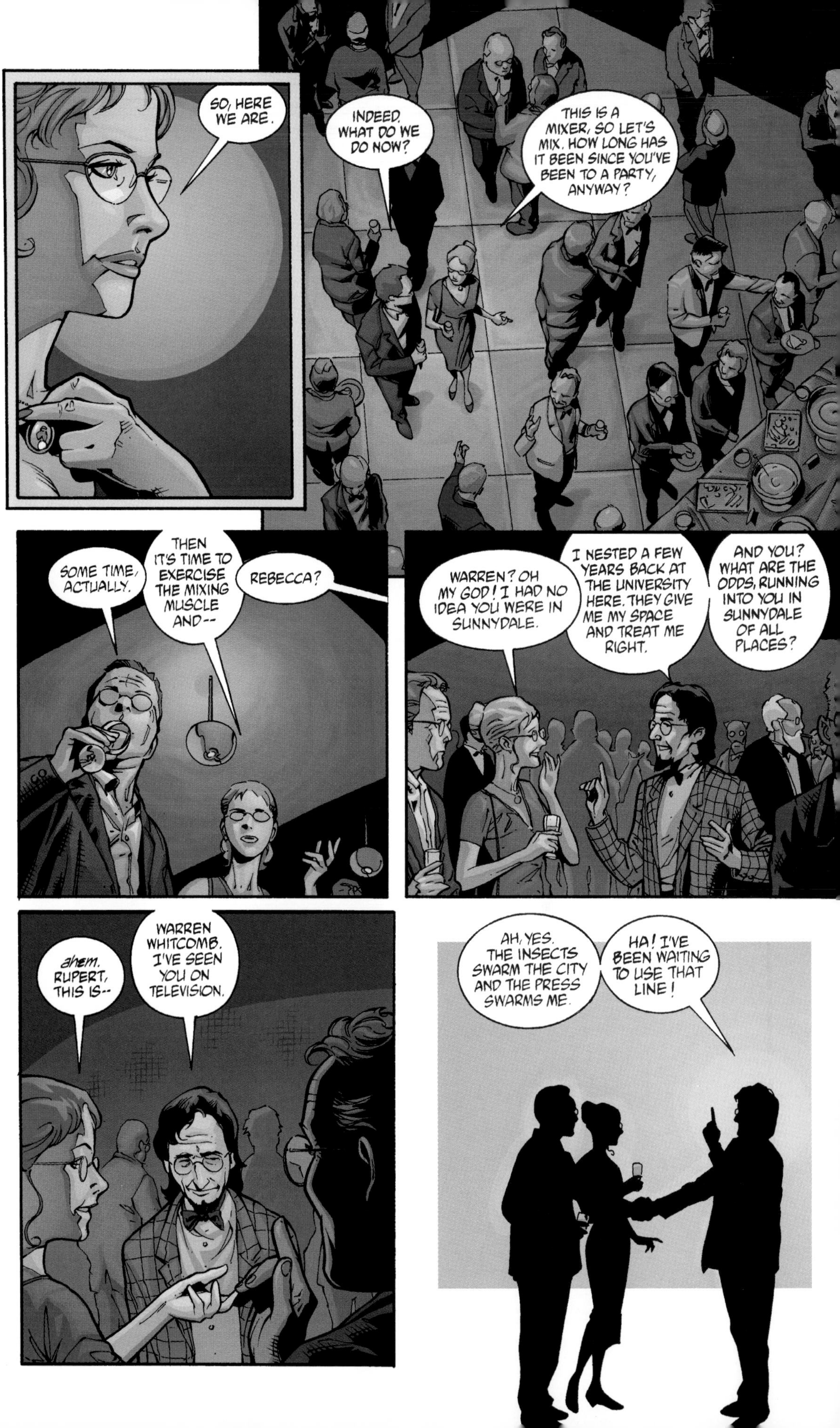
SO, HERE WE ARE.
INDEED. WHAT DO WE DO NOW?
THIS IS A MIXER, SO LET'S MIX. HOW LONG HAS IT BEEN SINCE YOU'VE BEEN TO A PARTY, ANYWAY?
SOME TIME, ACTUALLY.
THEN IT'S TIME TO EXERCISE THE MIXING MUSCLE AND--
REBECCA?
WARREN? OH MY GOD! I HAD NO IDEA YOU WERE IN SUNNYDALE.
I NESTED A FEW YEARS BACK AT THE UNIVERSITY HERE. THEY GIVE ME MY SPACE AND TREAT ME RIGHT.
AND YOU? WHAT ARE THE ODDS, RUNNING INTO YOU IN SUNNYDALE OF ALL PLACES?
ahem. RUPERT, THIS IS--
WARREN WHITCOMB. I'VE SEEN YOU ON TELEVISION.
AH, YES. THE INSECTS SWARM THE CITY AND THE PRESS SWARMS ME.
HA! I'VE BEEN WAITING TO USE THAT LINE!

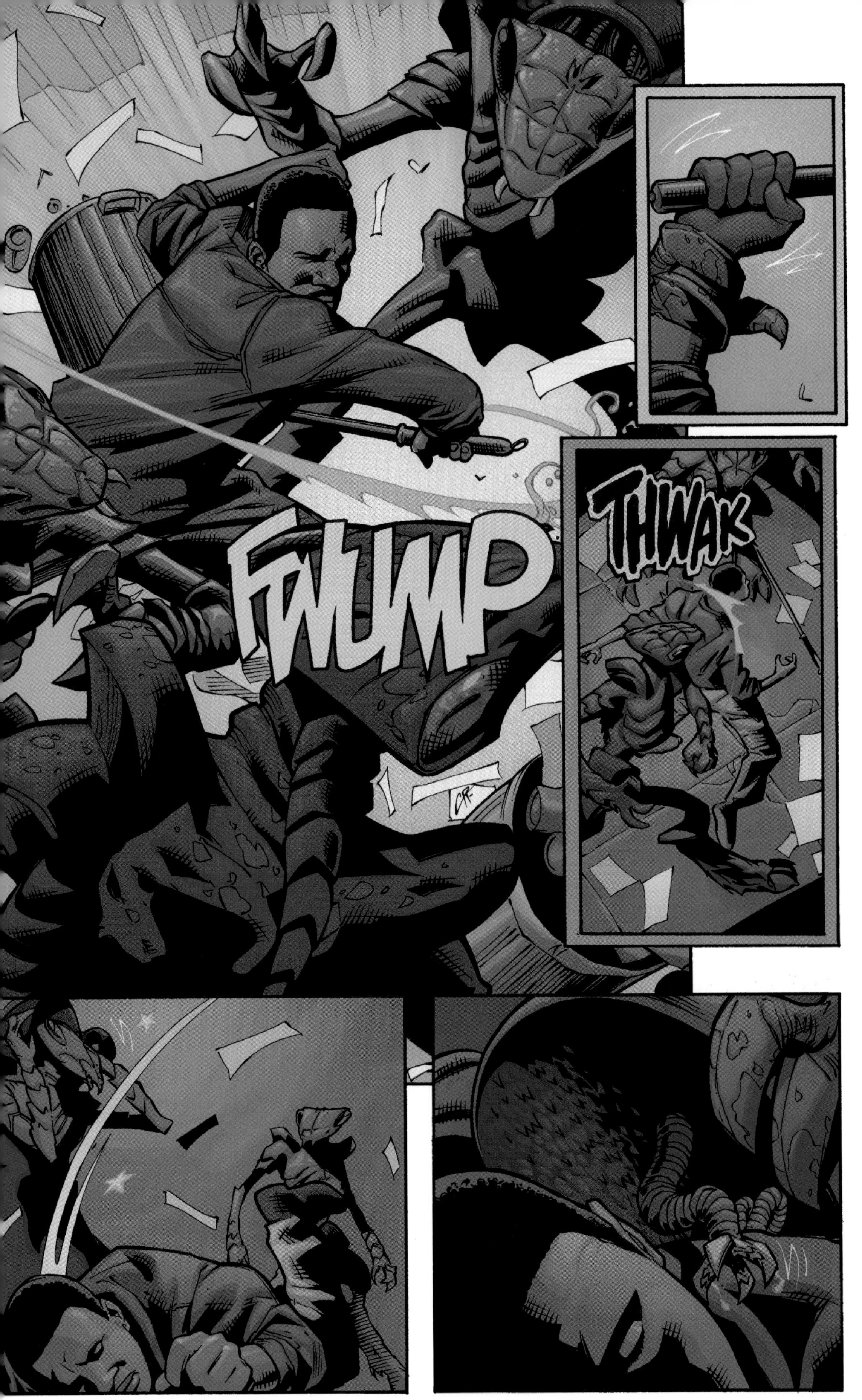
FWUMP
THWAK

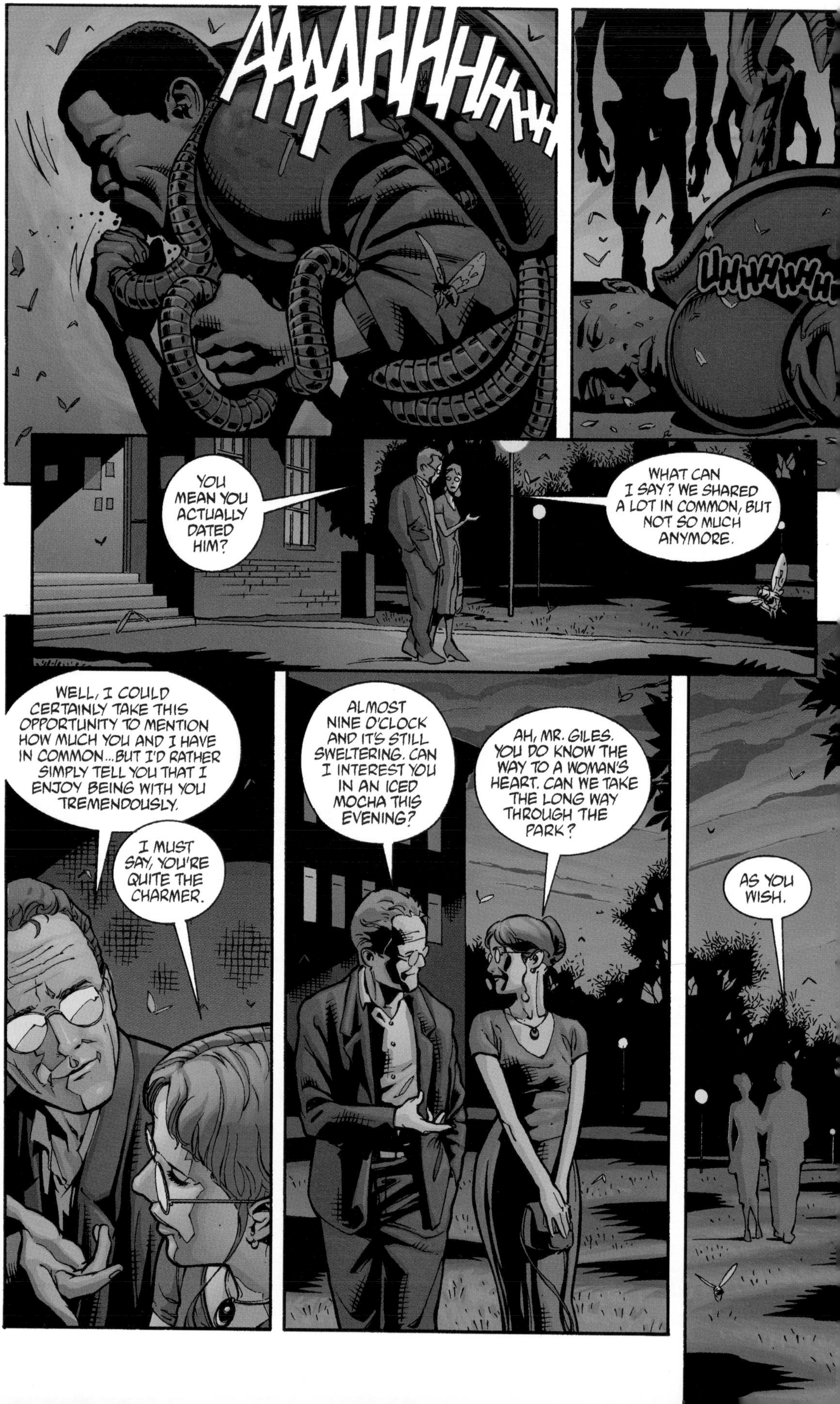
AAAAHHHHHHH
UHHHHHH
YOU MEAN YOU ACTUALLY DATED HIM?
WHAT CAN I SAY? WE SHARED A LOT IN COMMON, BUT NOT SO MUCH ANYMORE.
WELL, I COULD CERTAINLY TAKE THIS OPPORTUNITY TO MENTION HOW MUCH YOU AND I HAVE IN COMMON...BUT I'D RATHER SIMPLY TELL YOU THAT I ENJOY BEING WITH YOU TREMENDOUSLY.
I MUST SAY, YOU'RE QUITE THE CHARMER.
ALMOST NINE O'CLOCK AND IT'S STILL SWELTERING. CAN I INTEREST YOU IN AN ICED MOCHA THIS EVENING?
AH, MR. GILES. YOU DO KNOW THE WAY TO A WOMAN'S HEART. CAN WE TAKE THE LONG WAY THROUGH THE PARK?
AS YOU WISH.

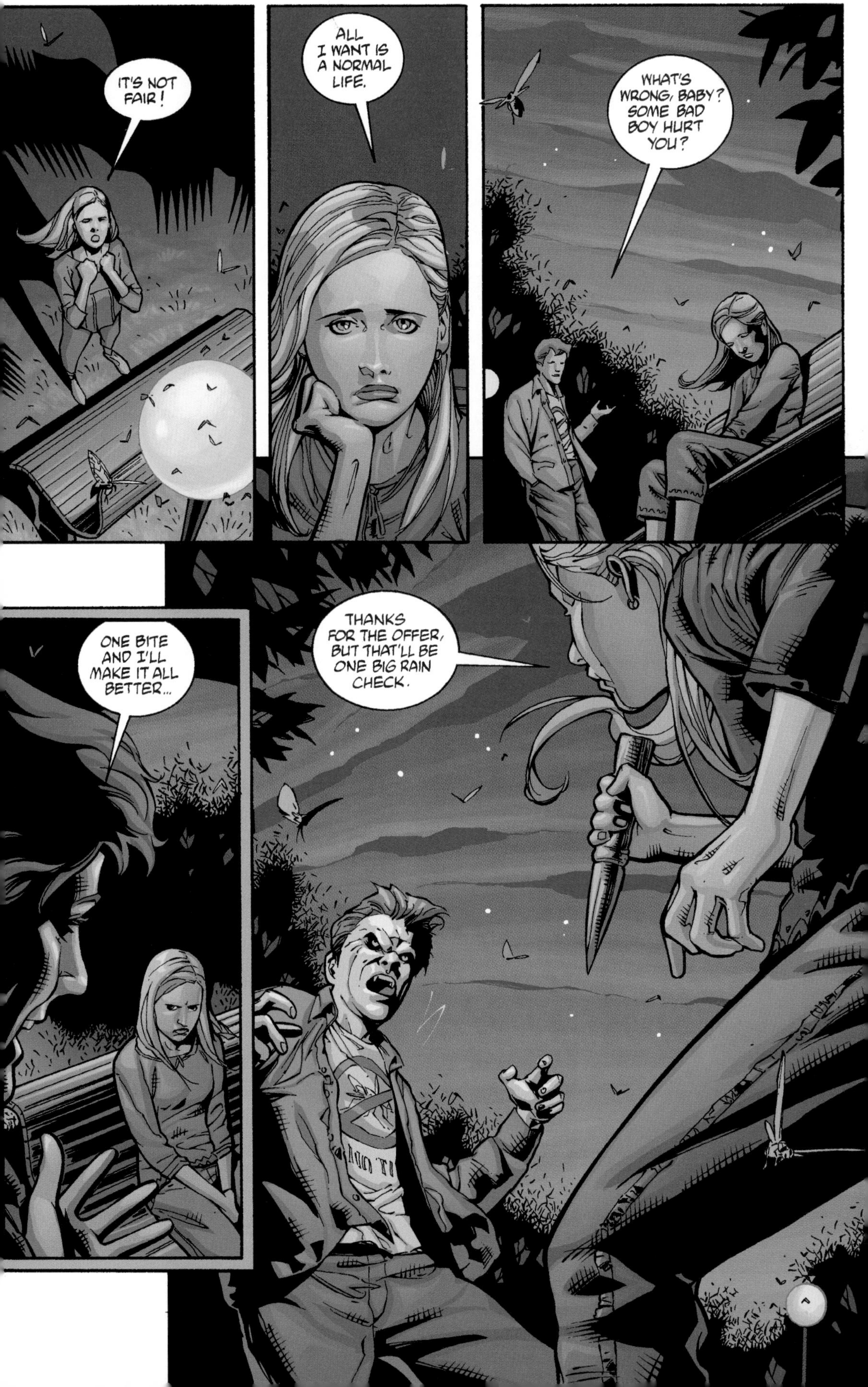
IT'S NOT FAIR!
ALL I WANT IS A NORMAL LIFE.
WHAT'S WRONG, BABY? SOME BAD BOY HURT YOU?
ONE BITE AND I'LL MAKE IT ALL BETTER...
THANKS FOR THE OFFER, BUT THAT'LL BE ONE BIG RAIN CHECK.

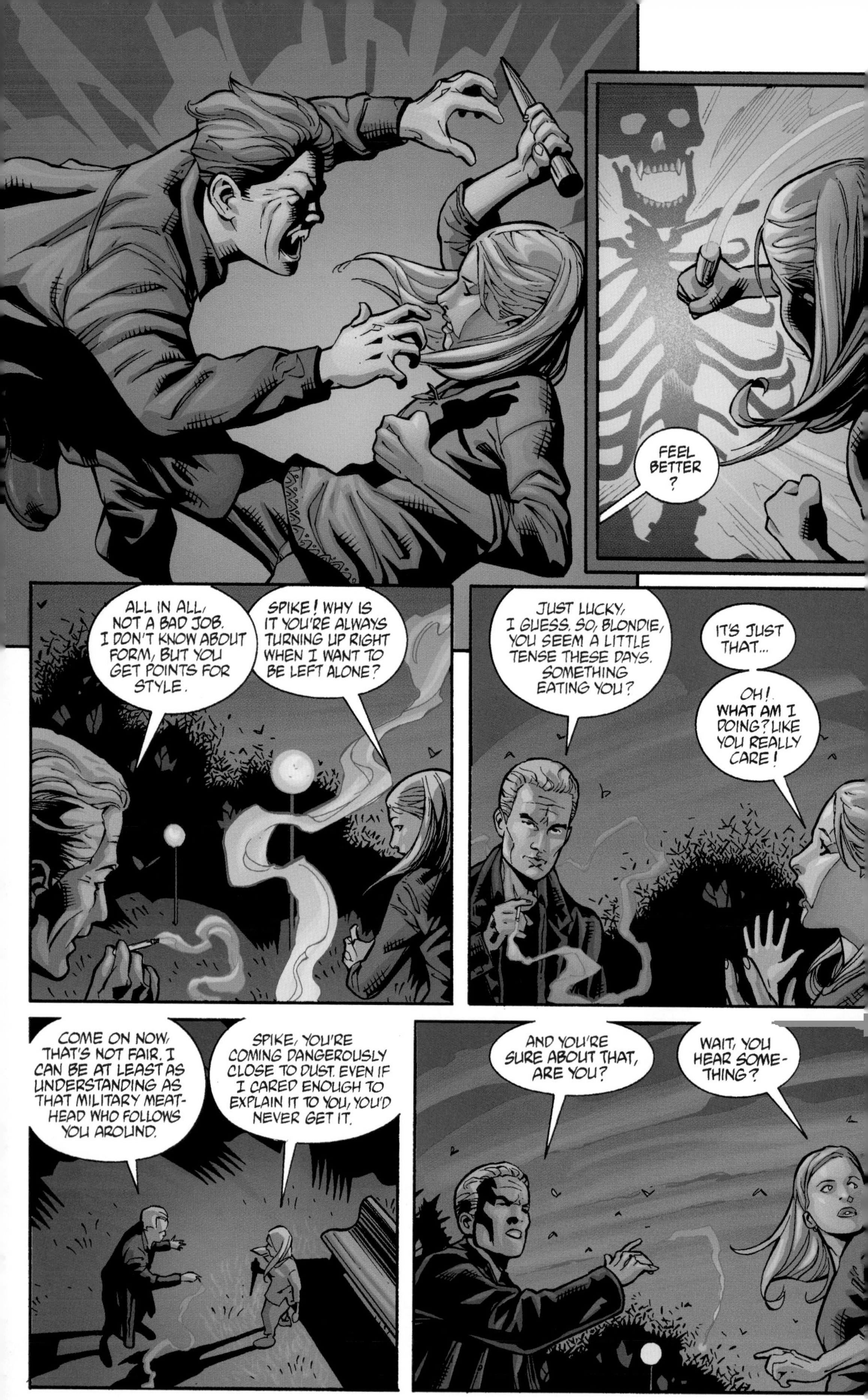
FEEL BETTER ?
ALL IN ALL, NOT A BAD JOB. I DON'T KNOW ABOUT FORM, BUT YOU GET POINTS FOR STYLE.
SPIKE! WHY IS IT YOU'RE ALWAYS TURNING UP RIGHT WHEN I WANT TO BE LEFT ALONE?
JUST LUCKY, I GUESS. SO, BLONDIE, YOU SEEM A LITTLE TENSE THESE DAYS. SOMETHING EATING YOU?
IT'S JUST THAT...
OH! WHAT AM I DOING? LIKE YOU REALLY CARE!
COME ON NOW, THAT'S NOT FAIR. I CAN BE AT LEAST AS UNDERSTANDING AS THAT MILITARY MEAT-HEAD WHO FOLLOWS YOU AROUND.
SPIKE, YOU'RE COMING DANGEROUSLY CLOSE TO DUST. EVEN IF I CARED ENOUGH TO EXPLAIN IT TO YOU, YOU'D NEVER GET IT.
AND YOU'RE SURE ABOUT THAT, ARE YOU?
WAIT, YOU HEAR SOME-THING?

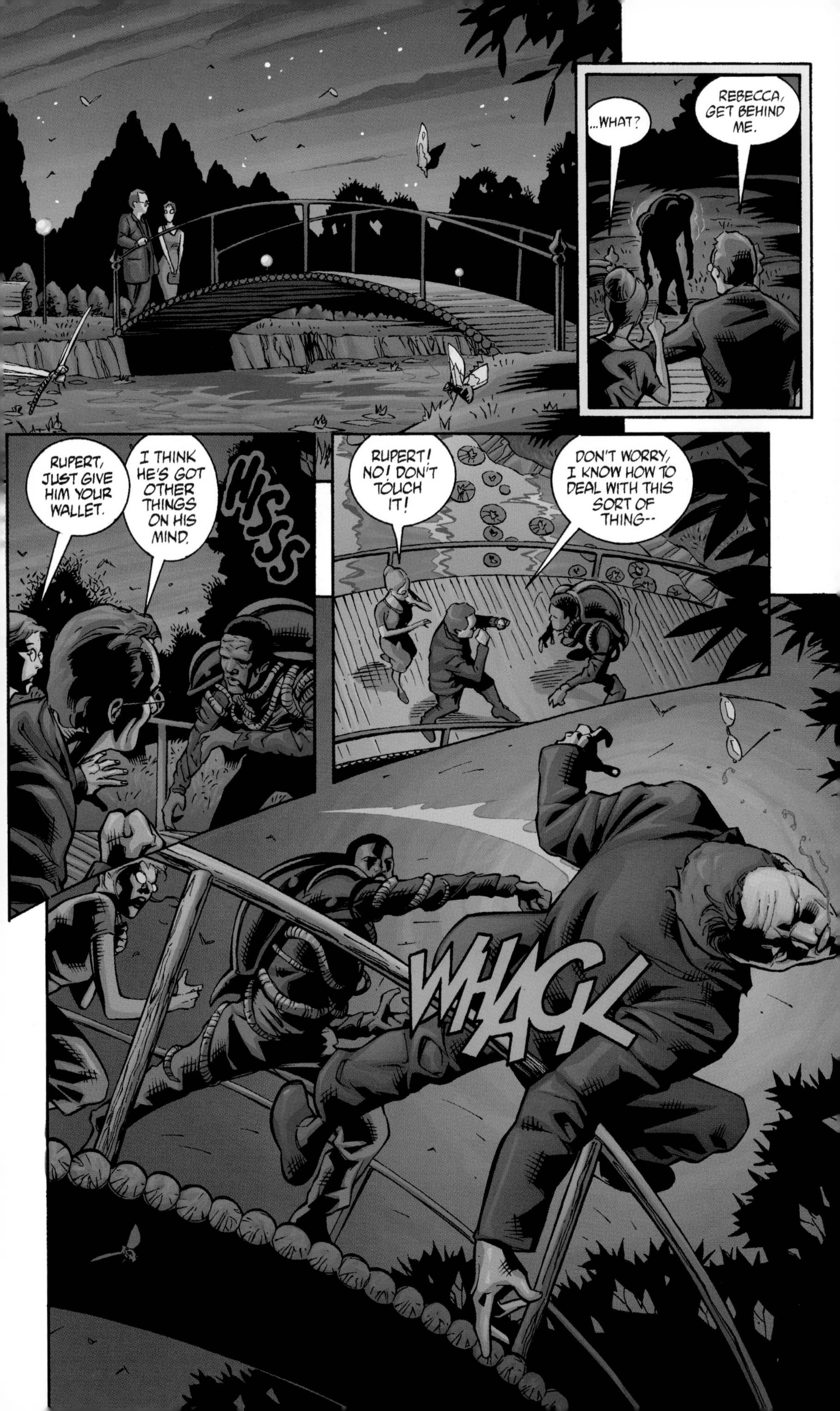
...WHAT?
REBECCA, GET BEHIND ME.
RUPERT, JUST GIVE HIM YOUR WALLET.
I THINK HE'S GOT OTHER THINGS ON HIS MIND.
HISSS
RUPERT! NO! DON'T TOUCH IT!
DON'T WORRY, I KNOW HOW TO DEAL WITH THIS SORT OF THING--
WHACK

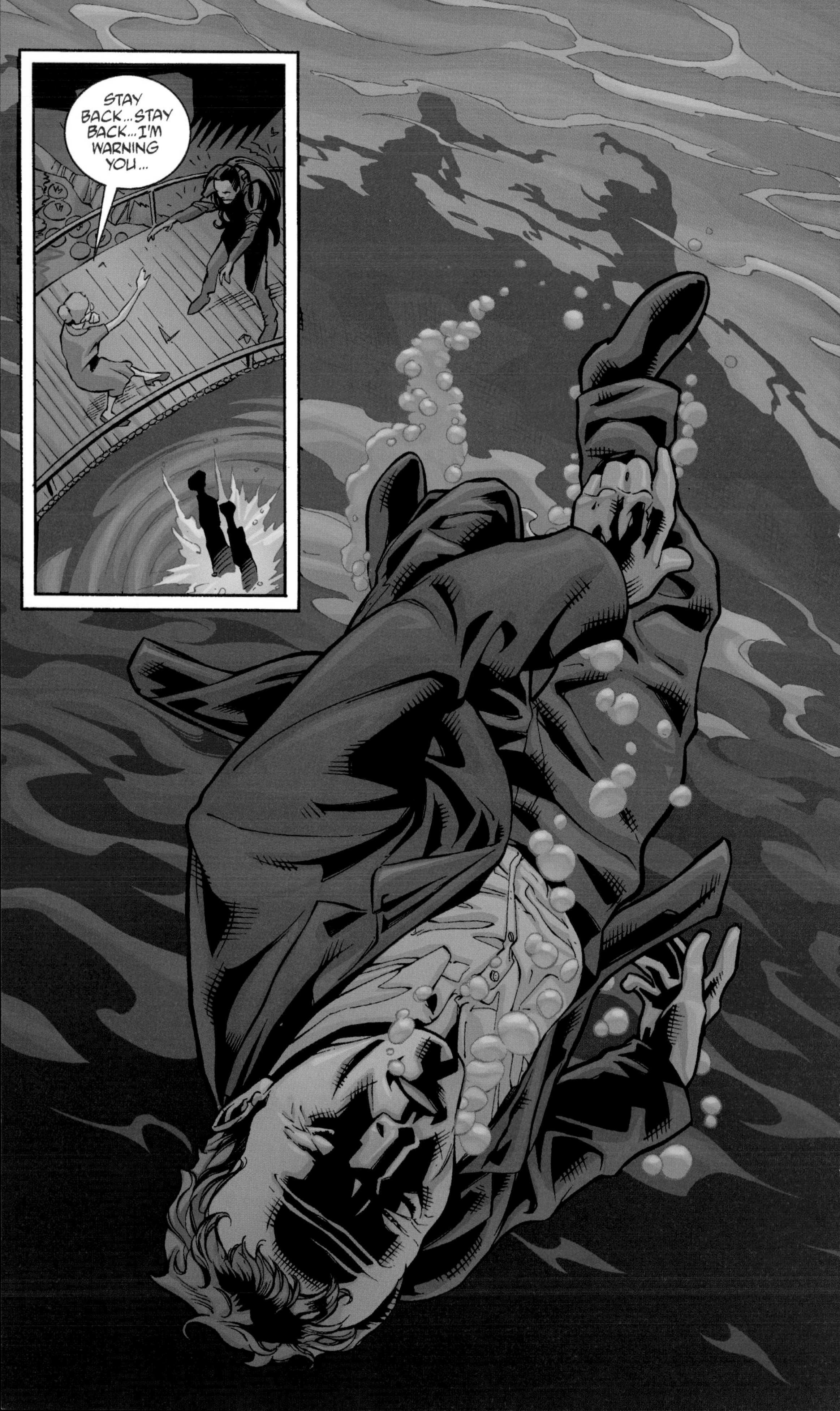
STAY BACK...STAY BACK...I'M WARNING YOU...

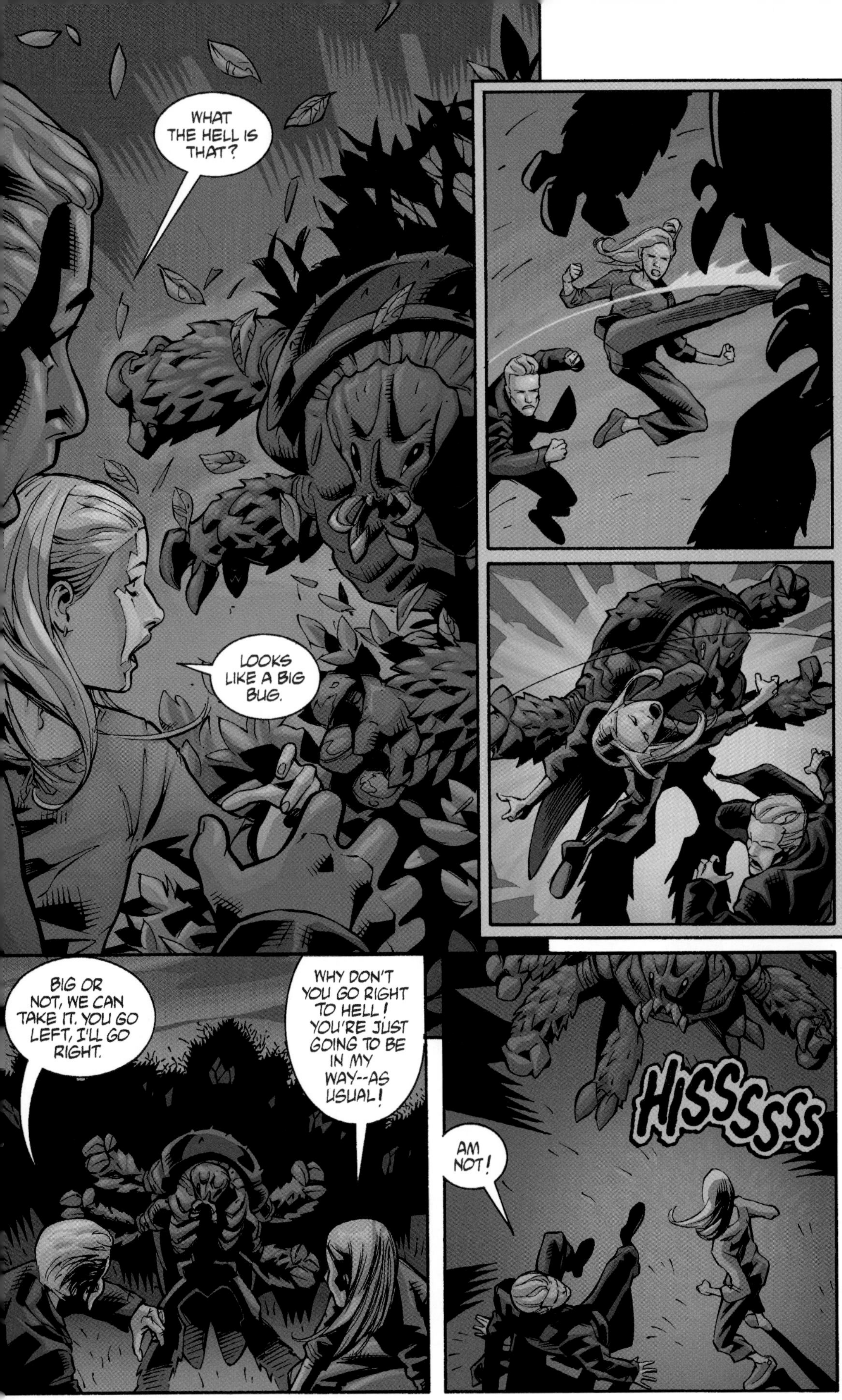

WHAT THE HELL IS THAT?
LOOKS LIKE A BIG BUG.
BIG OR NOT, WE CAN TAKE IT. YOU GO LEFT, I'LL GO RIGHT.
WHY DON'T YOU GO RIGHT TO HELL! YOU'RE JUST GOING TO BE IN MY WAY--AS USUAL!
HISSSSSS
AM NOT!

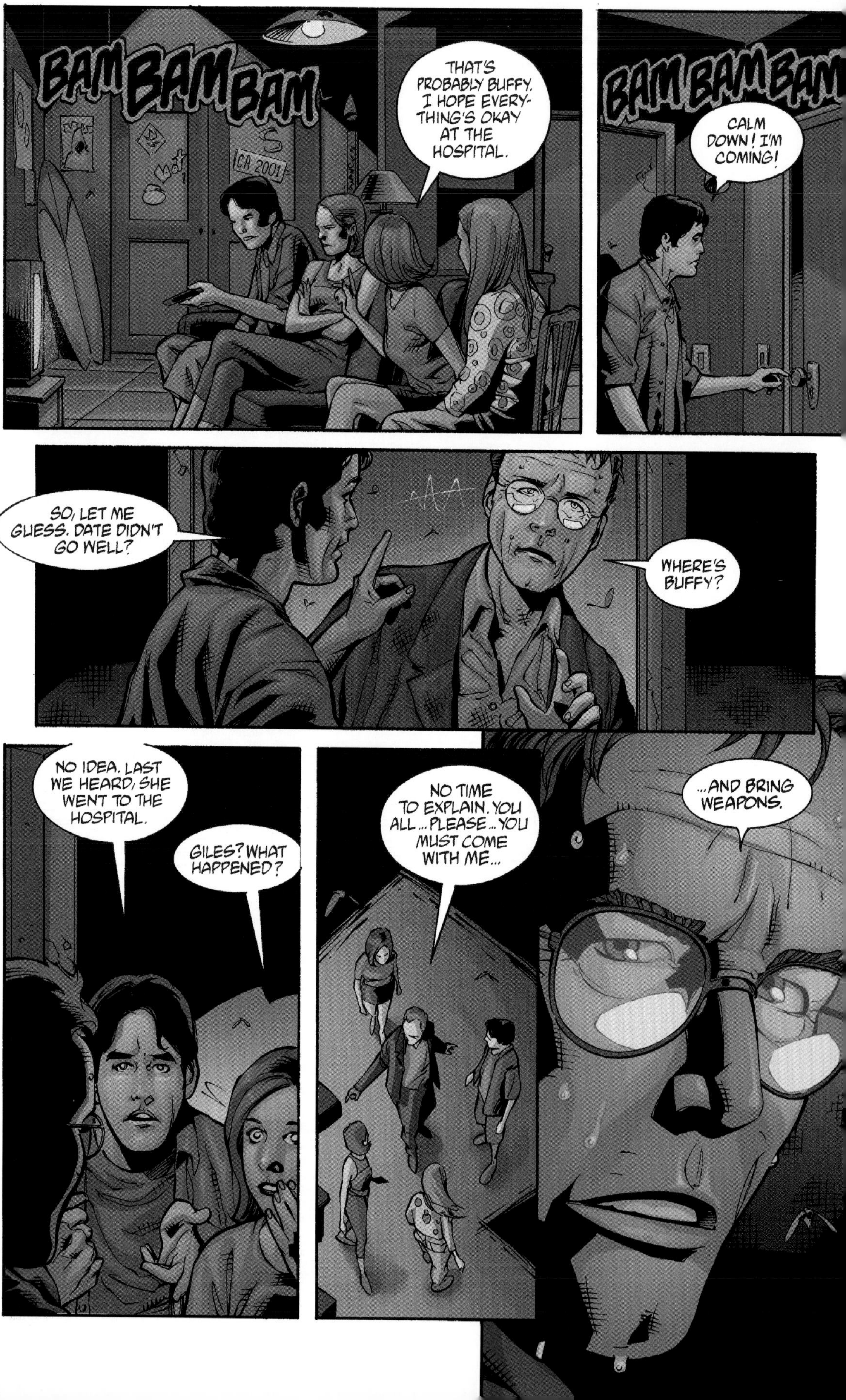
BAM BAM BAM
THAT'S PROBABLY BUFFY. I HOPE EVERYTHING'S OKAY AT THE HOSPITAL.
CA 2001
BAM BAM BAM
CALM DOWN! I'M COMING!
SO, LET ME GUESS. DATE DIDN'T GO WELL?
WHERE'S BUFFY?
NO IDEA. LAST WE HEARD, SHE WENT TO THE HOSPITAL.
GILES? WHAT HAPPENED?
NO TIME TO EXPLAIN. YOU ALL... PLEASE... YOU MUST COME WITH ME...
...AND BRING WEAPONS.

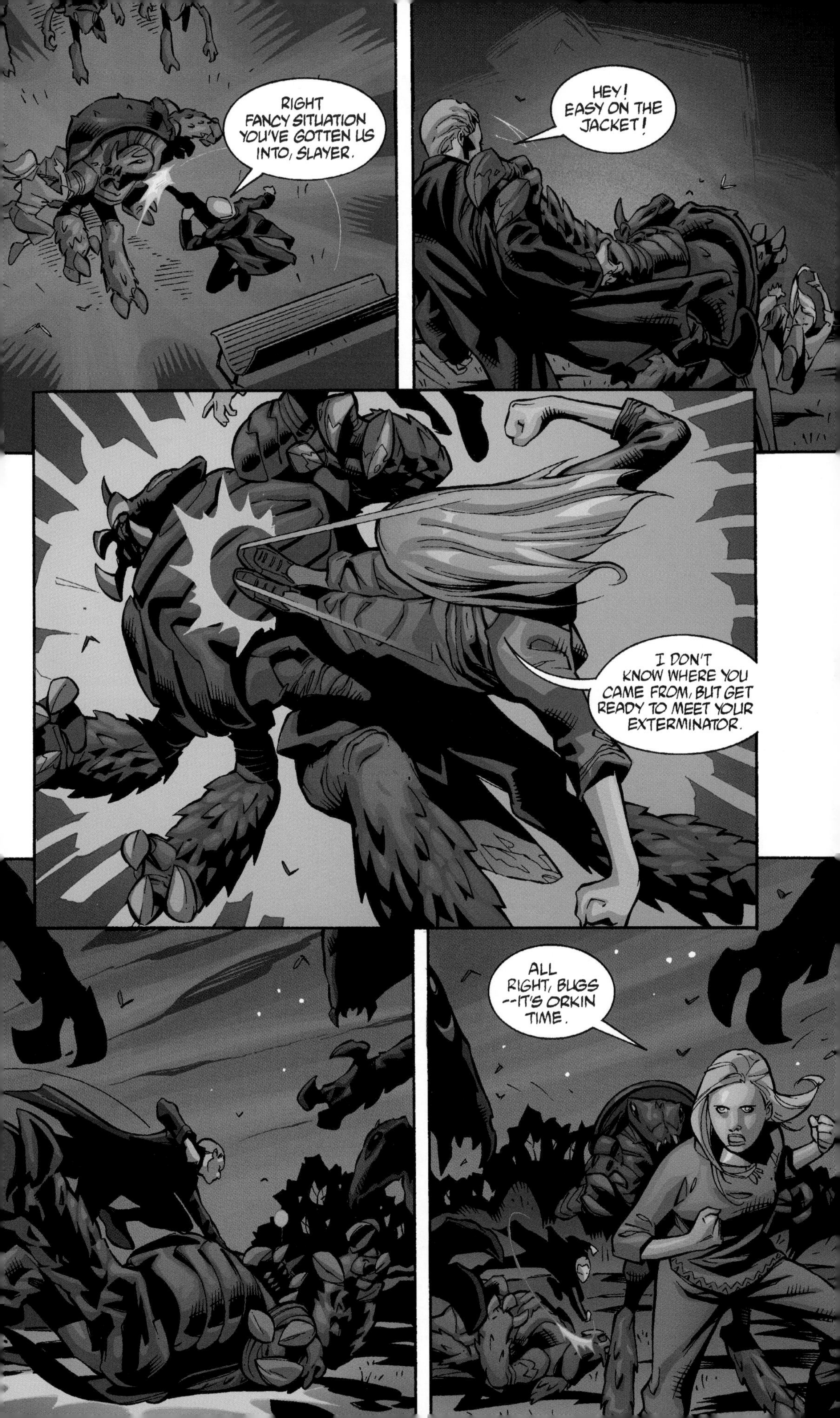
RIGHT FANCY SITUATION YOU'VE GOTTEN US INTO, SLAYER.
HEY! EASY ON THE JACKET!
I DON'T KNOW WHERE YOU CAME FROM, BUT GET READY TO MEET YOUR EXTERMINATOR.
ALL RIGHT, BUGS --IT'S ORKIN TIME.

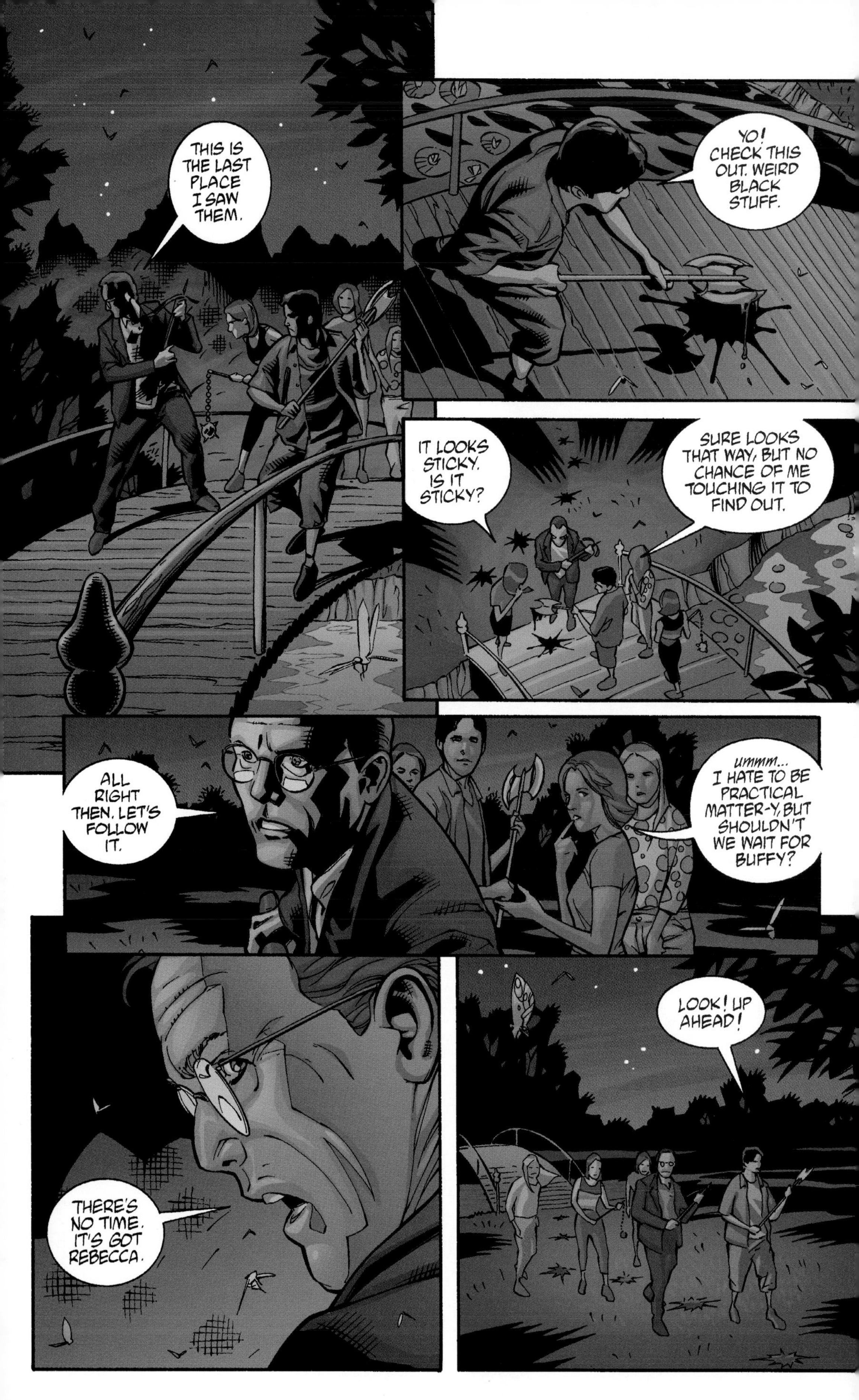
THIS IS THE LAST PLACE I SAW THEM.
YO! CHECK THIS OUT. WEIRD BLACK STUFF.
IT LOOKS STICKY. IS IT STICKY?
SURE LOOKS THAT WAY, BUT NO CHANCE OF ME TOUCHING IT TO FIND OUT.
ALL RIGHT THEN. LET'S FOLLOW IT.
ummm... I HATE TO BE PRACTICAL MATTER-Y, BUT SHOULDN'T WE WAIT FOR BUFFY?
THERE'S NO TIME. IT'S GOT REBECCA.
LOOK! UP AHEAD!

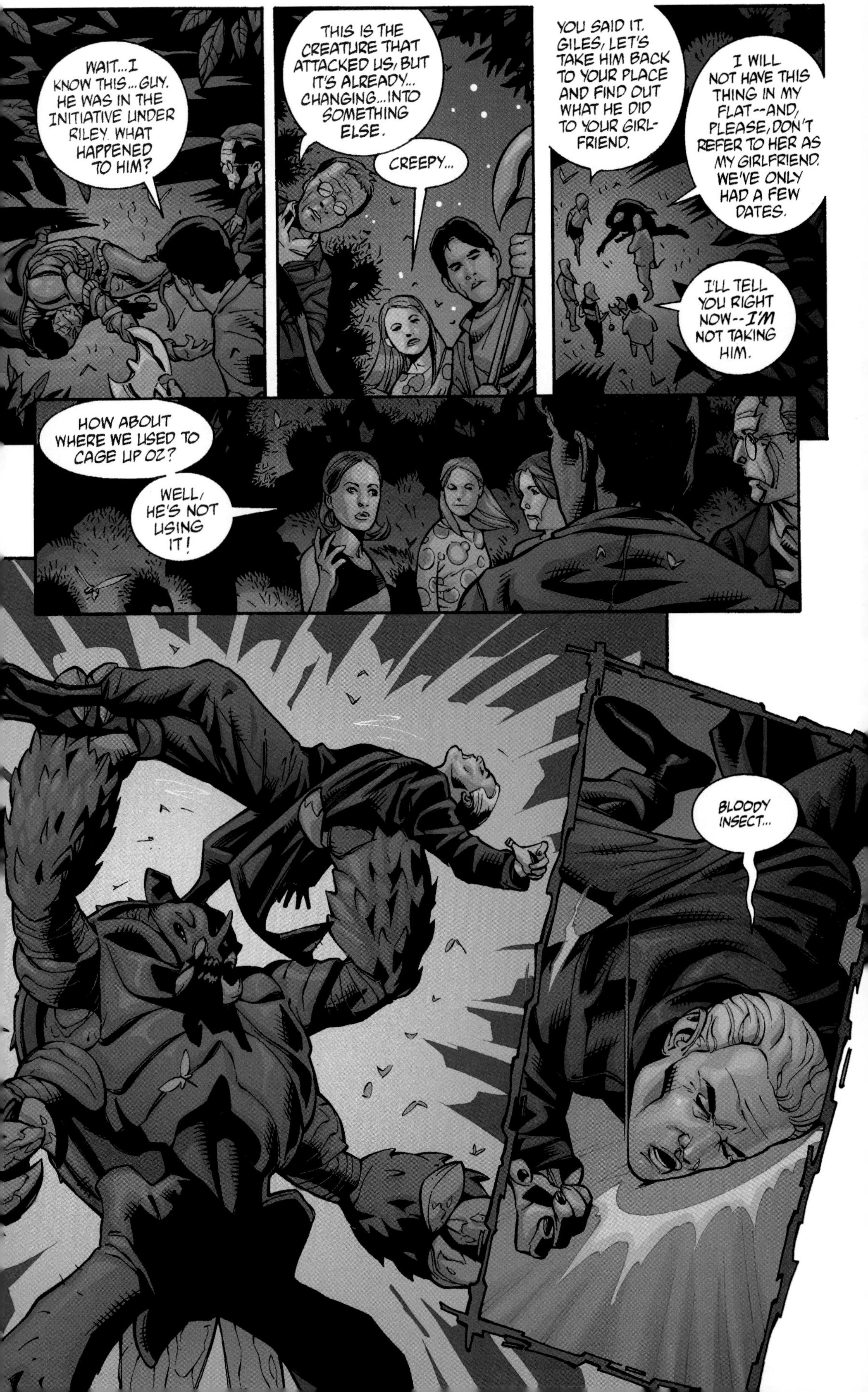
WAIT...I KNOW THIS...GUY. HE WAS IN THE INITIATIVE UNDER RILEY. WHAT HAPPENED TO HIM?
THIS IS THE CREATURE THAT ATTACKED US, BUT IT'S ALREADY... CHANGING...INTO SOMETHING ELSE.
CREEPY...
YOU SAID IT. GILES, LET'S TAKE HIM BACK TO YOUR PLACE AND FIND OUT WHAT HE DID TO YOUR GIRL-FRIEND.
I WILL NOT HAVE THIS THING IN MY FLAT--AND, PLEASE, DON'T REFER TO HER AS MY GIRLFRIEND. WE'VE ONLY HAD A FEW DATES.
I'LL TELL YOU RIGHT NOW--I'M NOT TAKING HIM.
HOW ABOUT WHERE WE USED TO CAGE UP OZ?
WELL, HE'S NOT USING IT!
BLOODY INSECT...

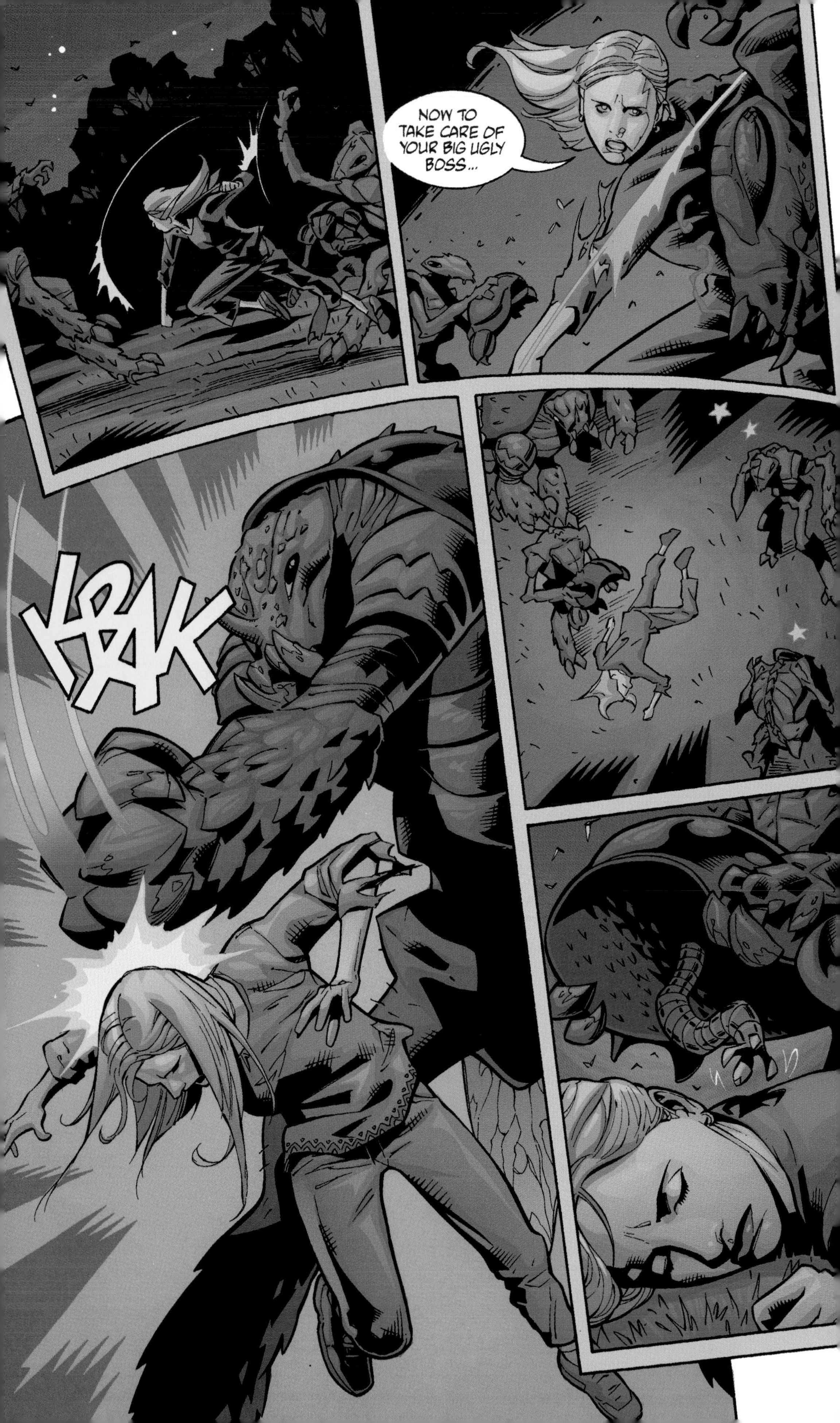
NOW TO TAKE CARE OF YOUR BIG UGLY BOSS...
KRAK

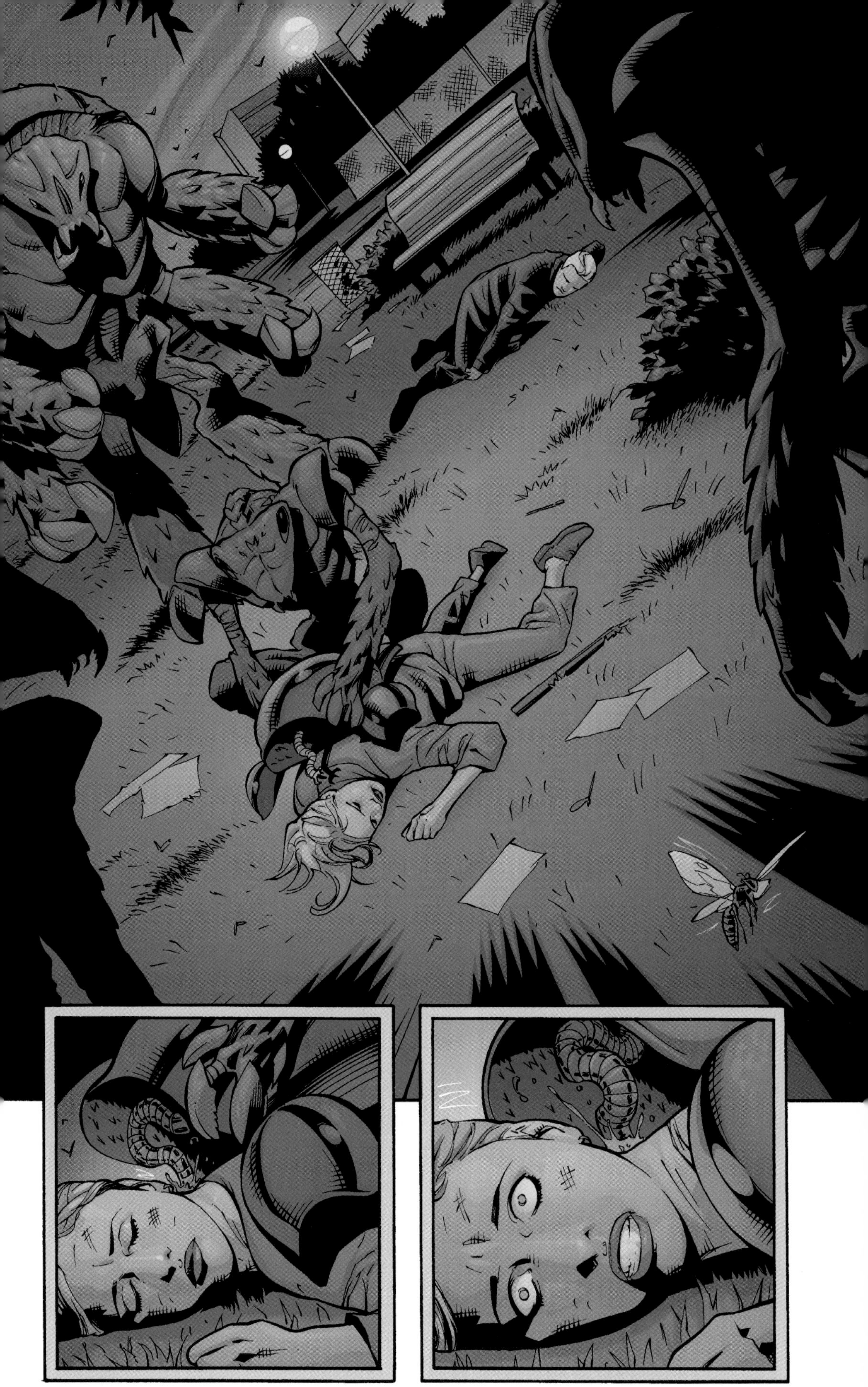

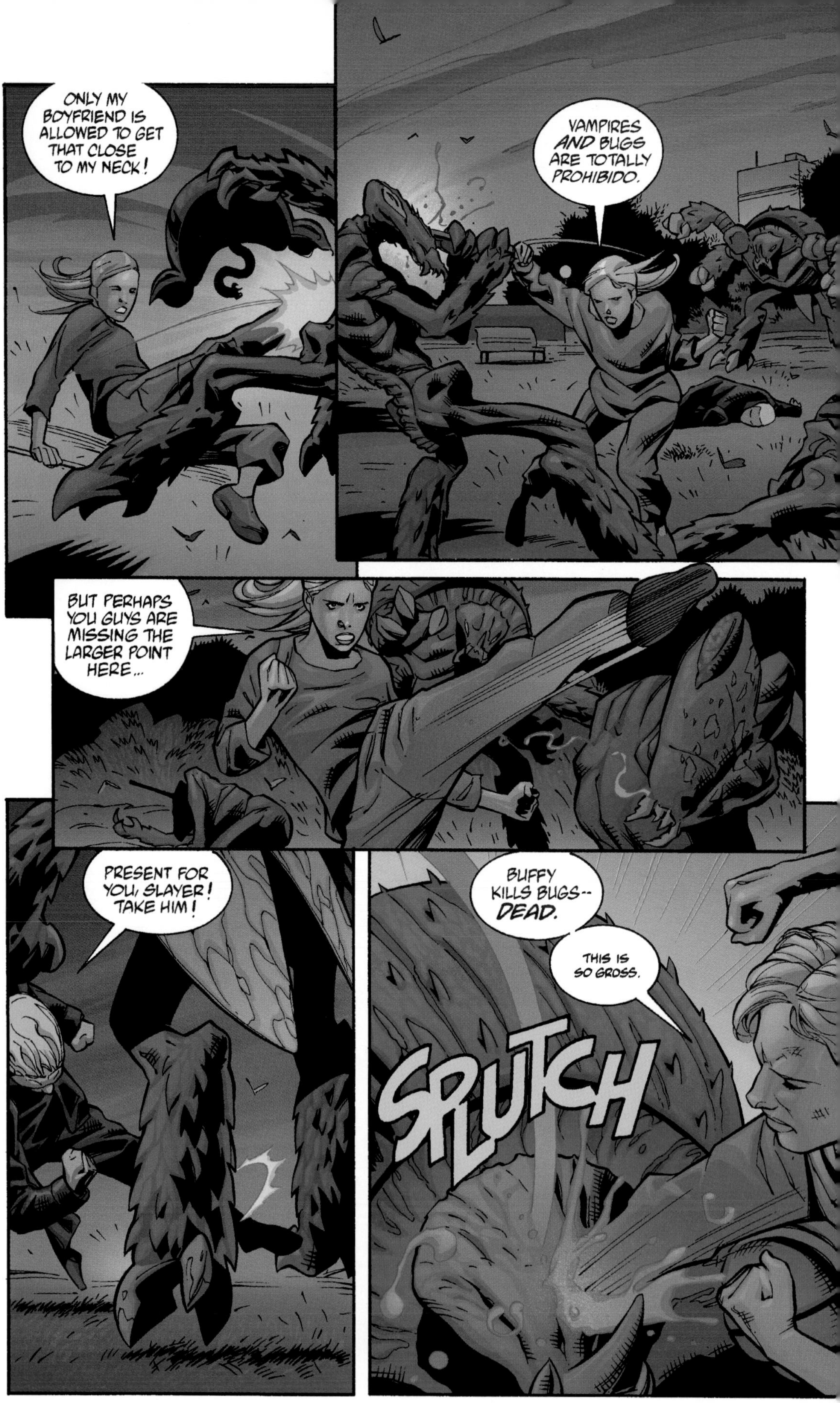
ONLY MY BOYFRIEND IS ALLOWED TO GET THAT CLOSE TO MY NECK!
VAMPIRES AND BUGS ARE TOTALLY PROHIBIDO.
BUT PERHAPS YOU GUYS ARE MISSING THE LARGER POINT HERE...
PRESENT FOR YOU, SLAYER! TAKE HIM!
BUFFY KILLS BUGS-- DEAD.
THIS IS SO GROSS.
SPLUTCH

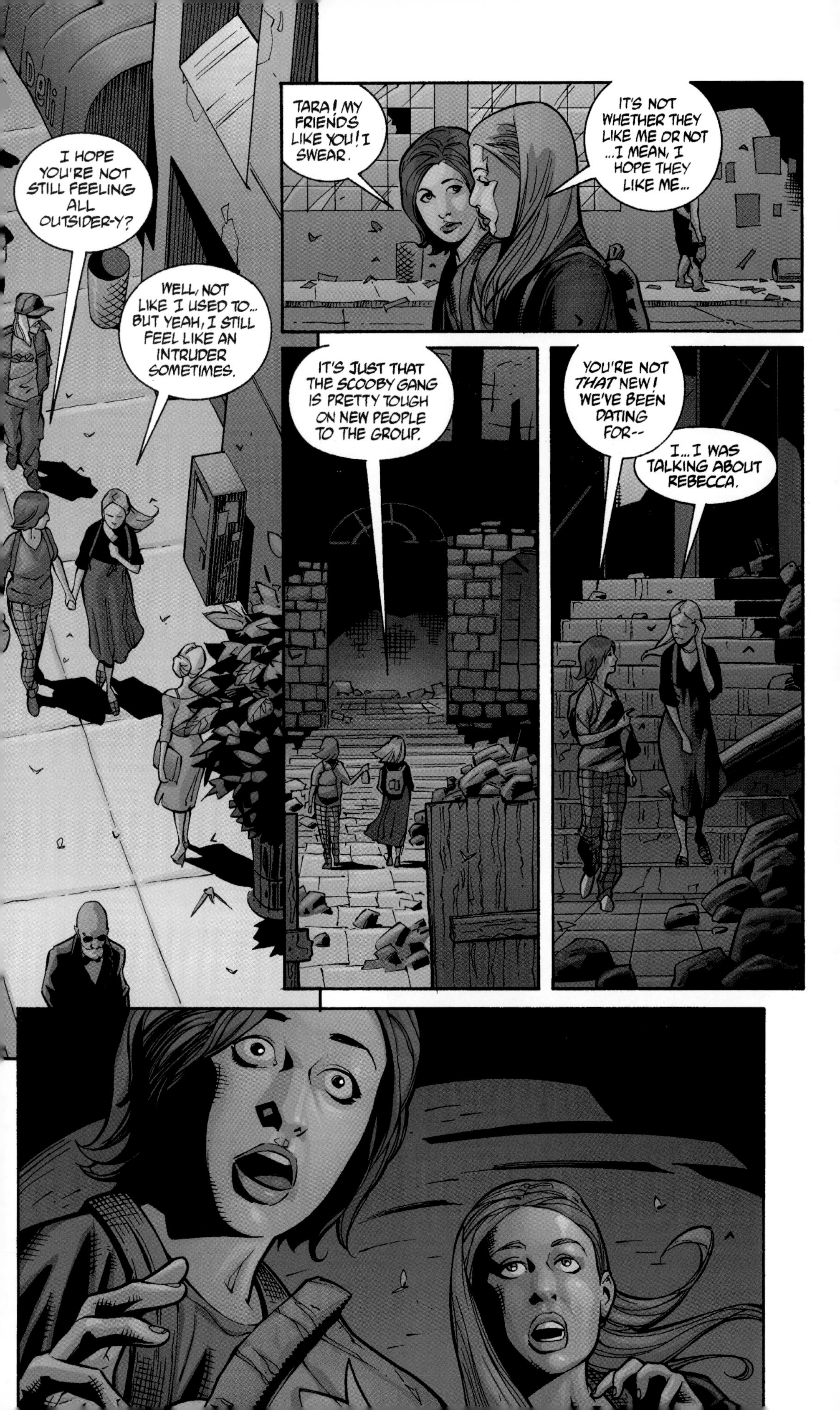

I HOPE YOU'RE NOT STILL FEELING ALL OUTSIDER-Y?
WELL, NOT LIKE I USED TO... BUT YEAH, I STILL FEEL LIKE AN INTRUDER SOMETIMES.
TARA! MY FRIENDS LIKE YOU! I SWEAR.
IT'S NOT WHETHER THEY LIKE ME OR NOT ...I MEAN, I HOPE THEY LIKE ME...
IT'S JUST THAT THE SCOOBY GANG IS PRETTY TOUGH ON NEW PEOPLE TO THE GROUP.
YOU'RE NOT THAT NEW! WE'VE BEEN DATING FOR--
I... I WAS TALKING ABOUT REBECCA.

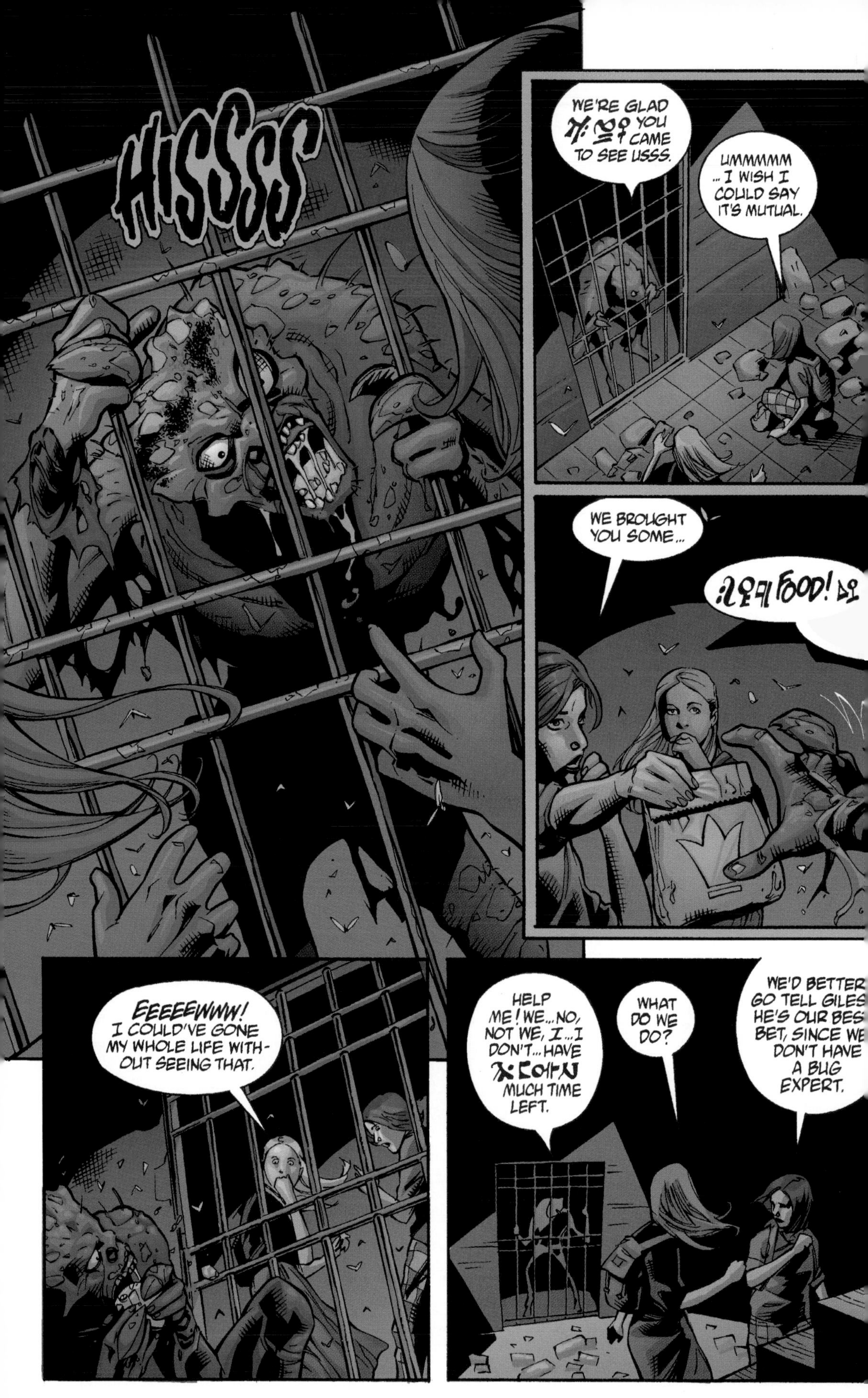
HISSSS
WE'RE GLAD YOU CAME TO SEE USSS.
UMMMMM ... I WISH I COULD SAY IT'S MUTUAL.
WE BROUGHT YOU SOME...
FOOD!
EEEEEWWW! I COULD'VE GONE MY WHOLE LIFE WITHOUT SEEING THAT.
HELP ME! WE... NO, NOT WE, I... I DON'T... HAVE MUCH TIME LEFT.
WHAT DO WE DO?
WE'D BETTER GO TELL GILES HE'S OUR BEST BET, SINCE WE DON'T HAVE A BUG EXPERT.

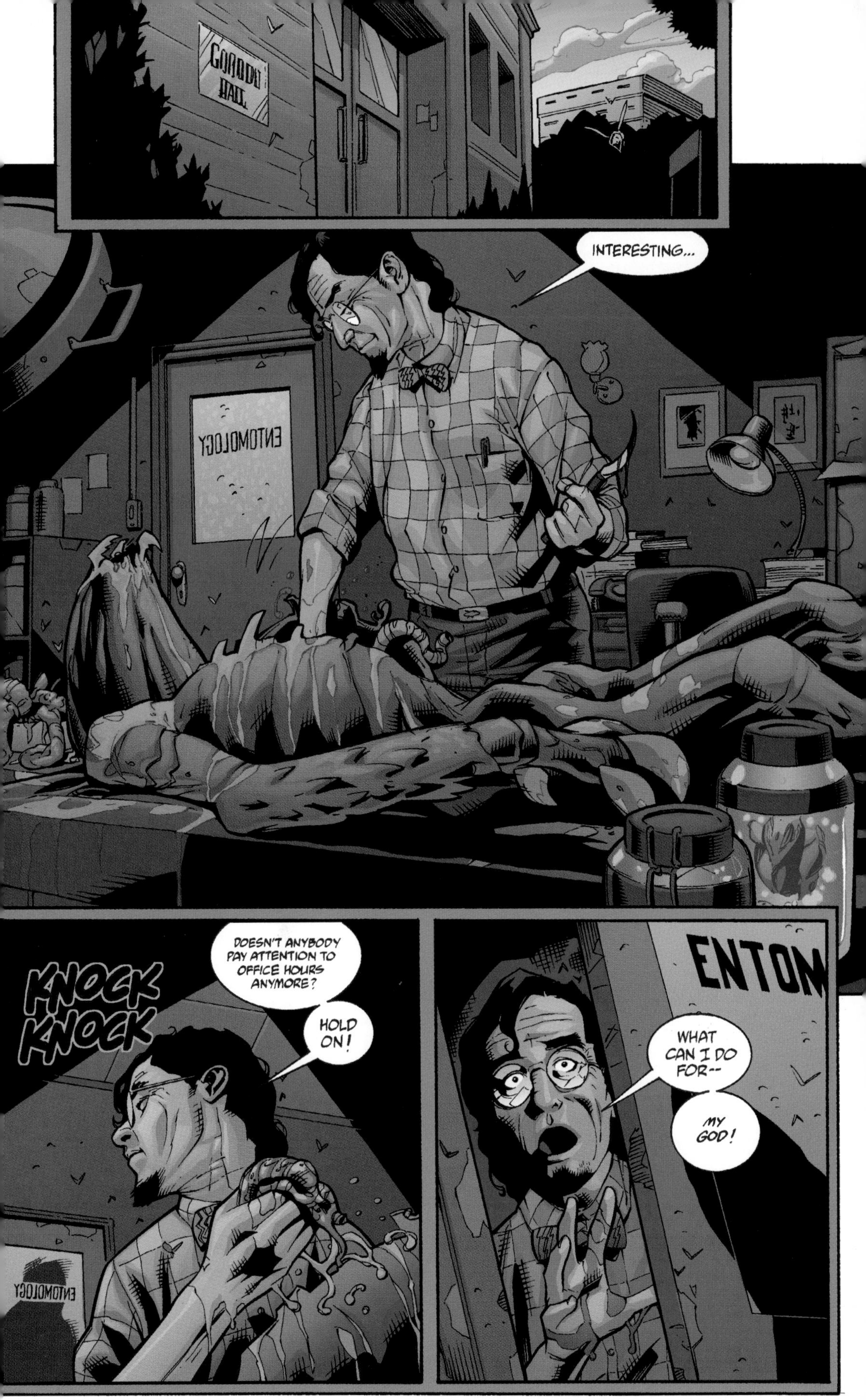
GORDON HALL
INTERESTING...
ENTOMOLOGY
KNOCK KNOCK
DOESN'T ANYBODY PAY ATTENTION TO OFFICE HOURS ANYMORE?
HOLD ON!
ENTOM
WHAT CAN I DO FOR--
MY GOD!

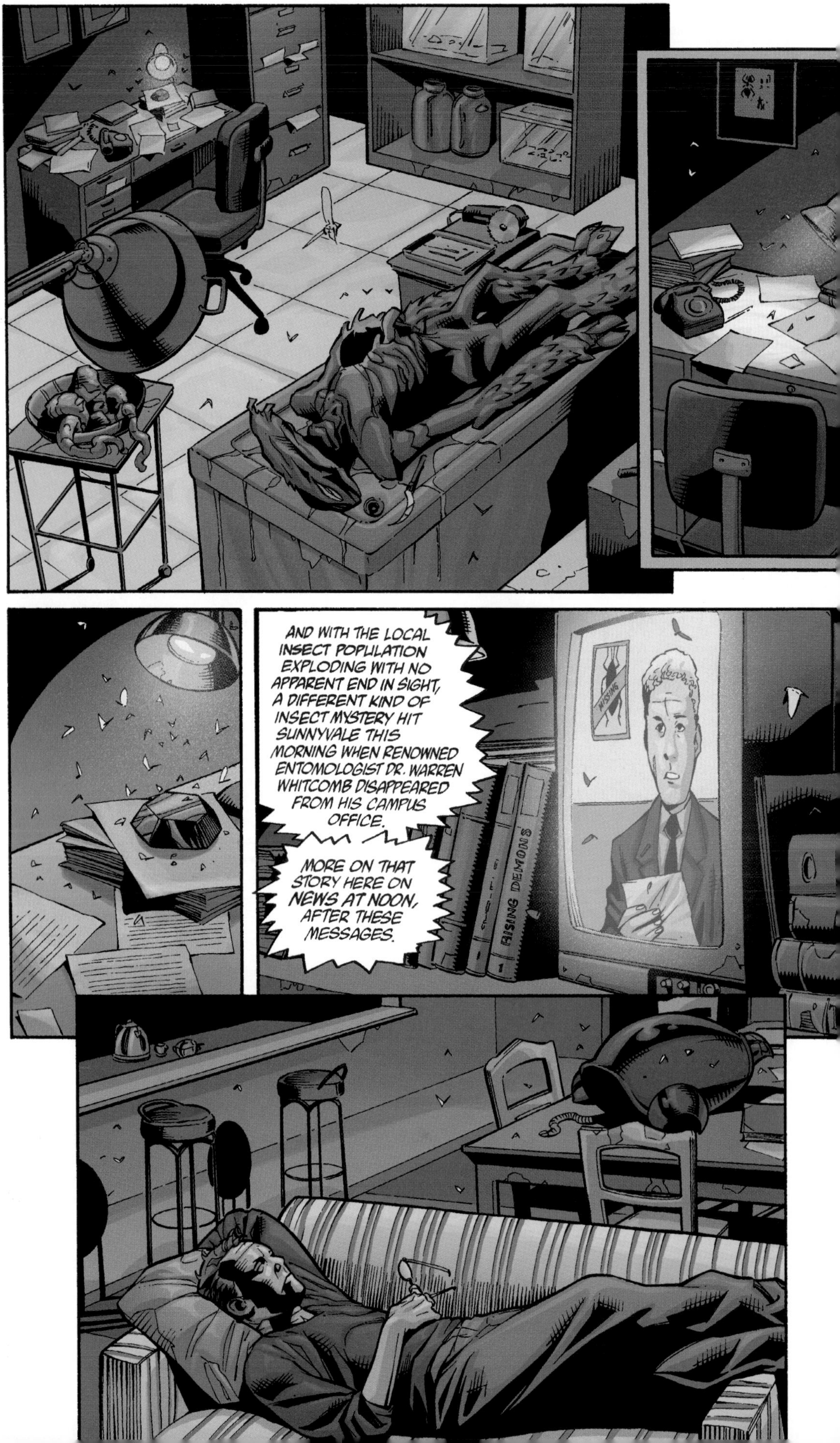
AND WITH THE LOCAL INSECT POPULATION EXPLODING WITH NO APPARENT END IN SIGHT, A DIFFERENT KIND OF INSECT MYSTERY HIT SUNNYVALE THIS MORNING WHEN RENOWNED ENTOMOLOGIST DR. WARREN WHITCOMB DISAPPEARED FROM HIS CAMPUS OFFICE.
MORE ON THAT STORY HERE ON NEWS AT NOON, AFTER THESE MESSAGES.
MISSING
RISING DEMONS

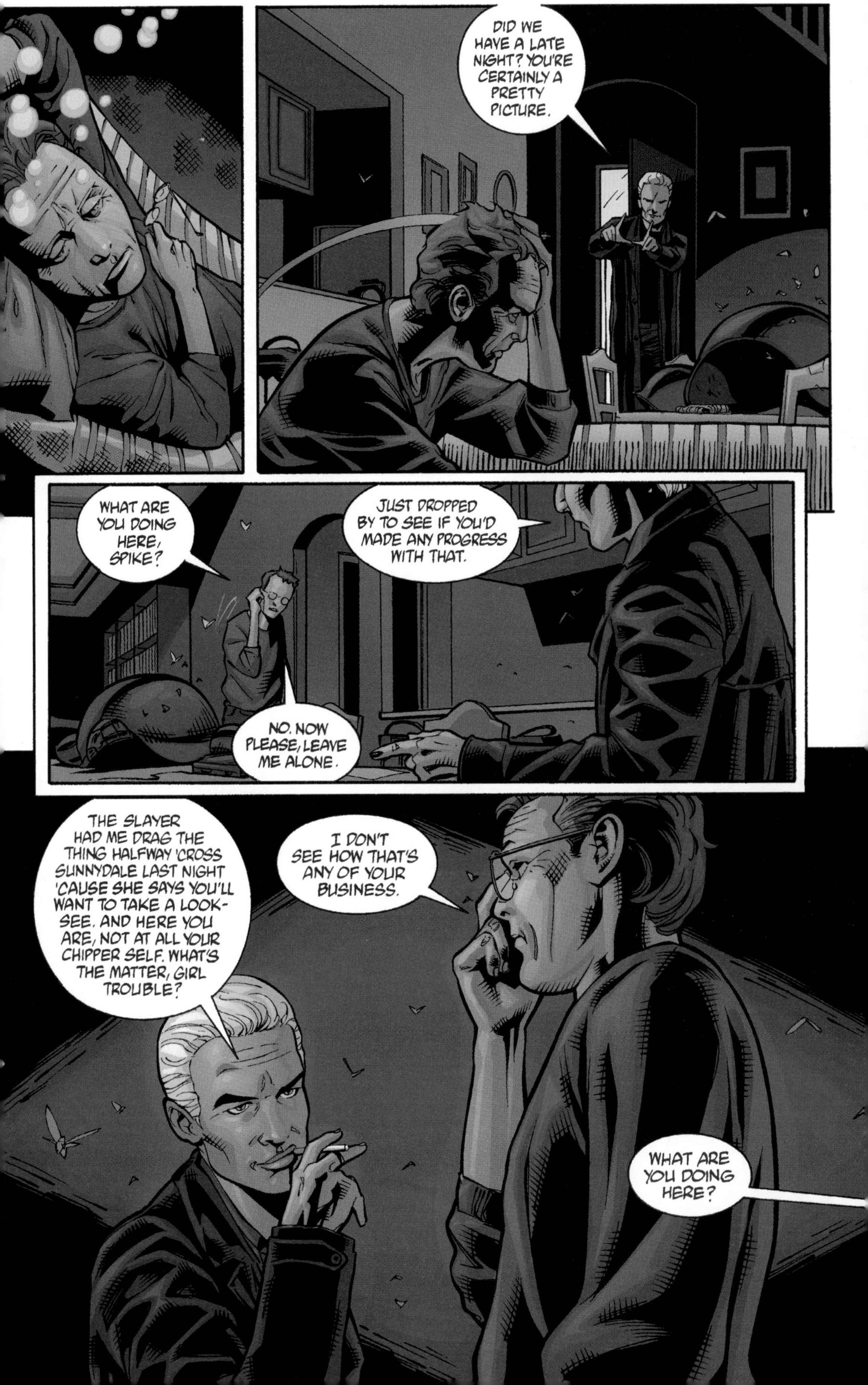
DID WE HAVE A LATE NIGHT? YOU'RE CERTAINLY A PRETTY PICTURE.
WHAT ARE YOU DOING HERE, SPIKE?
JUST DROPPED BY TO SEE IF YOU'D MADE ANY PROGRESS WITH THAT.
NO. NOW PLEASE, LEAVE ME ALONE.
THE SLAYER HAD ME DRAG THE THING HALFWAY 'CROSS SUNNYDALE LAST NIGHT 'CAUSE SHE SAYS YOU'LL WANT TO TAKE A LOOK-SEE. AND HERE YOU ARE, NOT AT ALL YOUR CHIPPER SELF. WHAT'S THE MATTER, GIRL TROUBLE?
I DON'T SEE HOW THAT'S ANY OF YOUR BUSINESS.
WHAT ARE YOU DOING HERE?

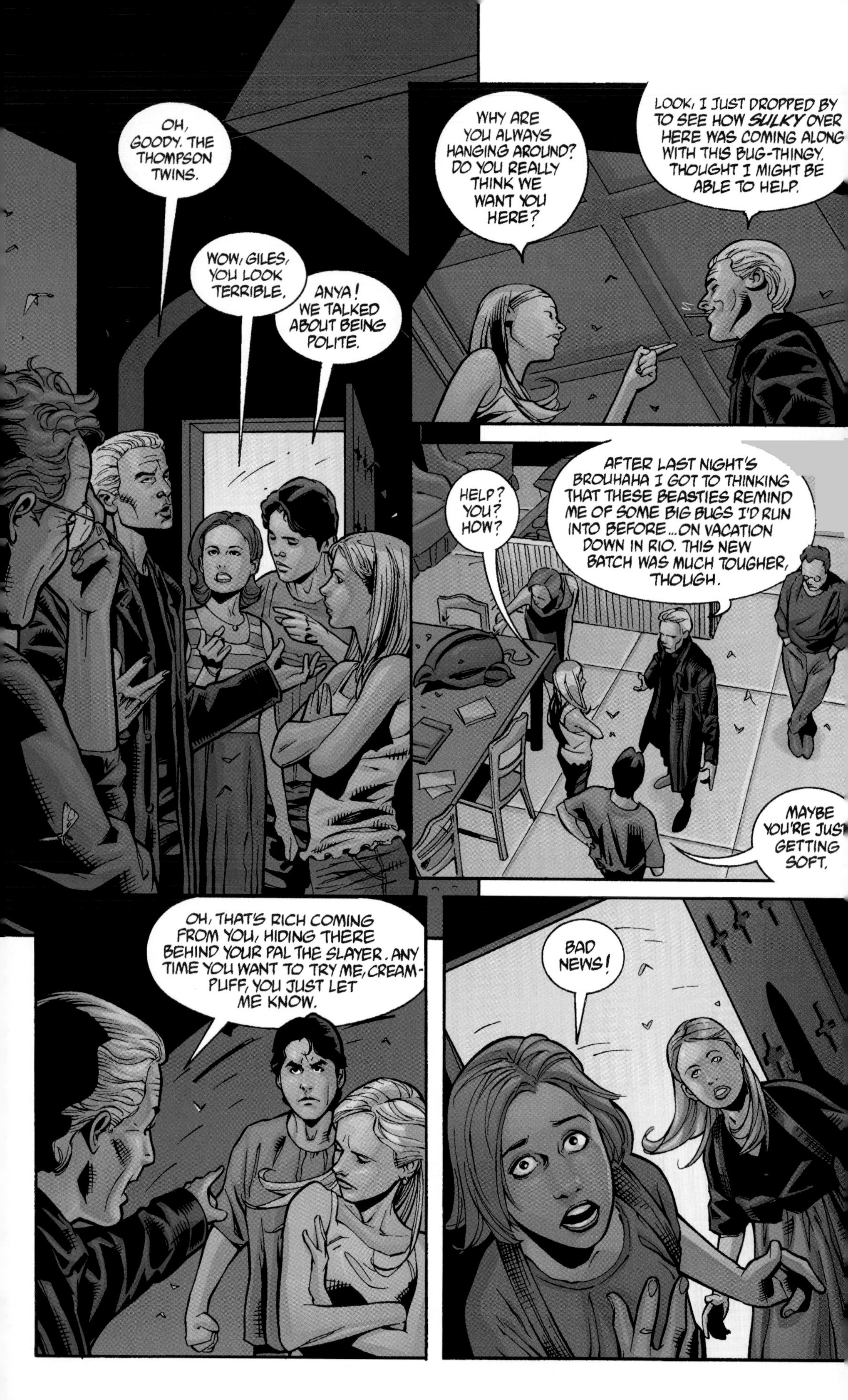
OH, GOODY. THE THOMPSON TWINS.
WOW, GILES, YOU LOOK TERRIBLE.
ANYA! WE TALKED ABOUT BEING POLITE.
WHY ARE YOU ALWAYS HANGING AROUND? DO YOU REALLY THINK WE WANT YOU HERE?
LOOK, I JUST DROPPED BY TO SEE HOW *SULKY* OVER HERE WAS COMING ALONG WITH THIS BUG-THINGY. THOUGHT I MIGHT BE ABLE TO HELP.
HELP? YOU? HOW?
AFTER LAST NIGHT'S BROUHAHA I GOT TO THINKING THAT THESE BEASTIES REMIND ME OF SOME BIG BUGS I'D RUN INTO BEFORE...ON VACATION DOWN IN RIO. THIS NEW BATCH WAS MUCH TOUGHER, THOUGH.
MAYBE YOU'RE JUST GETTING SOFT.
OH, THAT'S RICH COMING FROM YOU, HIDING THERE BEHIND YOUR PAL THE SLAYER. ANY TIME YOU WANT TO TRY ME, CREAM-PUFF, YOU JUST LET ME KNOW.
BAD NEWS!

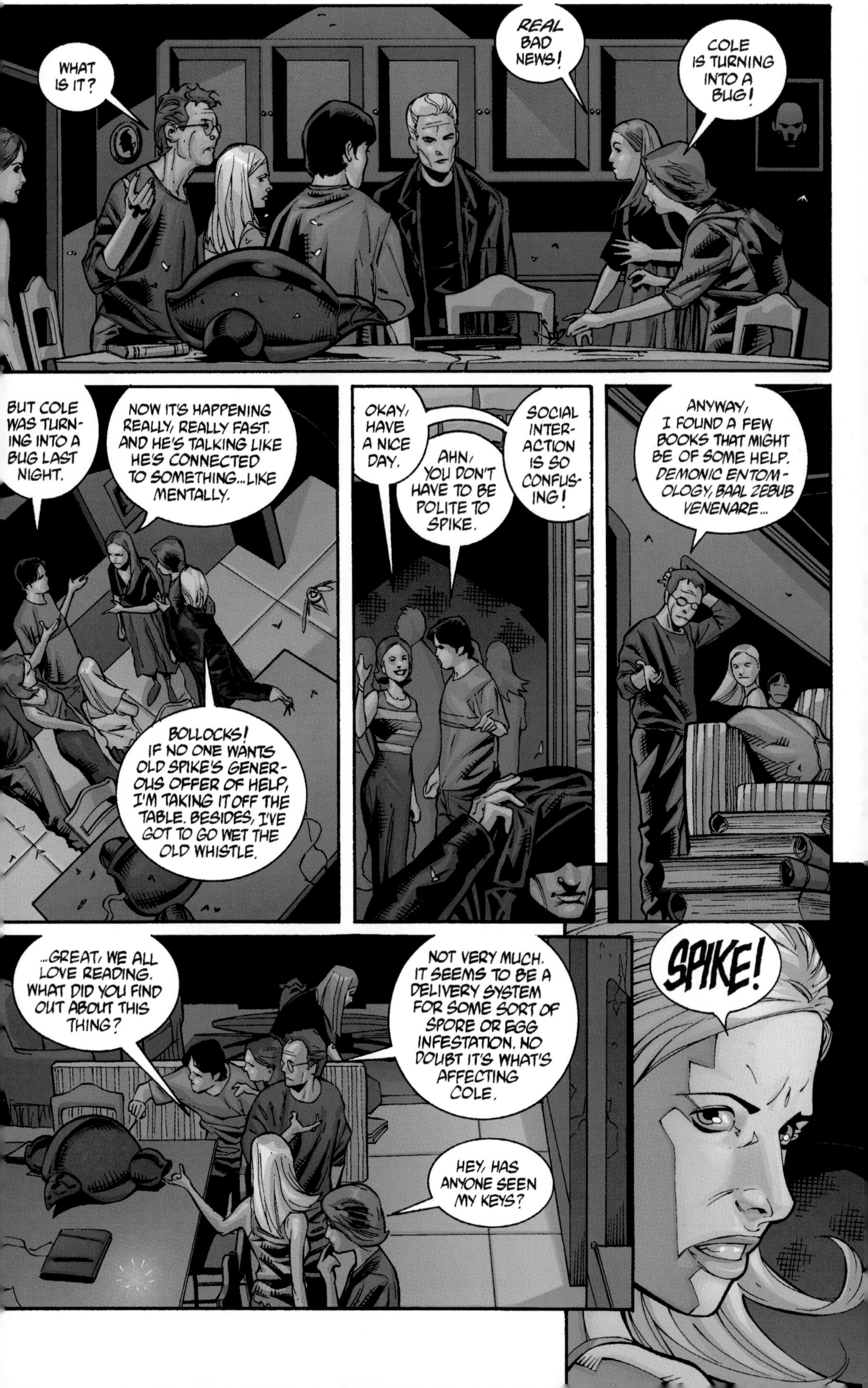
WHAT IS IT?
REAL BAD NEWS!
COLE IS TURNING INTO A BUG!
BUT COLE WAS TURNING INTO A BUG LAST NIGHT.
NOW IT'S HAPPENING REALLY, REALLY FAST. AND HE'S TALKING LIKE HE'S CONNECTED TO SOMETHING...LIKE MENTALLY.
BOLLOCKS! IF NO ONE WANTS OLD SPIKE'S GENEROUS OFFER OF HELP, I'M TAKING IT OFF THE TABLE. BESIDES, I'VE GOT TO GO WET THE OLD WHISTLE.
OKAY, HAVE A NICE DAY.
SOCIAL INTERACTION IS SO CONFUSING!
AHN, YOU DON'T HAVE TO BE POLITE TO SPIKE.
ANYWAY, I FOUND A FEW BOOKS THAT MIGHT BE OF SOME HELP. DEMONIC ENTOMOLOGY, BAAL ZEBUB VENENARE...
...GREAT, WE ALL LOVE READING. WHAT DID YOU FIND OUT ABOUT THIS THING?
NOT VERY MUCH. IT SEEMS TO BE A DELIVERY SYSTEM FOR SOME SORT OF SPORE OR EGG INFESTATION. NO DOUBT IT'S WHAT'S AFFECTING COLE.
HEY, HAS ANYONE SEEN MY KEYS?
SPIKE!

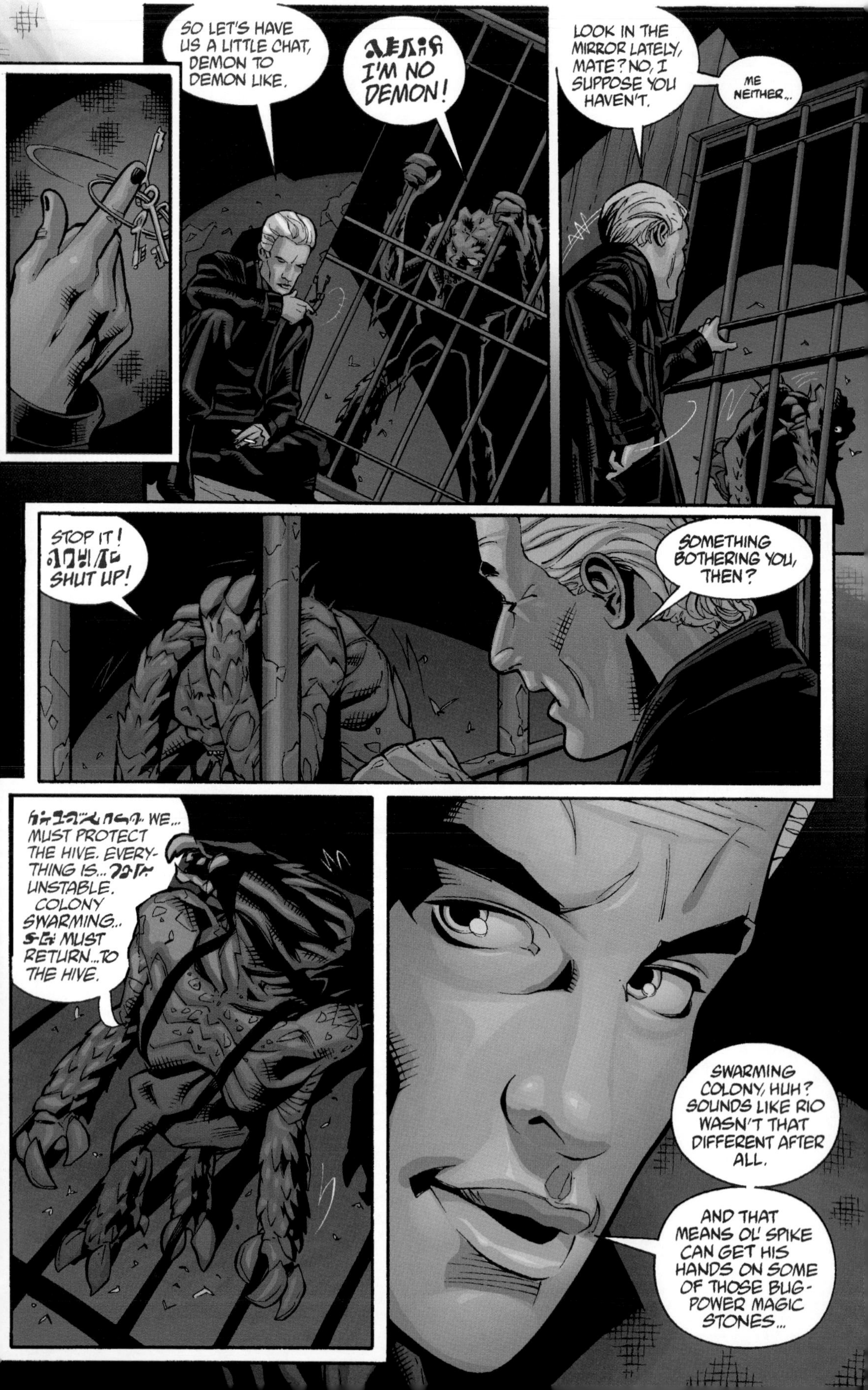

SO LET'S HAVE US A LITTLE CHAT, DEMON TO DEMON LIKE.
I'M NO DEMON!
LOOK IN THE MIRROR LATELY, MATE? NO, I SUPPOSE YOU HAVEN'T.
ME NEITHER...
STOP IT! SHUT UP!
SOMETHING BOTHERING YOU, THEN?
WE... MUST PROTECT THE HIVE. EVERYTHING IS... UNSTABLE. COLONY SWARMING... MUST RETURN... TO THE HIVE.
SWARMING COLONY, HUH? SOUNDS LIKE RIO WASN'T THAT DIFFERENT AFTER ALL.
AND THAT MEANS OL' SPIKE CAN GET HIS HANDS ON SOME OF THOSE BUG-POWER MAGIC STONES...

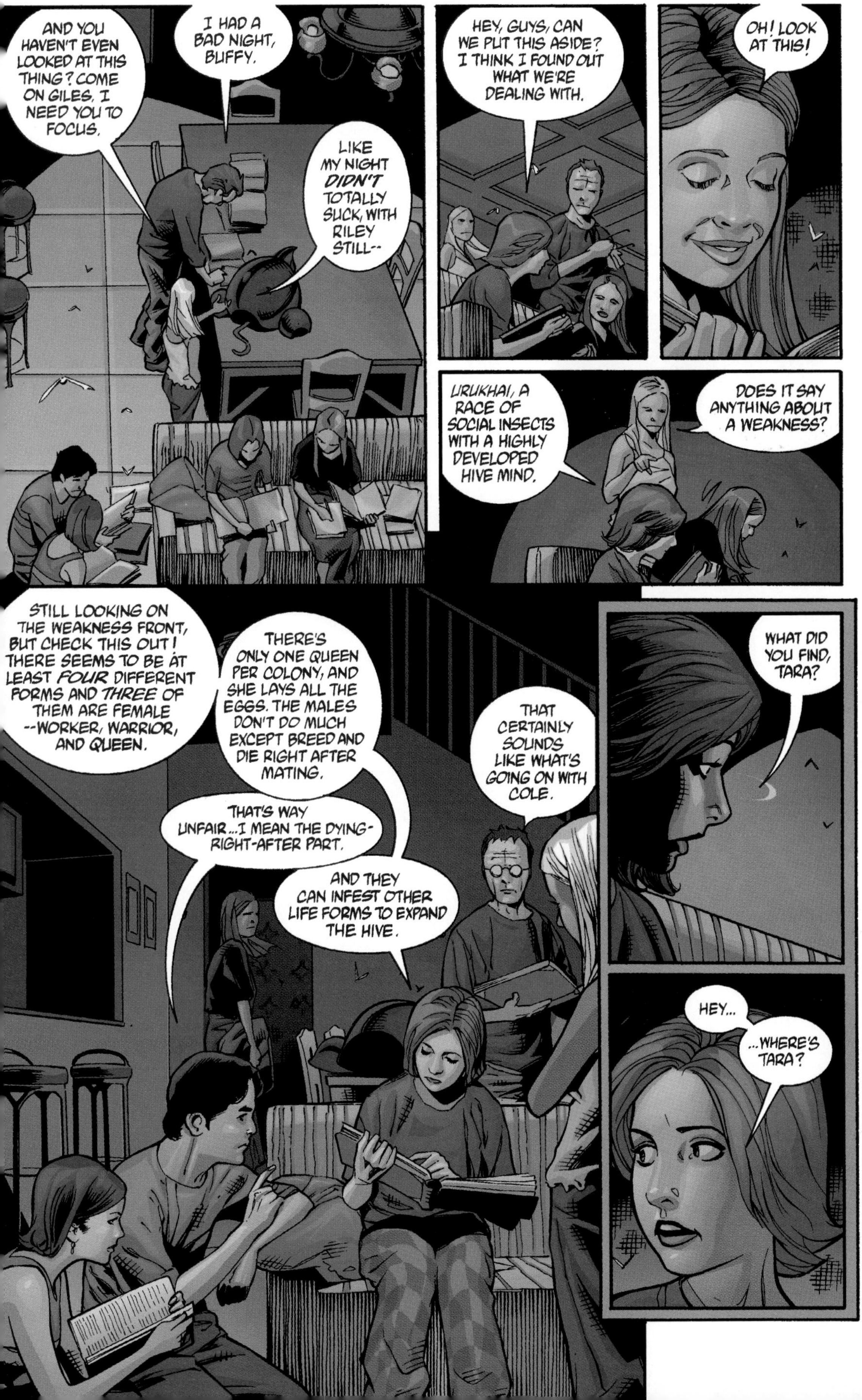
AND YOU HAVEN'T EVEN LOOKED AT THIS THING? COME ON GILES. I NEED YOU TO FOCUS.
I HAD A BAD NIGHT, BUFFY.
LIKE MY NIGHT *DIDN'T* TOTALLY SUCK, WITH RILEY STILL--
HEY, GUYS, CAN WE PUT THIS ASIDE? I THINK I FOUND OUT WHAT WE'RE DEALING WITH.
OH! LOOK AT THIS!
URUKHAI, A RACE OF SOCIAL INSECTS WITH A HIGHLY DEVELOPED HIVE MIND.
DOES IT SAY ANYTHING ABOUT A WEAKNESS?
STILL LOOKING ON THE WEAKNESS FRONT, BUT CHECK THIS OUT! THERE SEEMS TO BE AT LEAST *FOUR* DIFFERENT FORMS AND *THREE* OF THEM ARE FEMALE --WORKER, WARRIOR, AND QUEEN.
THERE'S ONLY ONE QUEEN PER COLONY, AND SHE LAYS ALL THE EGGS. THE MALES DON'T DO MUCH EXCEPT BREED AND DIE RIGHT AFTER MATING.
THAT'S WAY UNFAIR...I MEAN THE DYING-RIGHT-AFTER PART.
AND THEY CAN INFEST OTHER LIFE FORMS TO EXPAND THE HIVE.
THAT CERTAINLY SOUNDS LIKE WHAT'S GOING ON WITH COLE.
WHAT DID YOU FIND, TARA?
HEY...
...WHERE'S TARA?

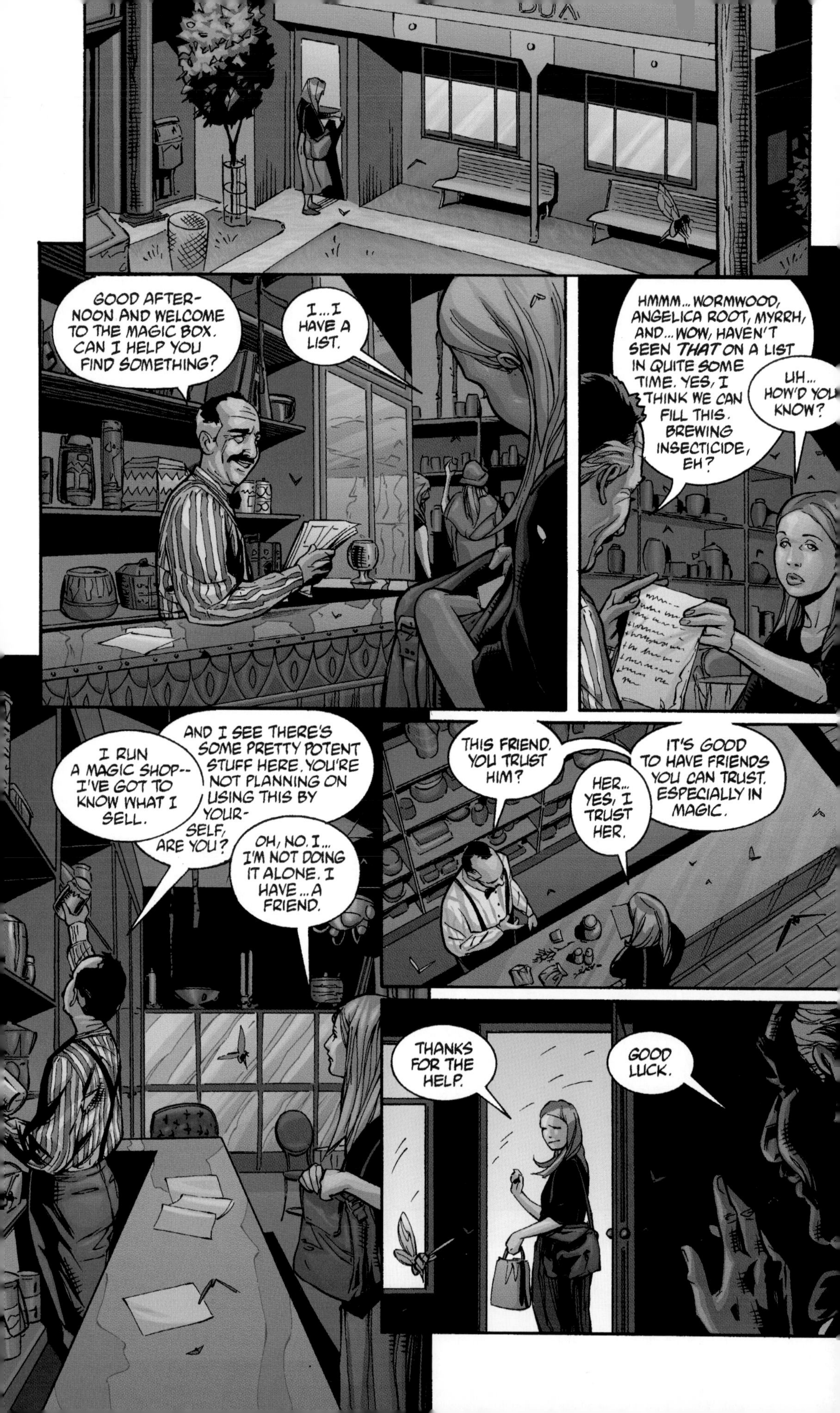
GOOD AFTER-NOON AND WELCOME TO THE MAGIC BOX. CAN I HELP YOU FIND SOMETHING?
I...I HAVE A LIST.
HMMM... WORMWOOD, ANGELICA ROOT, MYRRH, AND... WOW, HAVEN'T SEEN *THAT* ON A LIST IN QUITE SOME TIME. YES, I THINK WE CAN FILL THIS. BREWING INSECTICIDE, EH?
UH... HOW'D YOU KNOW?
I RUN A MAGIC SHOP-- I'VE GOT TO KNOW WHAT I SELL.
AND I SEE THERE'S SOME PRETTY POTENT STUFF HERE. YOU'RE NOT PLANNING ON USING THIS BY YOUR-SELF, ARE YOU?
OH, NO. I... I'M NOT DOING IT ALONE. I HAVE... A FRIEND.
THIS FRIEND. YOU TRUST HIM?
HER... YES, I TRUST HER.
IT'S GOOD TO HAVE FRIENDS YOU CAN TRUST. ESPECIALLY IN MAGIC.
THANKS FOR THE HELP.
GOOD LUCK.

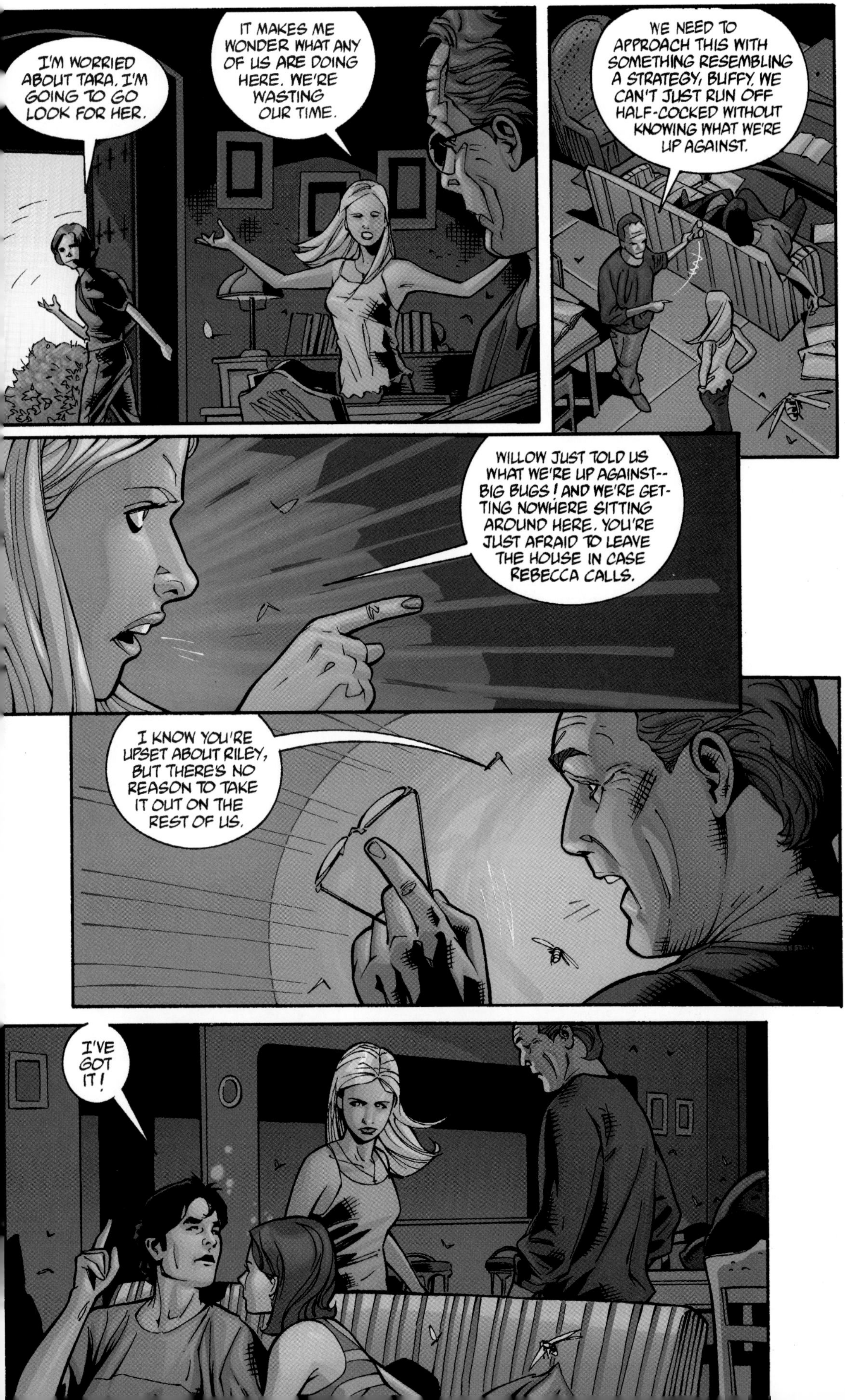
I'M WORRIED ABOUT TARA. I'M GOING TO GO LOOK FOR HER.
IT MAKES ME WONDER WHAT ANY OF US ARE DOING HERE. WE'RE WASTING OUR TIME.
WE NEED TO APPROACH THIS WITH SOMETHING RESEMBLING A STRATEGY, BUFFY. WE CAN'T JUST RUN OFF HALF-COCKED WITHOUT KNOWING WHAT WE'RE UP AGAINST.
WILLOW JUST TOLD US WHAT WE'RE UP AGAINST-- BIG BUGS! AND WE'RE GETTING NOWHERE SITTING AROUND HERE. YOU'RE JUST AFRAID TO LEAVE THE HOUSE IN CASE REBECCA CALLS.
I KNOW YOU'RE UPSET ABOUT RILEY, BUT THERE'S NO REASON TO TAKE IT OUT ON THE REST OF US.
I'VE GOT IT!

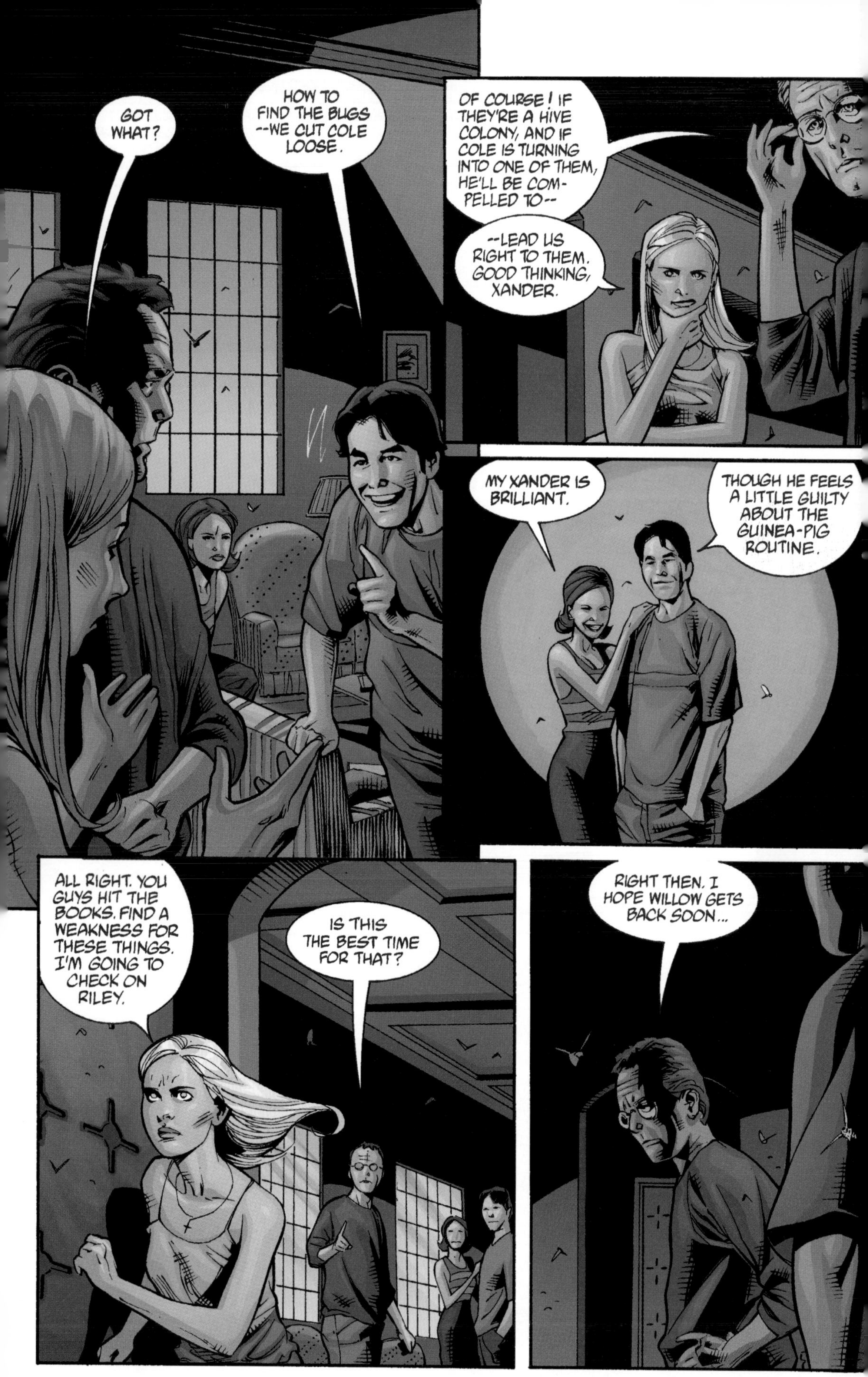
GOT WHAT?
HOW TO FIND THE BUGS --WE CUT COLE LOOSE.
OF COURSE! IF THEY'RE A HIVE COLONY, AND IF COLE IS TURNING INTO ONE OF THEM, HE'LL BE COMPELLED TO--
--LEAD US RIGHT TO THEM. GOOD THINKING, XANDER.
MY XANDER IS BRILLIANT.
THOUGH HE FEELS A LITTLE GUILTY ABOUT THE GUINEA-PIG ROUTINE.
ALL RIGHT. YOU GUYS HIT THE BOOKS. FIND A WEAKNESS FOR THESE THINGS. I'M GOING TO CHECK ON RILEY.
IS THIS THE BEST TIME FOR THAT?
RIGHT THEN. I HOPE WILLOW GETS BACK SOON...

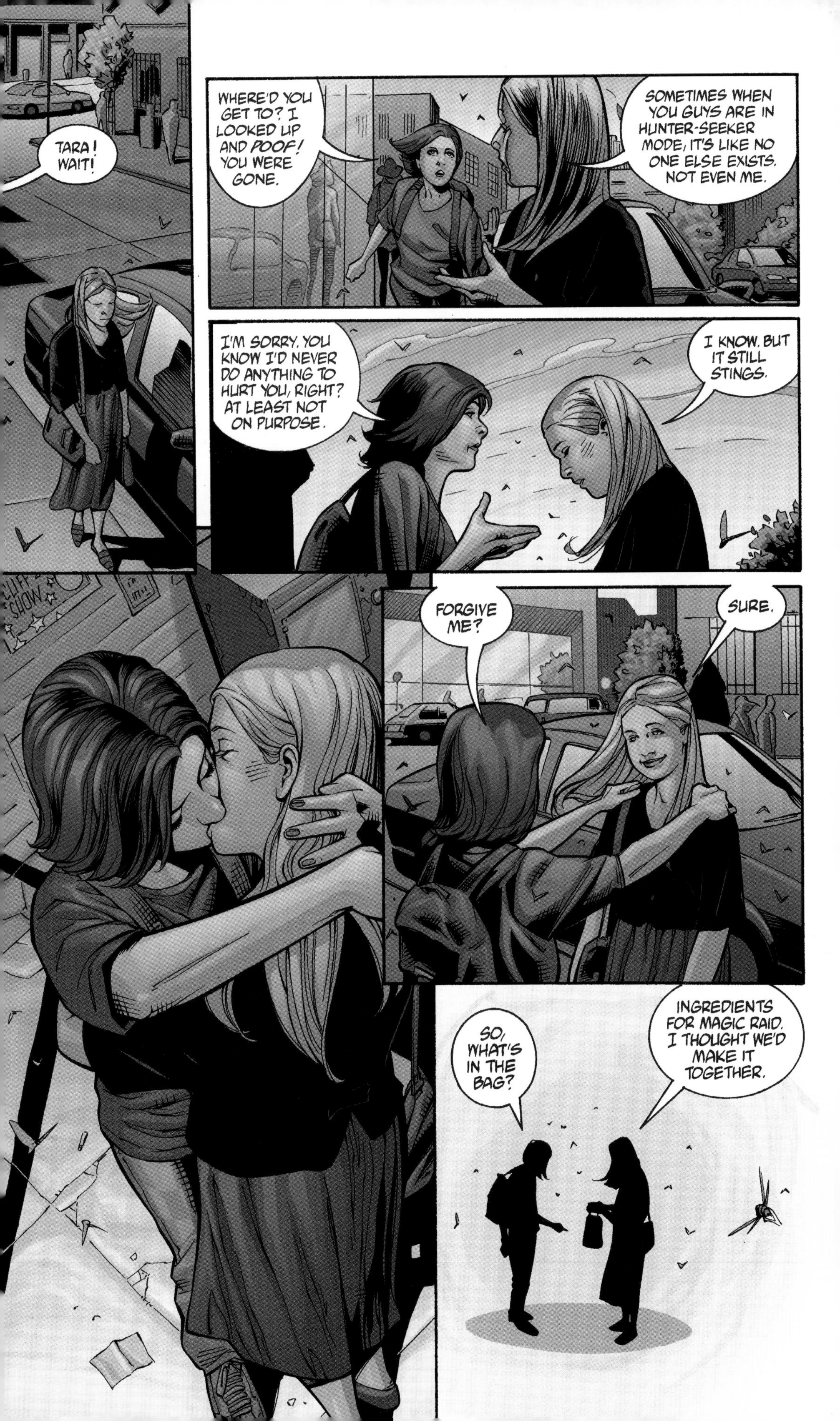
TARA! WAIT!
WHERE'D YOU GET TO? I LOOKED UP AND POOF! YOU WERE GONE.
SOMETIMES WHEN YOU GUYS ARE IN HUNTER-SEEKER MODE, IT'S LIKE NO ONE ELSE EXISTS. NOT EVEN ME.
I'M SORRY. YOU KNOW I'D NEVER DO ANYTHING TO HURT YOU, RIGHT? AT LEAST NOT ON PURPOSE.
I KNOW. BUT IT STILL STINGS.
FORGIVE ME?
SURE.
SO, WHAT'S IN THE BAG?
INGREDIENTS FOR MAGIC RAID. I THOUGHT WE'D MAKE IT TOGETHER.

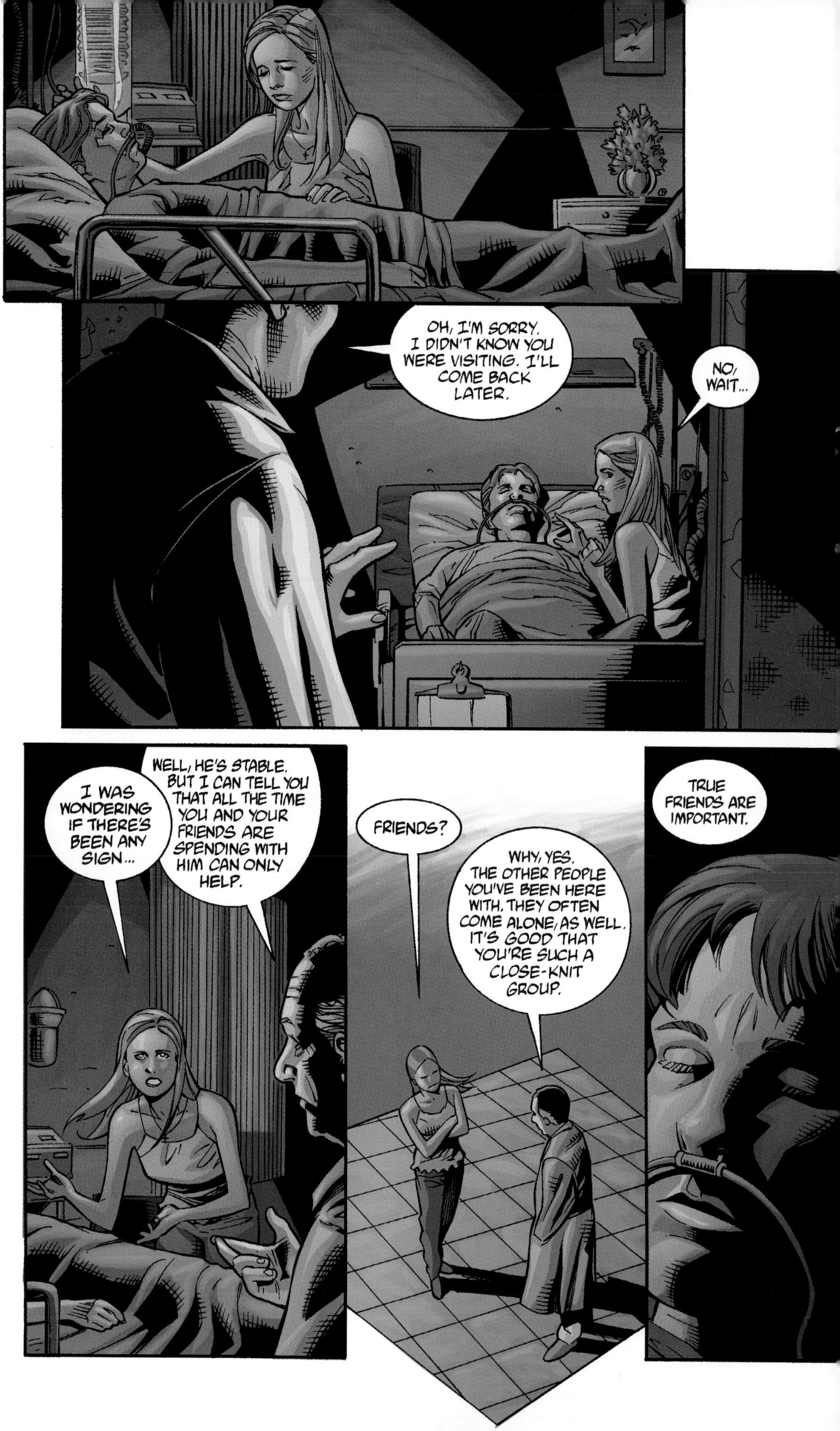
OH, I'M SORRY. I DIDN'T KNOW YOU WERE VISITING. I'LL COME BACK LATER.
NO, WAIT...
I WAS WONDERING IF THERE'S BEEN ANY SIGN...
WELL, HE'S STABLE. BUT I CAN TELL YOU THAT ALL THE TIME YOU AND YOUR FRIENDS ARE SPENDING WITH HIM CAN ONLY HELP.
FRIENDS?
WHY, YES. THE OTHER PEOPLE YOU'VE BEEN HERE WITH. THEY OFTEN COME ALONE, AS WELL. IT'S GOOD THAT YOU'RE SUCH A CLOSE-KNIT GROUP.
TRUE FRIENDS ARE IMPORTANT.

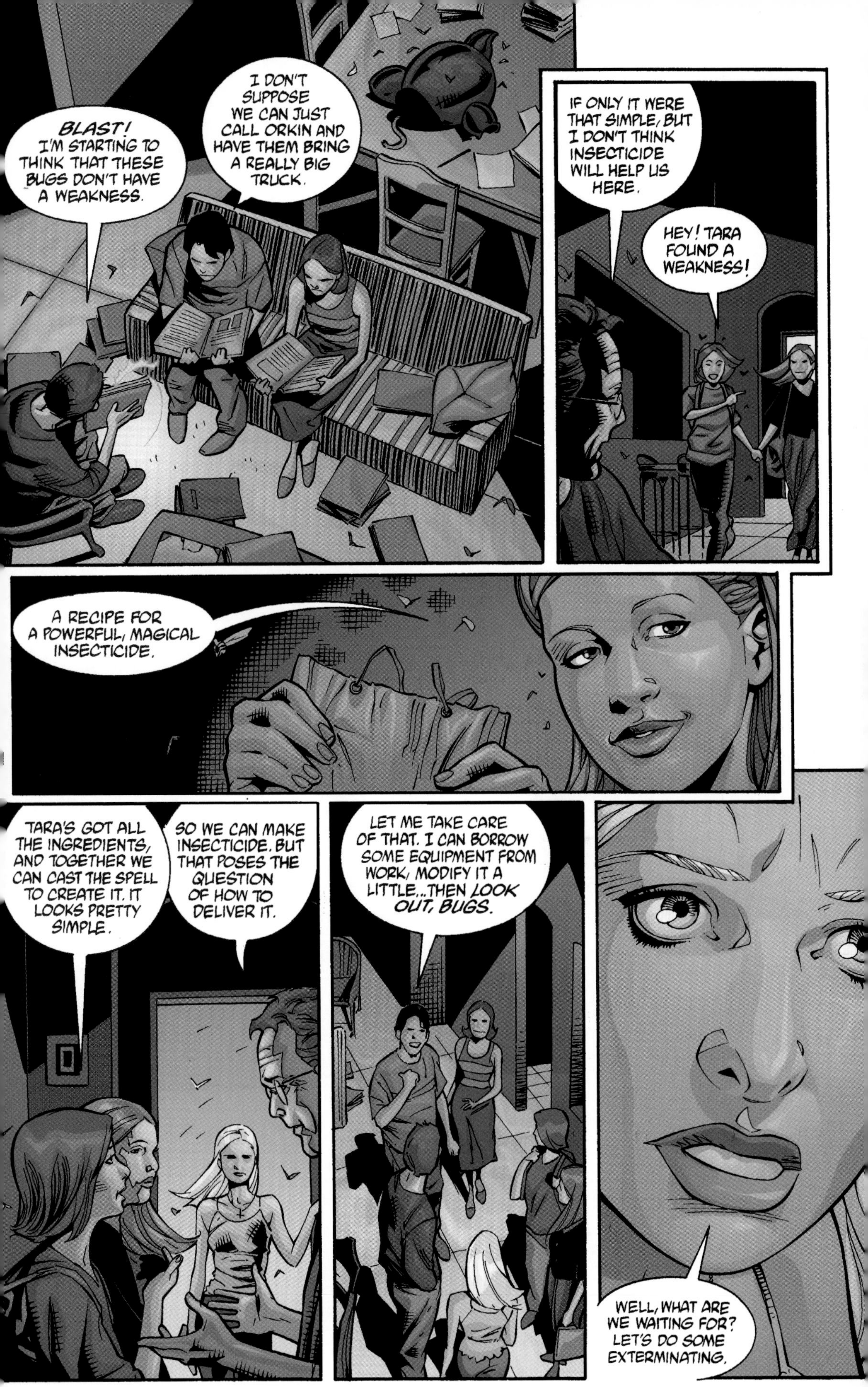
BLAST! I'M STARTING TO THINK THAT THESE BUGS DON'T HAVE A WEAKNESS.
I DON'T SUPPOSE WE CAN JUST CALL ORKIN AND HAVE THEM BRING A REALLY BIG TRUCK.
IF ONLY IT WERE THAT SIMPLE, BUT I DON'T THINK INSECTICIDE WILL HELP US HERE.
HEY! TARA FOUND A WEAKNESS!
A RECIPE FOR A POWERFUL, MAGICAL INSECTICIDE.
TARA'S GOT ALL THE INGREDIENTS, AND TOGETHER WE CAN CAST THE SPELL TO CREATE IT. IT LOOKS PRETTY SIMPLE.
SO WE CAN MAKE INSECTICIDE. BUT THAT POSES THE QUESTION OF HOW TO DELIVER IT.
LET ME TAKE CARE OF THAT. I CAN BORROW SOME EQUIPMENT FROM WORK, MODIFY IT A LITTLE...THEN LOOK OUT, BUGS.
WELL, WHAT ARE WE WAITING FOR? LET'S DO SOME EXTERMINATING.

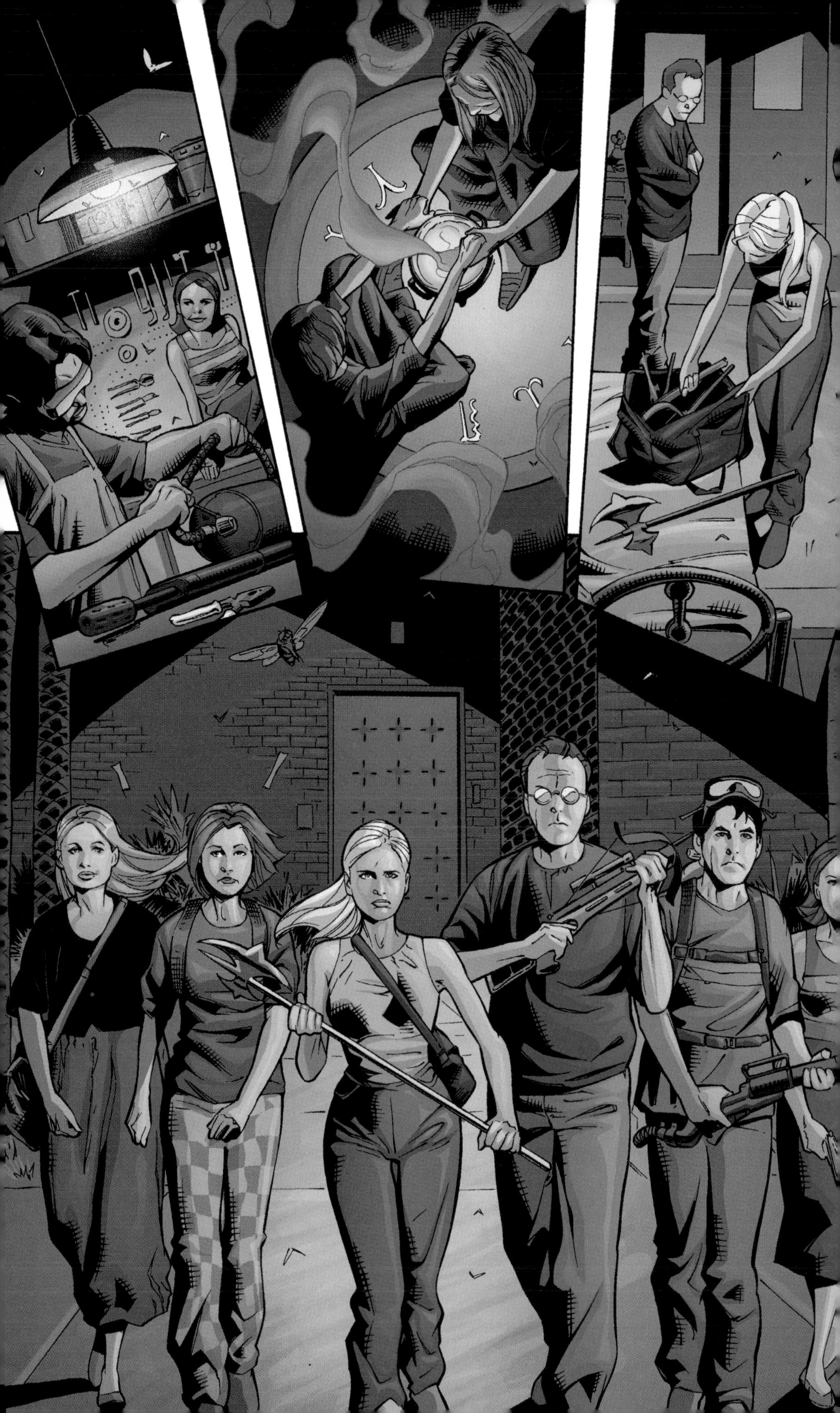

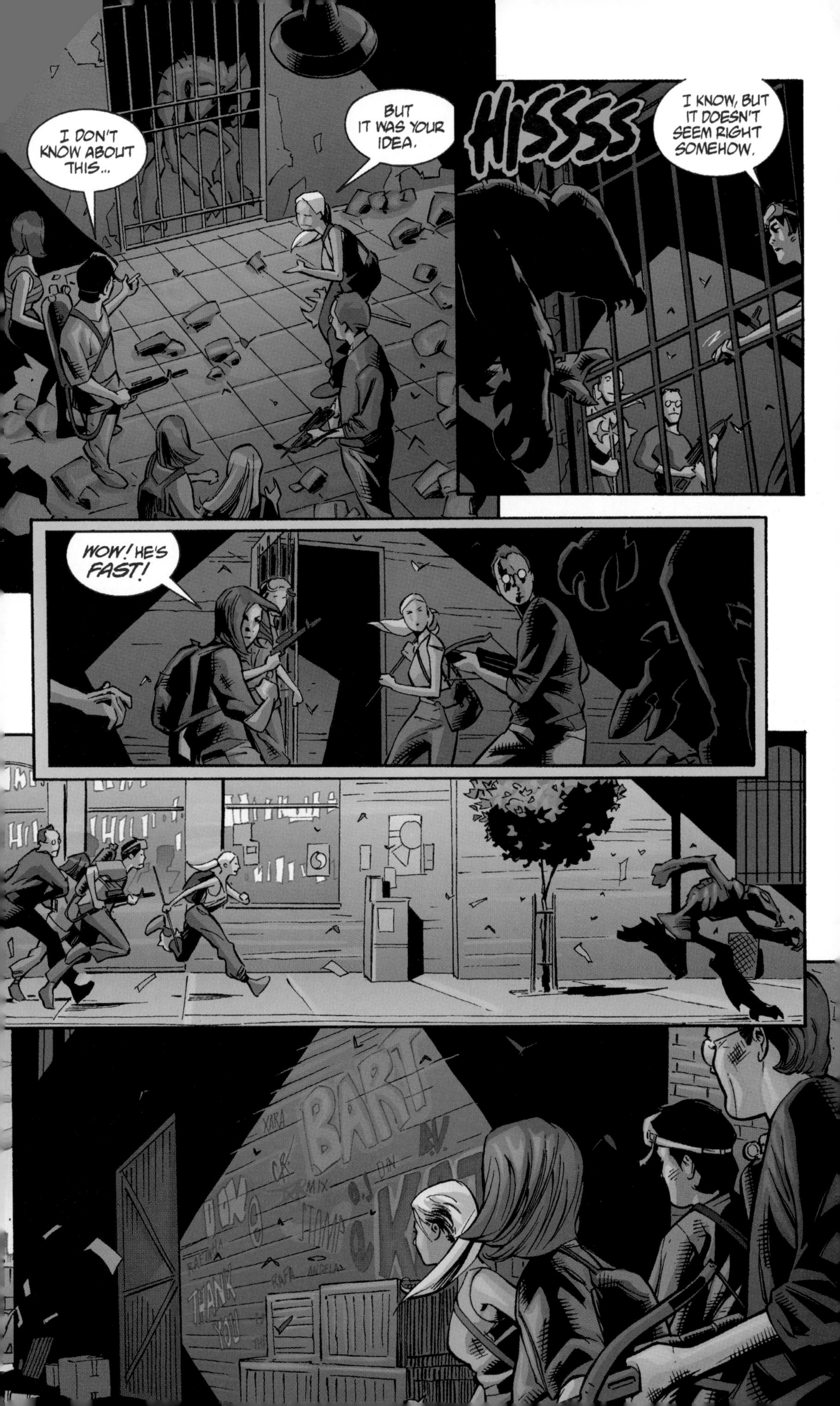
I DON'T KNOW ABOUT THIS...
BUT IT WAS YOUR IDEA.
HISSSS
I KNOW, BUT IT DOESN'T SEEM RIGHT SOMEHOW.
WOW! HE'S FAST!
BART

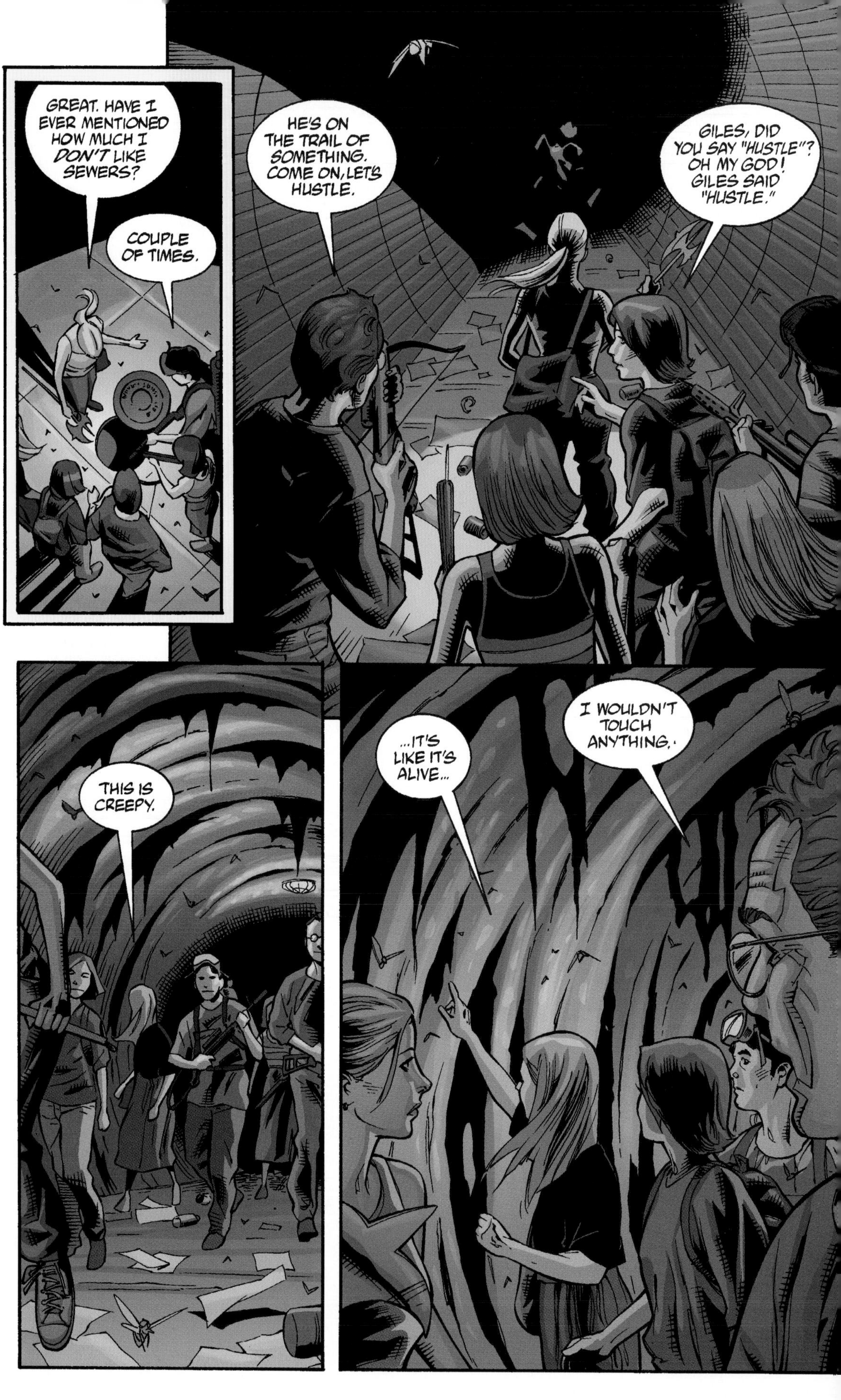
GREAT. HAVE I EVER MENTIONED HOW MUCH I *DON'T* LIKE SEWERS?
COUPLE OF TIMES.
HE'S ON THE TRAIL OF SOMETHING. COME ON, LET'S HUSTLE.
GILES, DID YOU SAY "HUSTLE"? OH MY GOD! GILES SAID "HUSTLE."
THIS IS CREEPY.
...IT'S LIKE IT'S ALIVE...
I WOULDN'T TOUCH ANYTHING.

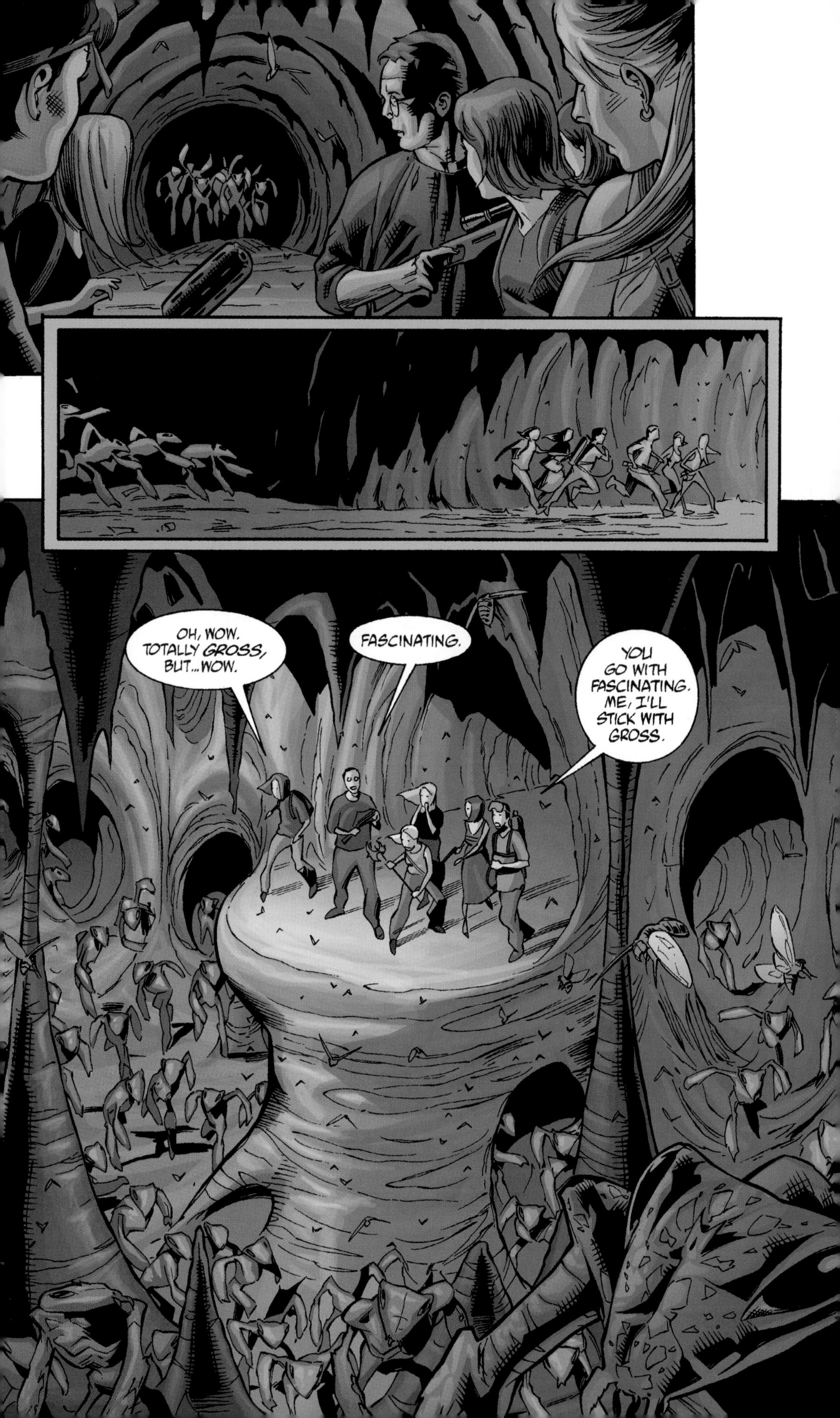
OH, WOW. TOTALLY *GROSS*, BUT...WOW.
FASCINATING.
YOU GO WITH FASCINATING. ME, I'LL STICK WITH GROSS.

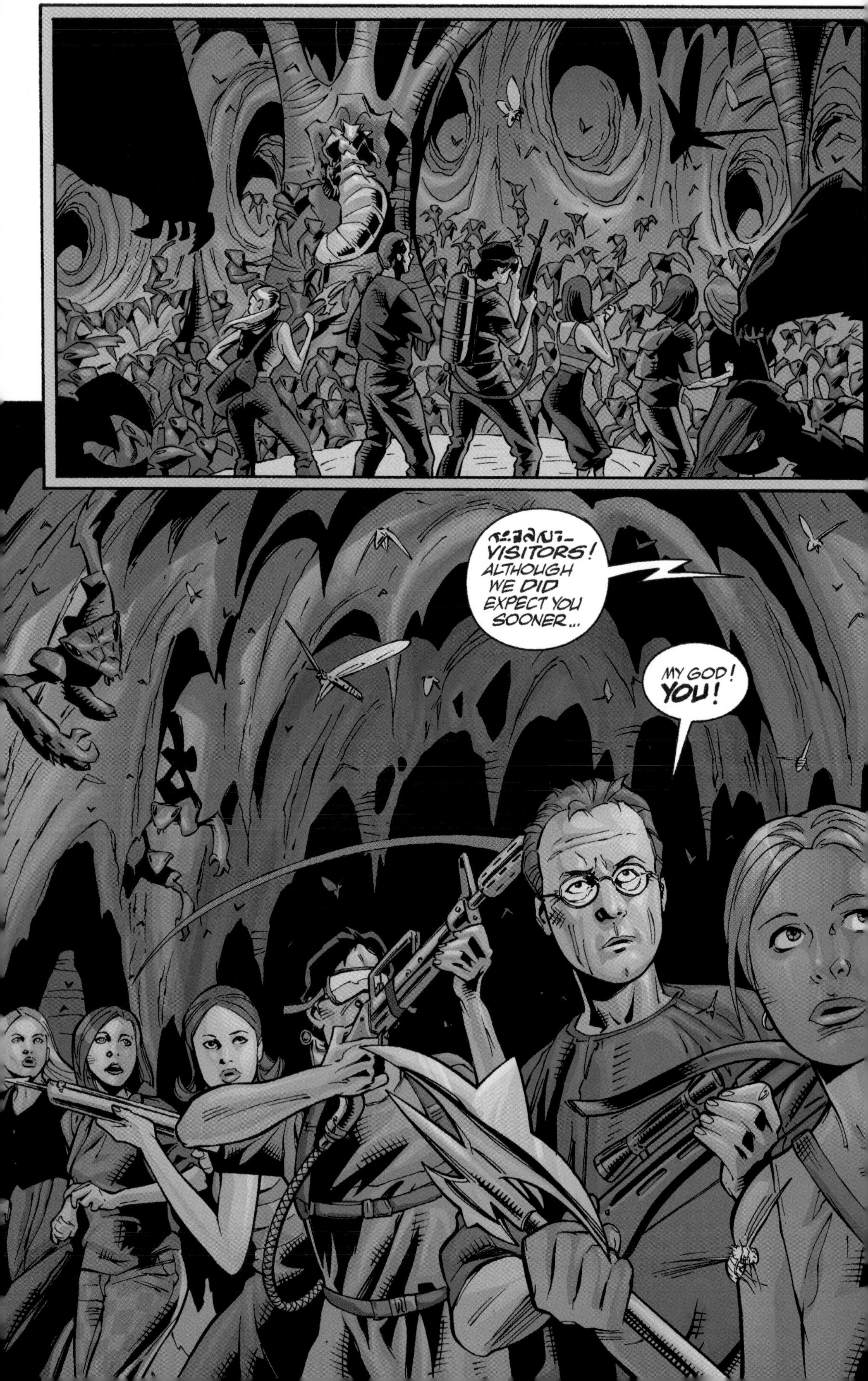
VISITORS! ALTHOUGH WE DID EXPECT YOU SOONER...
MY GOD! YOU!

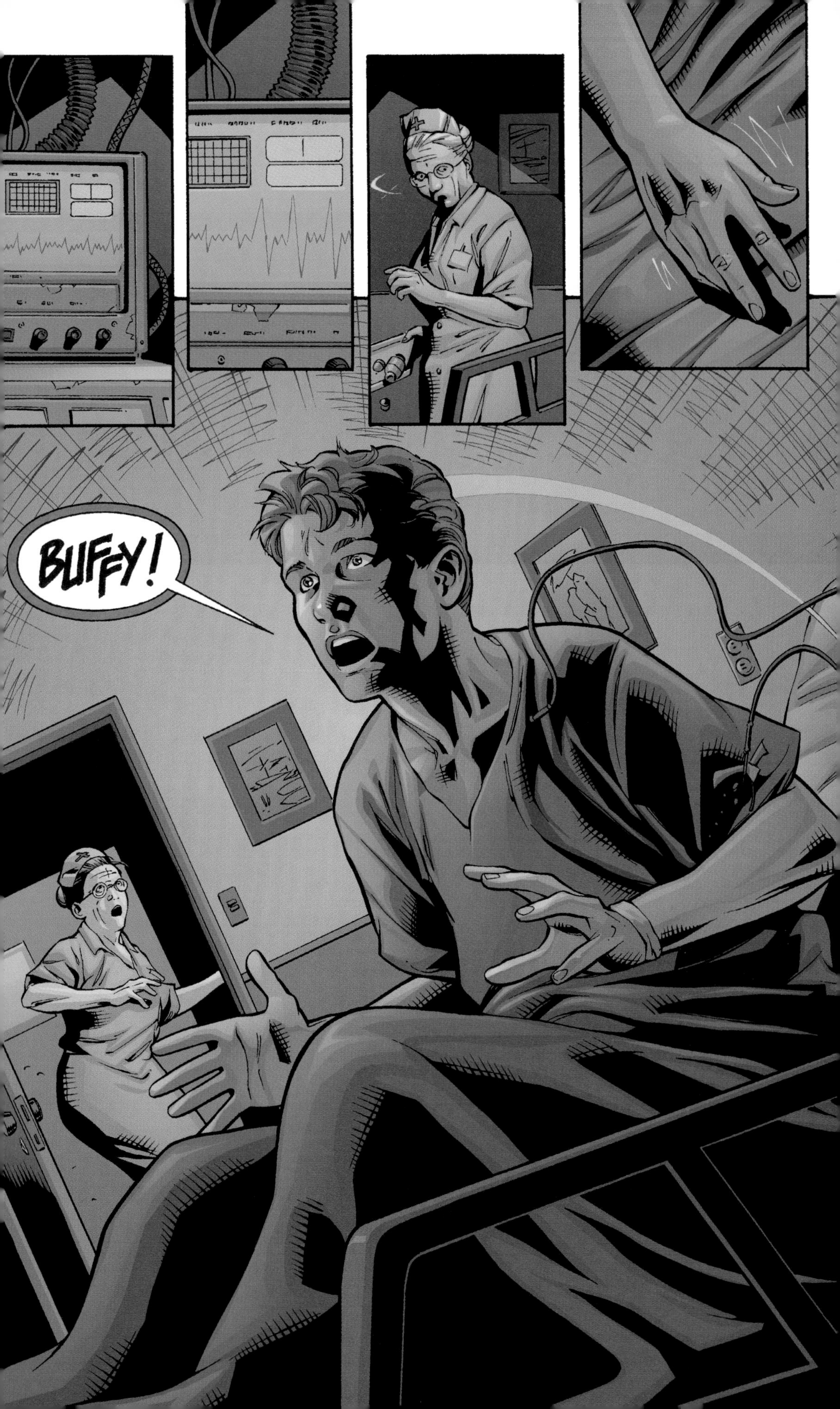
BUFFY!

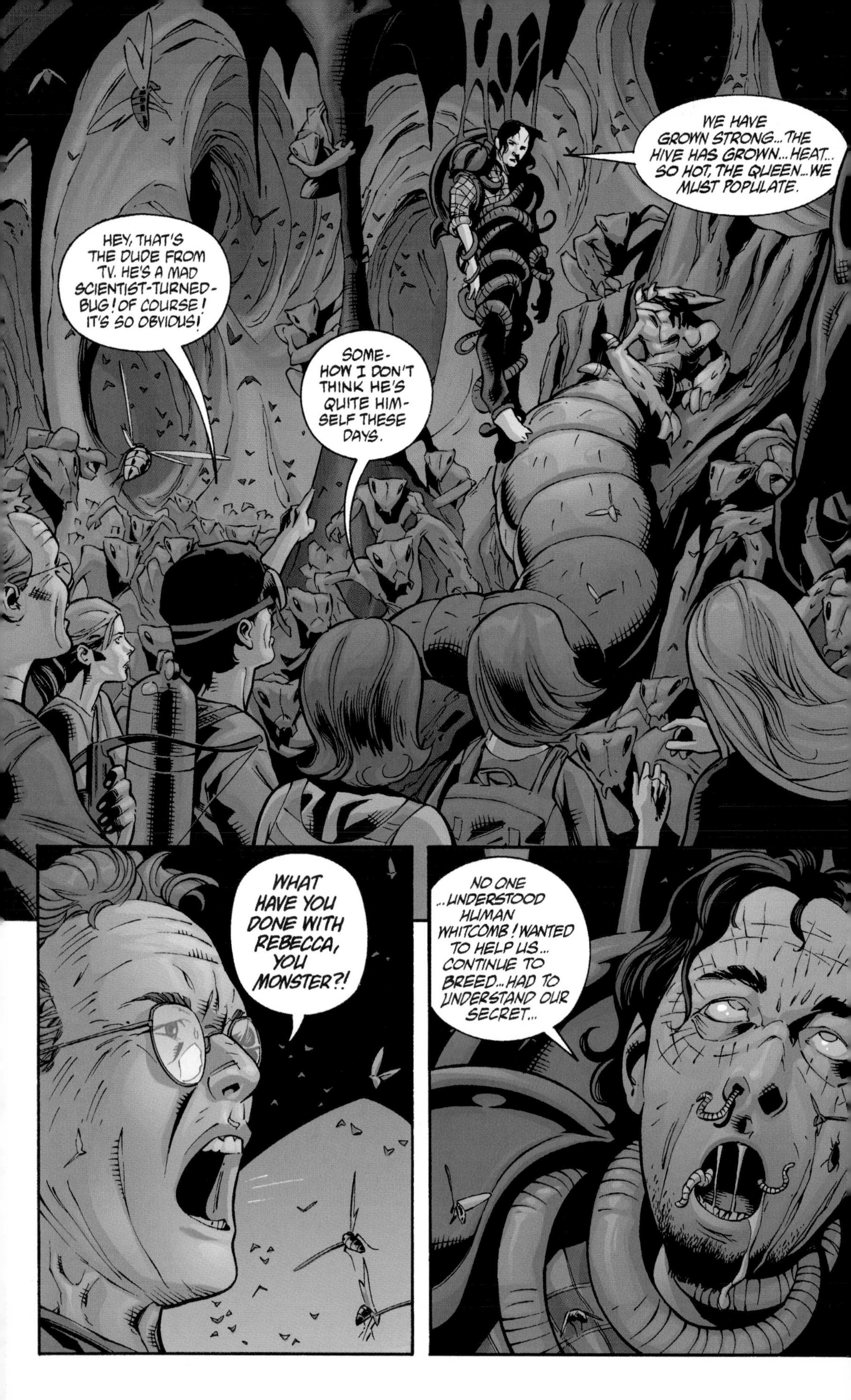
WE HAVE GROWN STRONG... THE HIVE HAS GROWN... HEAT... SO HOT, THE QUEEN... WE MUST POPULATE.
HEY, THAT'S THE DUDE FROM TV. HE'S A MAD SCIENTIST-TURNED-BUG! OF COURSE! IT'S SO OBVIOUS!
SOME-HOW I DON'T THINK HE'S QUITE HIM-SELF THESE DAYS.
WHAT HAVE YOU DONE WITH REBECCA, YOU MONSTER?!
NO ONE ...UNDERSTOOD HUMAN WHITCOMB! WANTED TO HELP US... CONTINUE TO BREED... HAD TO UNDERSTAND OUR SECRET...

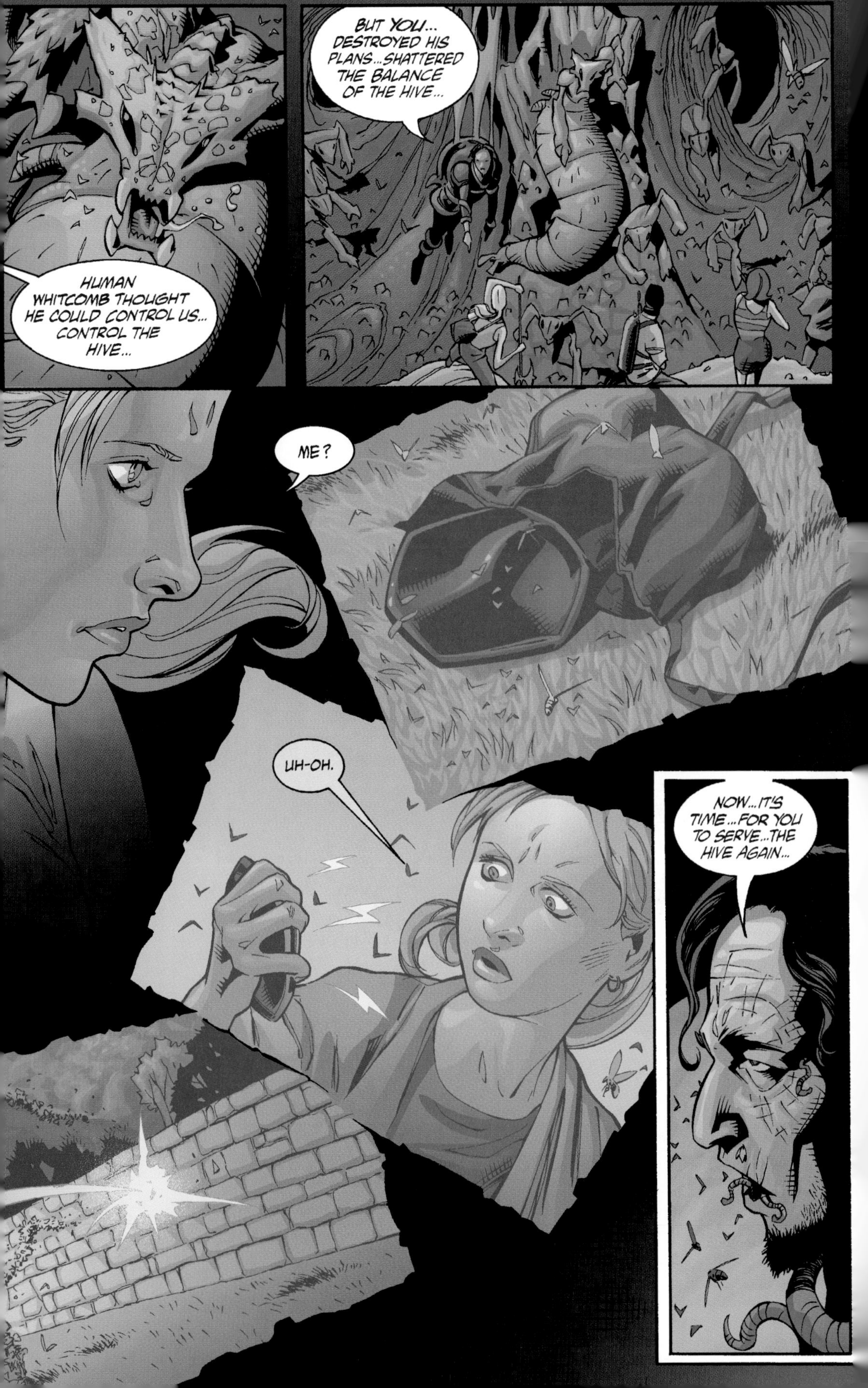
HUMAN WHITCOMB THOUGHT HE COULD CONTROL US... CONTROL THE HIVE...
BUT YOU... DESTROYED HIS PLANS...SHATTERED THE BALANCE OF THE HIVE...
ME?
UH-OH.
NOW...IT'S TIME...FOR YOU TO SERVE...THE HIVE AGAIN...

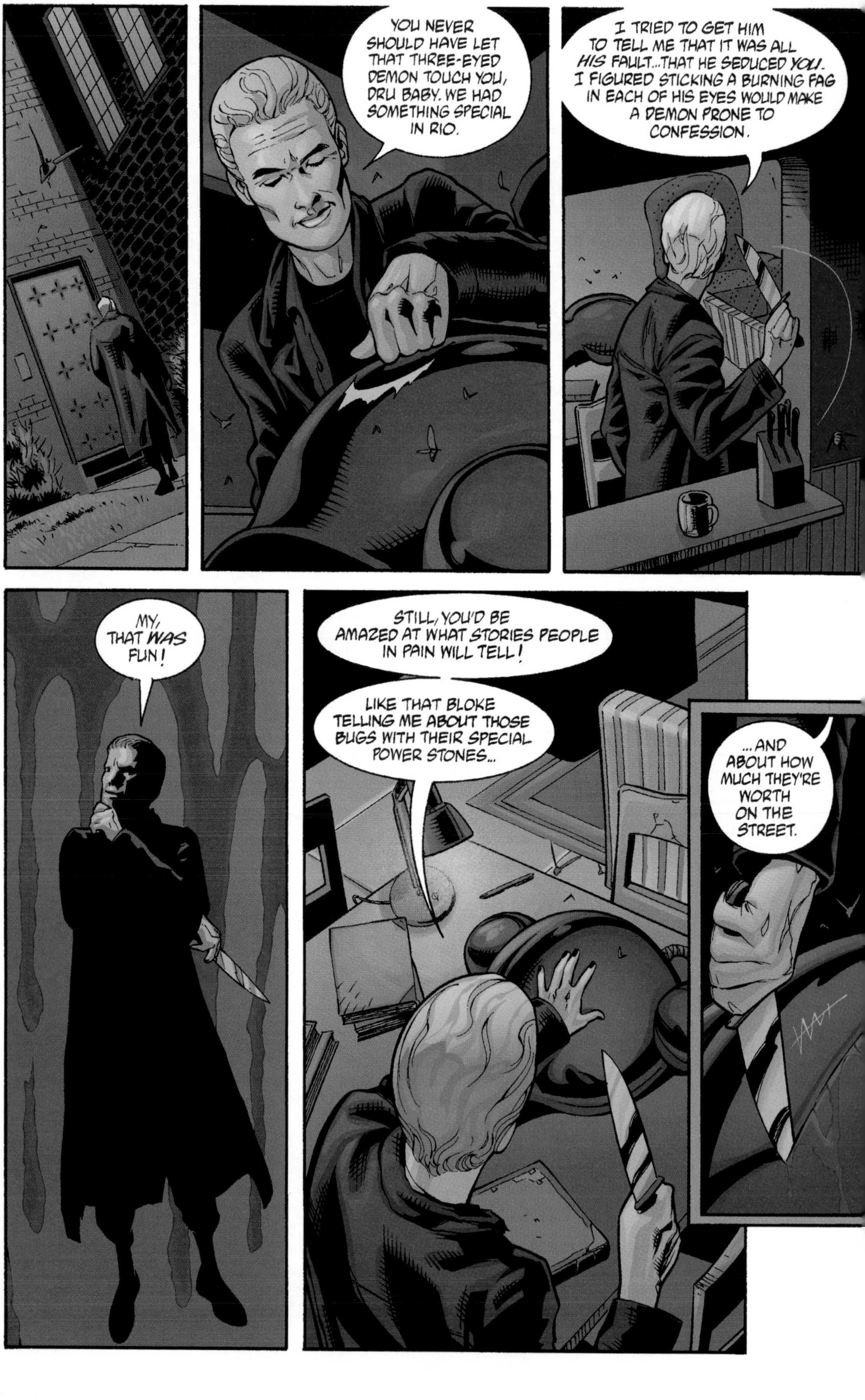
YOU NEVER SHOULD HAVE LET THAT THREE-EYED DEMON TOUCH YOU, DRU BABY. WE HAD SOMETHING SPECIAL IN RIO.
I TRIED TO GET HIM TO TELL ME THAT IT WAS ALL *HIS* FAULT...THAT HE SEDUCED *YOU*. I FIGURED STICKING A BURNING FAG IN EACH OF HIS EYES WOULD MAKE A DEMON PRONE TO CONFESSION.
MY, THAT *WAS* FUN!
STILL, YOU'D BE AMAZED AT WHAT STORIES PEOPLE IN PAIN WILL TELL!
LIKE THAT BLOKE TELLING ME ABOUT THOSE BUGS WITH THEIR SPECIAL POWER STONES...
...AND ABOUT HOW MUCH THEY'RE WORTH ON THE STREET.

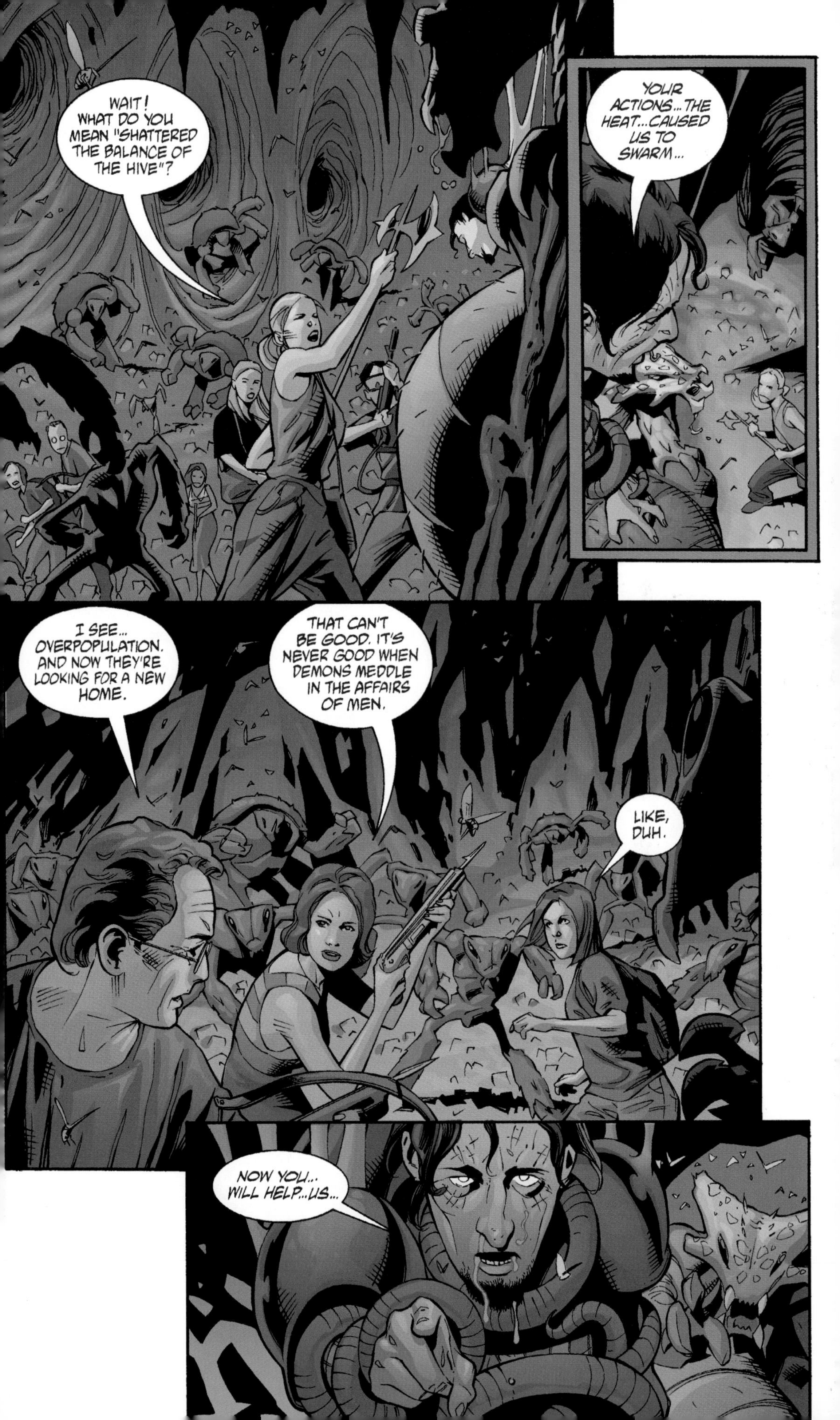
WAIT! WHAT DO YOU MEAN "SHATTERED THE BALANCE OF THE HIVE"?
YOUR ACTIONS...THE HEAT...CAUSED US TO SWARM...
I SEE... OVERPOPULATION. AND NOW THEY'RE LOOKING FOR A NEW HOME.
THAT CAN'T BE GOOD. IT'S NEVER GOOD WHEN DEMONS MEDDLE IN THE AFFAIRS OF MEN.
LIKE, DUH.
NOW YOU... WILL HELP...US...

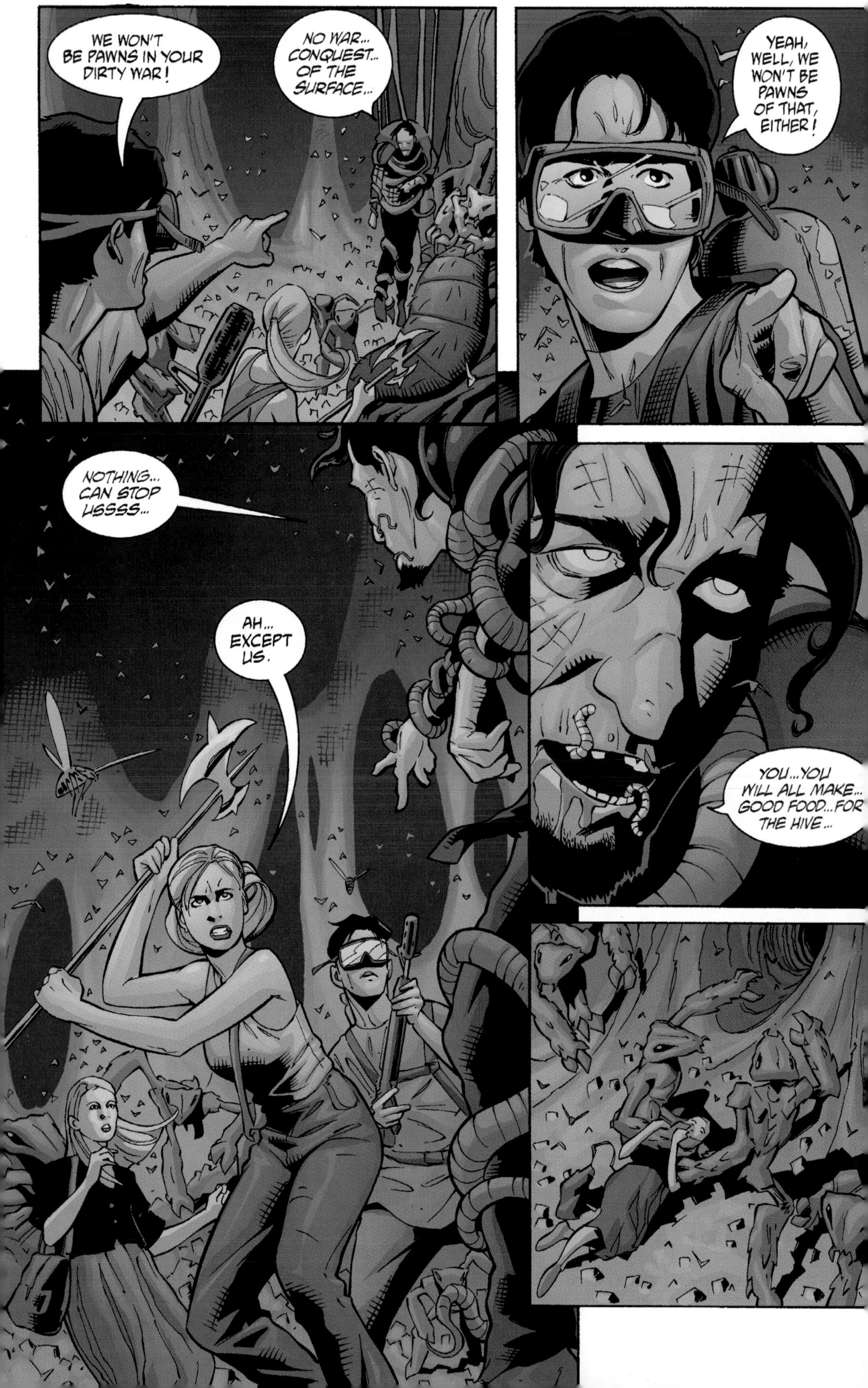
WE WON'T BE PAWNS IN YOUR DIRTY WAR!
NO WAR... CONQUEST... OF THE SURFACE...
YEAH, WELL, WE WON'T BE PAWNS OF THAT, EITHER!
NOTHING... CAN STOP USSSS...
AH... EXCEPT US.
YOU...YOU WILL ALL MAKE... GOOD FOOD...FOR THE HIVE...

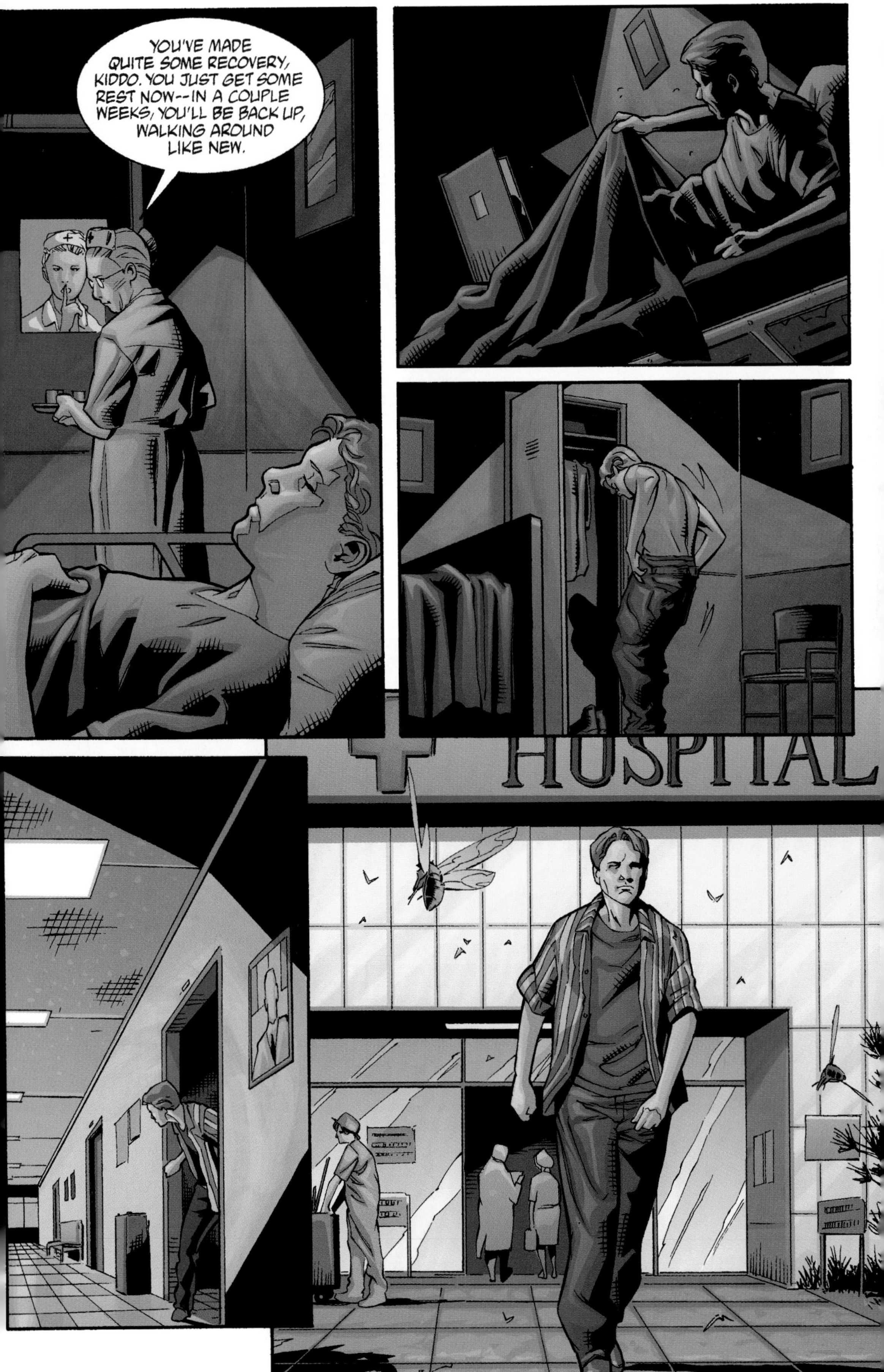
YOU'VE MADE QUITE SOME RECOVERY, KIDDO. YOU JUST GET SOME REST NOW--IN A COUPLE WEEKS, YOU'LL BE BACK UP, WALKING AROUND LIKE NEW.
HOSPITAL

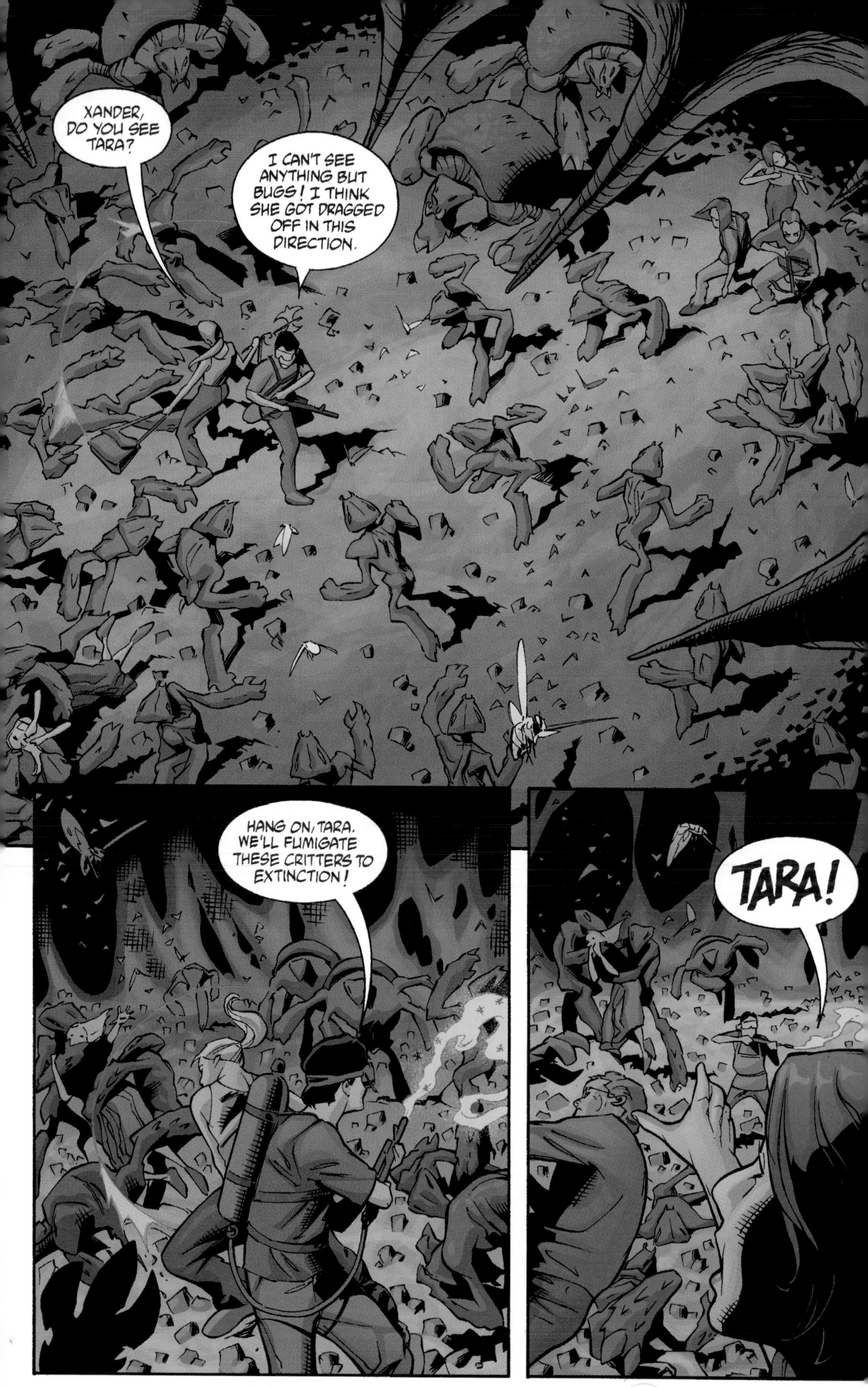
XANDER, DO YOU SEE TARA?
I CAN'T SEE ANYTHING BUT BUGS! I THINK SHE GOT DRAGGED OFF IN THIS DIRECTION.
HANG ON, TARA. WE'LL FUMIGATE THESE CRITTERS TO EXTINCTION!
TARA!

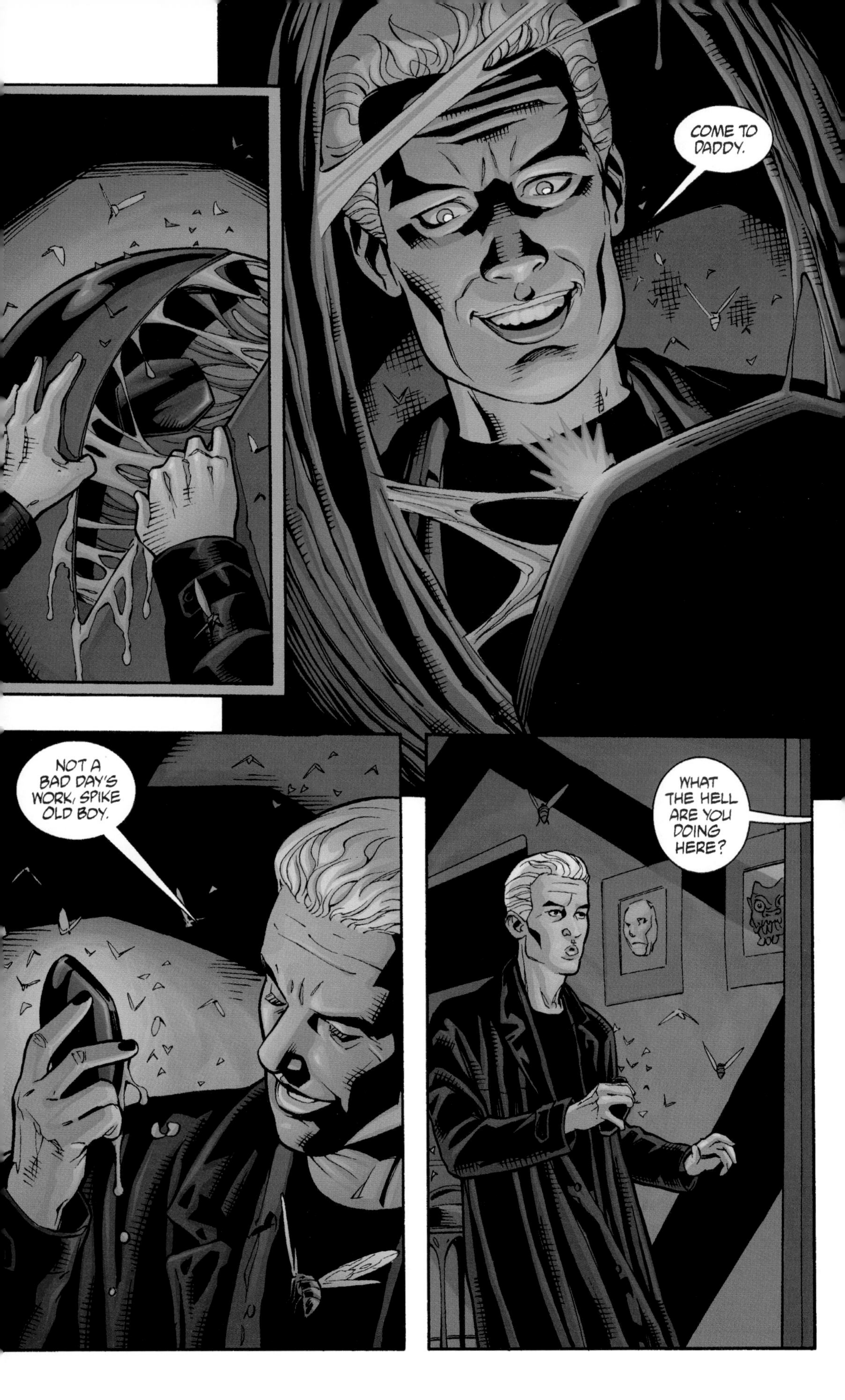
COME TO DADDY.
NOT A BAD DAY'S WORK, SPIKE OLD BOY.
WHAT THE HELL ARE YOU DOING HERE?

WELL, WELL. ENJOY YOUR BEAUTY SLEEP? I HATE TO BE THE ONE TO BREAK THE NEWS, BUT IT REALLY DIDN'T DO ALL THAT MUCH FOR YOU.

DON'T MESS WITH ME, SPIKE. I'M NOT IN THE MOOD. WHAT ARE YOU UP TO?

A LITTLE RABBLE-ROUSING, A LITTLE TROUBLE-MAKING... BASICALLY AS MUCH BADNESS AS I CAN MANAGE WITH THIS DEBILITATING CHIP IN MY HEAD.

YOU WANT THAT CHIP OUT SO BAD...

...LET'S BLOW IT OUT.

OKAY, OKAY. TRUTH IS, JUST CAME BY TO GET THIS.

WHAT THE HELL IS THAT?

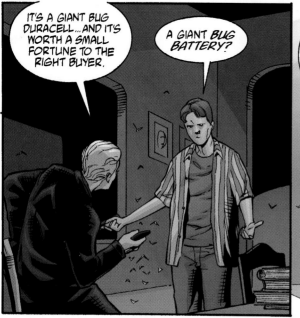

IT'S A GIANT BUG DURACELL... AND IT'S WORTH A SMALL FORTUNE TO THE RIGHT BUYER.

A GIANT BUG BATTERY?

OH, RIGHT. SLEEPING BEAUTY HERE MISSED ALL THE ACTION WHILE ME AND THE SLAYER BEEN KEEPING SUNNYDALE SAFE FROM INFESTATION.

WELL THEN FILL ME IN.

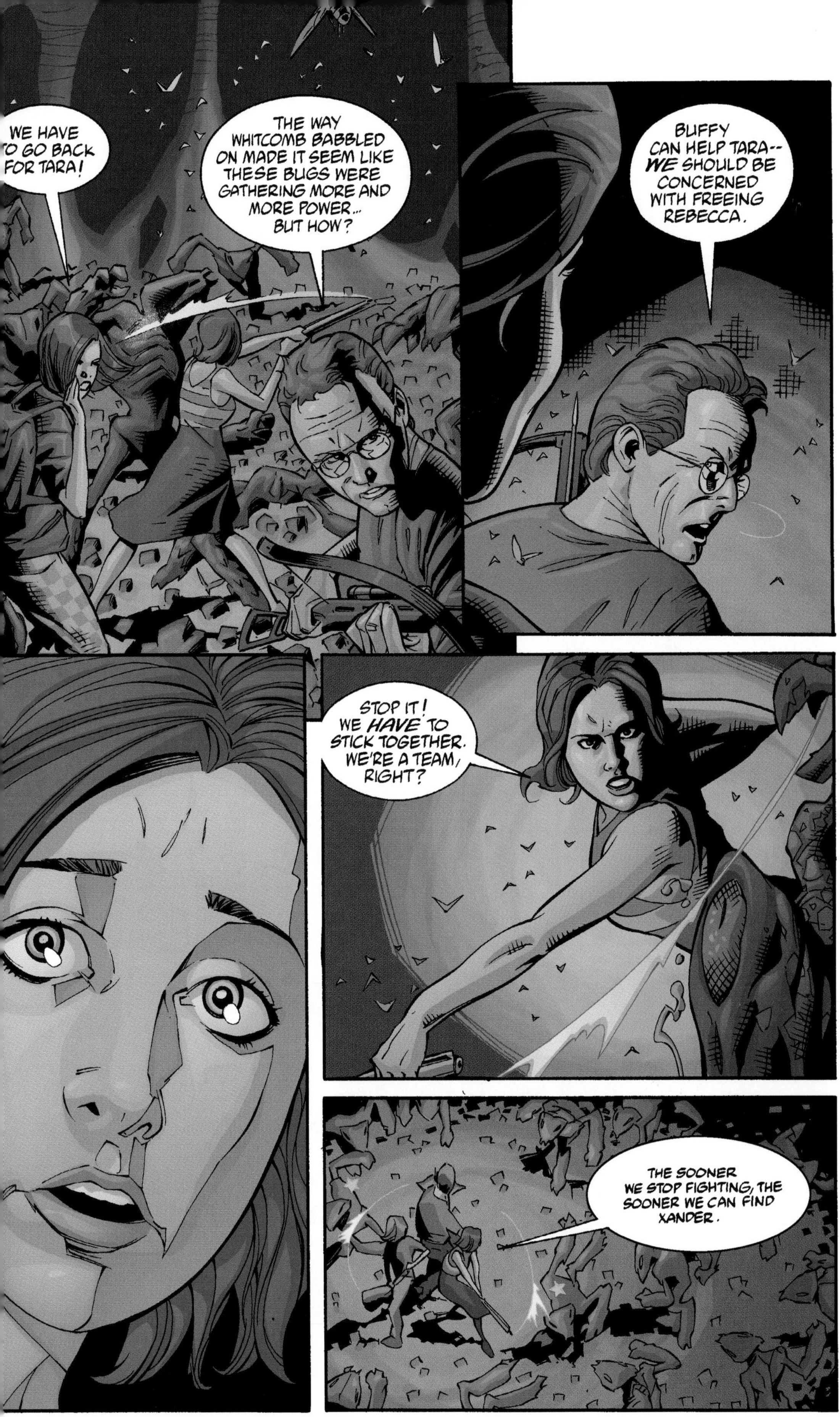
WE HAVE TO GO BACK FOR TARA!
THE WAY WHITCOMB BABBLED ON MADE IT SEEM LIKE THESE BUGS WERE GATHERING MORE AND MORE POWER... BUT HOW?
BUFFY CAN HELP TARA-- WE SHOULD BE CONCERNED WITH FREEING REBECCA.
STOP IT! WE HAVE TO STICK TOGETHER. WE'RE A TEAM, RIGHT?
THE SOONER WE STOP FIGHTING, THE SOONER WE CAN FIND XANDER.

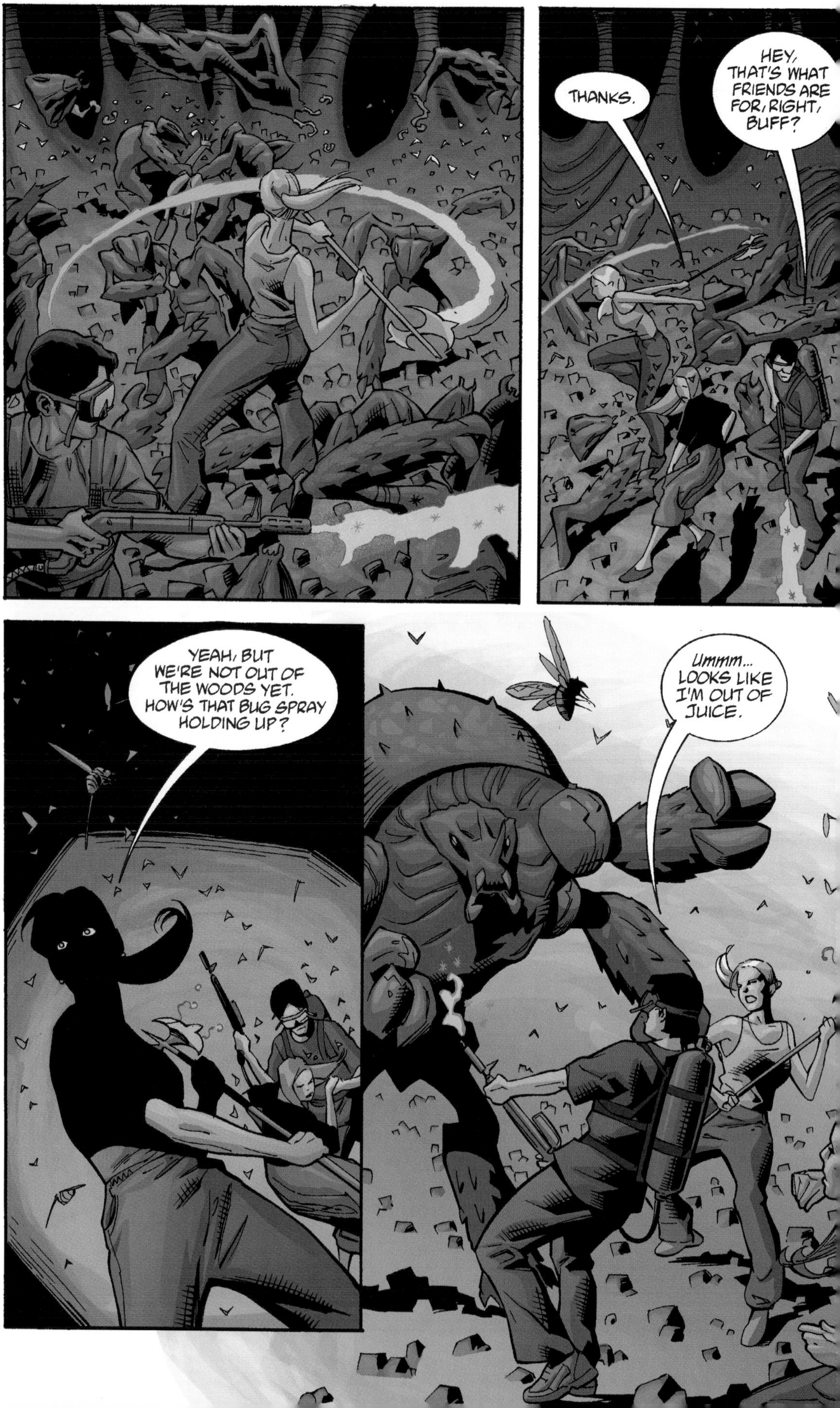
THANKS.
HEY, THAT'S WHAT FRIENDS ARE FOR, RIGHT, BUFF?
YEAH, BUT WE'RE NOT OUT OF THE WOODS YET. HOW'S THAT BUG SPRAY HOLDING UP?
Ummm... LOOKS LIKE I'M OUT OF JUICE.

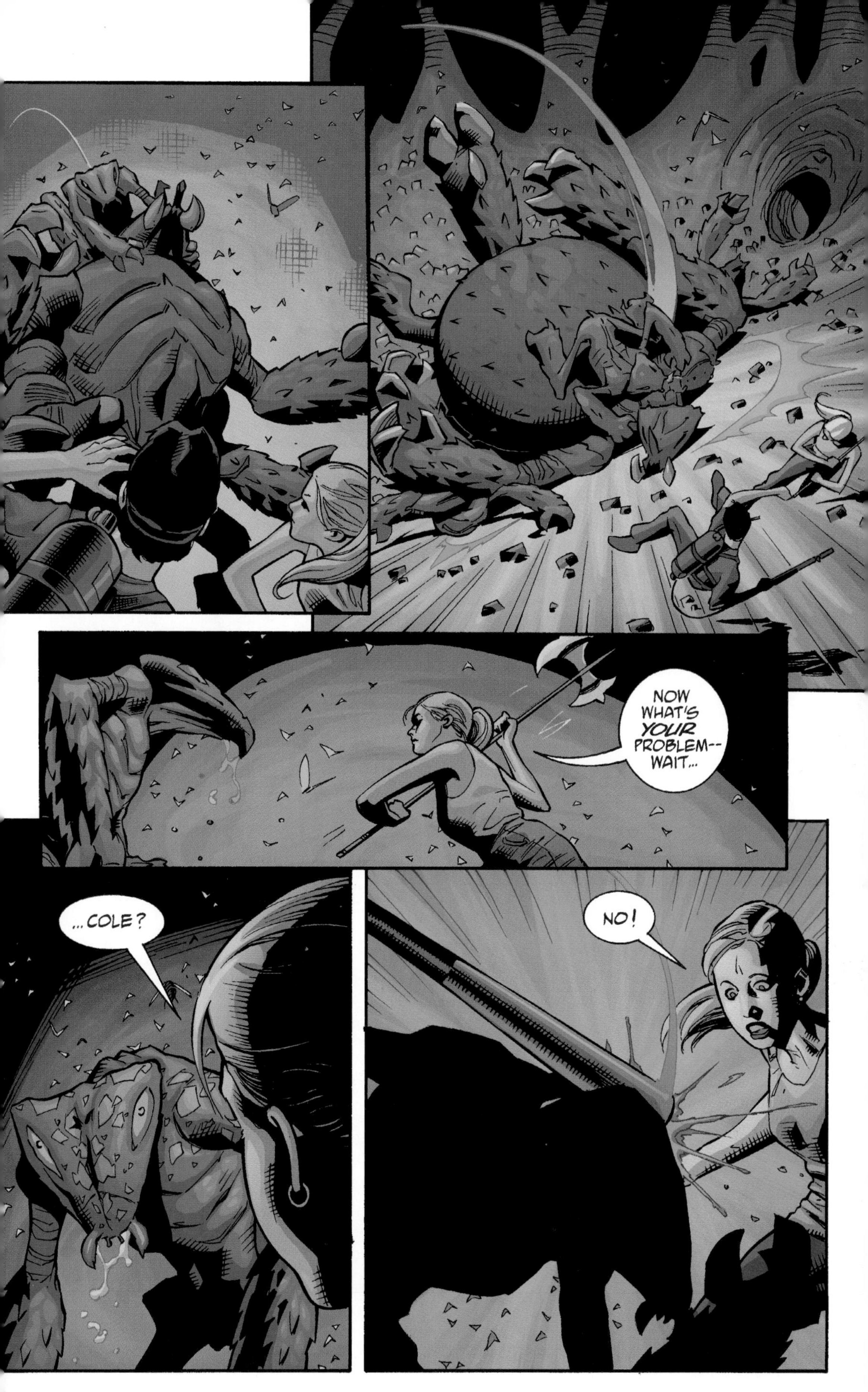
NOW WHAT'S *YOUR* PROBLEM-- WAIT...
...COLE?
NO!

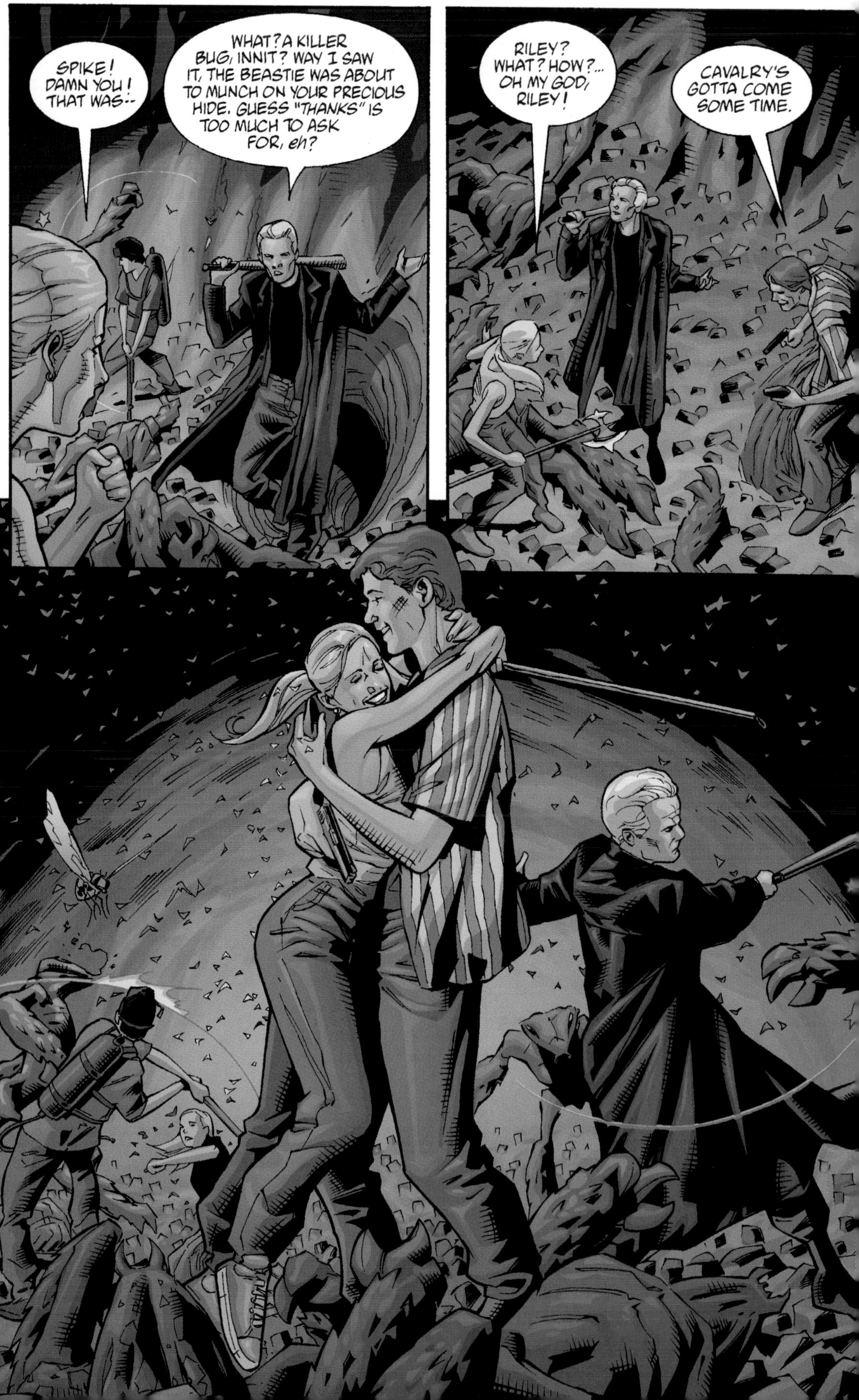
SPIKE! DAMN YOU! THAT WAS--
WHAT? A KILLER BUG, INNIT? WAY I SAW IT, THE BEASTIE WAS ABOUT TO MUNCH ON YOUR PRECIOUS HIDE. GUESS "THANKS" IS TOO MUCH TO ASK FOR, eh?
RILEY? WHAT? HOW?... OH MY GOD, RILEY!
CAVALRY'S GOTTA COME SOME TIME.

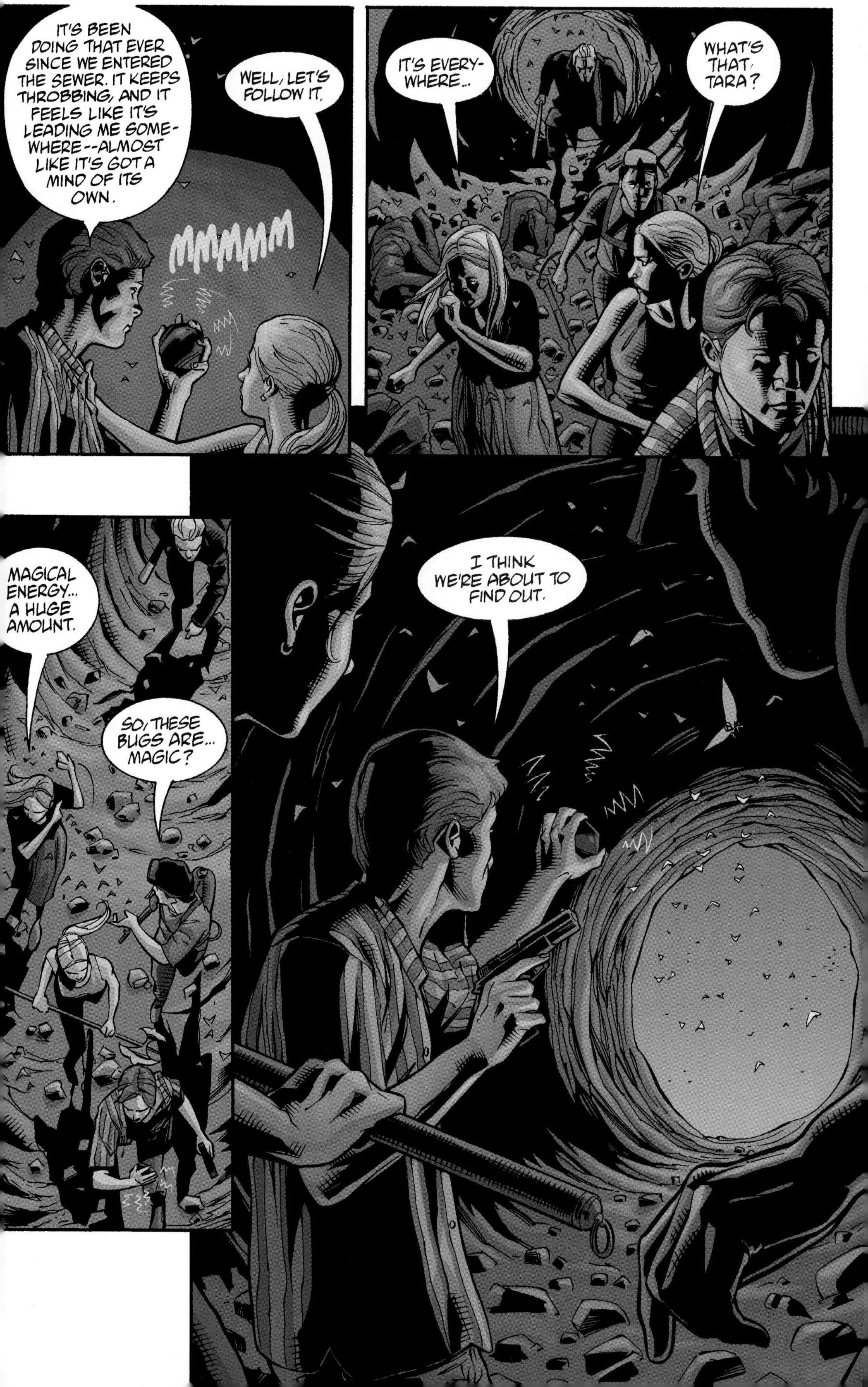
IT'S BEEN DOING THAT EVER SINCE WE ENTERED THE SEWER. IT KEEPS THROBBING, AND IT FEELS LIKE IT'S LEADING ME SOMEWHERE--ALMOST LIKE IT'S GOT A MIND OF ITS OWN.
WELL, LET'S FOLLOW IT.
MMMMM
IT'S EVERYWHERE...
WHAT'S THAT, TARA?
MAGICAL ENERGY... A HUGE AMOUNT.
SO, THESE BUGS ARE... MAGIC?
I THINK WE'RE ABOUT TO FIND OUT.

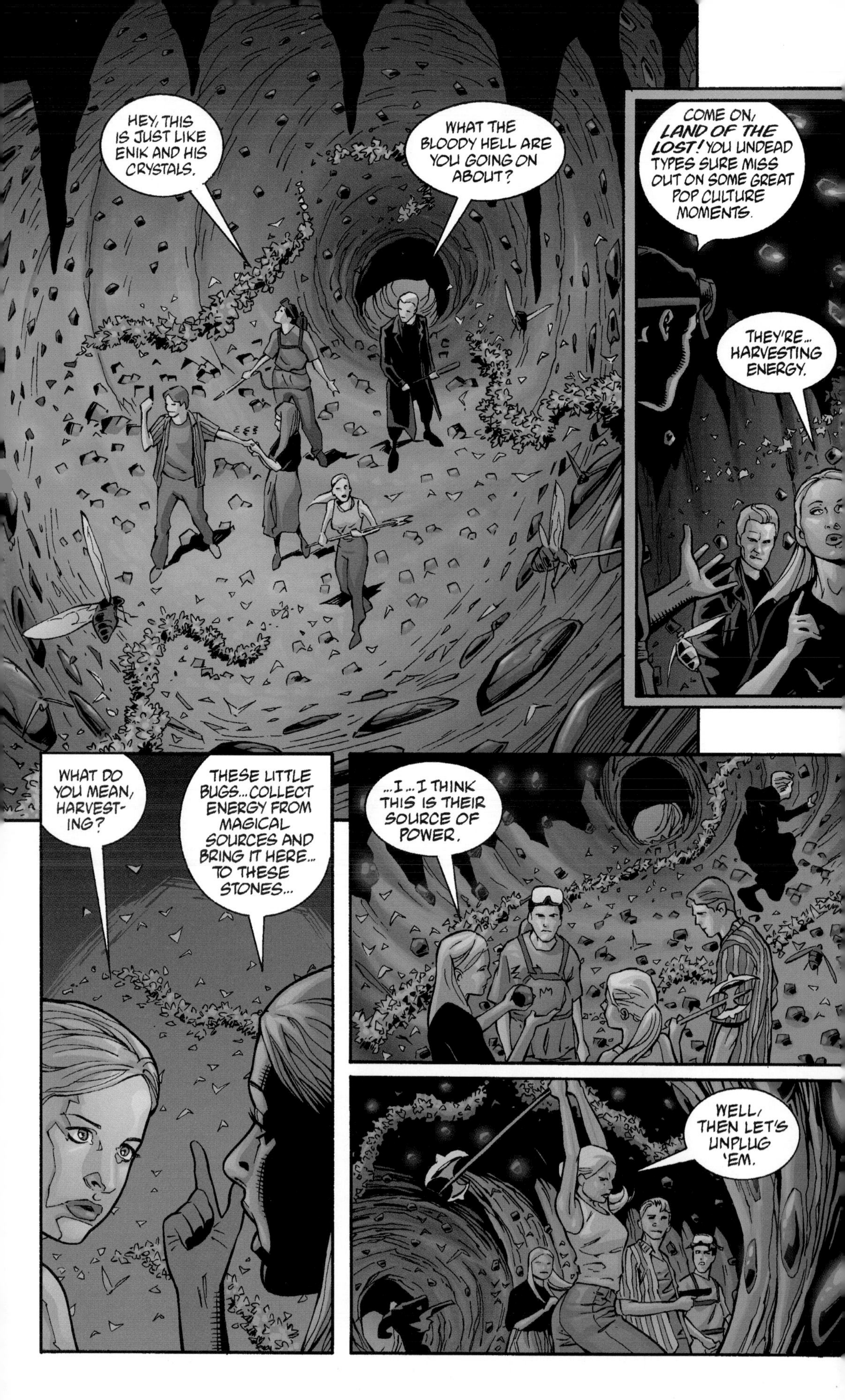
HEY, THIS IS JUST LIKE ENIK AND HIS CRYSTALS.
WHAT THE BLOODY HELL ARE YOU GOING ON ABOUT?
COME ON, LAND OF THE LOST! YOU UNDEAD TYPES SURE MISS OUT ON SOME GREAT POP CULTURE MOMENTS.
THEY'RE... HARVESTING ENERGY.
WHAT DO YOU MEAN, HARVESTING?
THESE LITTLE BUGS... COLLECT ENERGY FROM MAGICAL SOURCES AND BRING IT HERE... TO THESE STONES...
...I... I THINK THIS IS THEIR SOURCE OF POWER.
WELL, THEN LET'S UNPLUG 'EM.

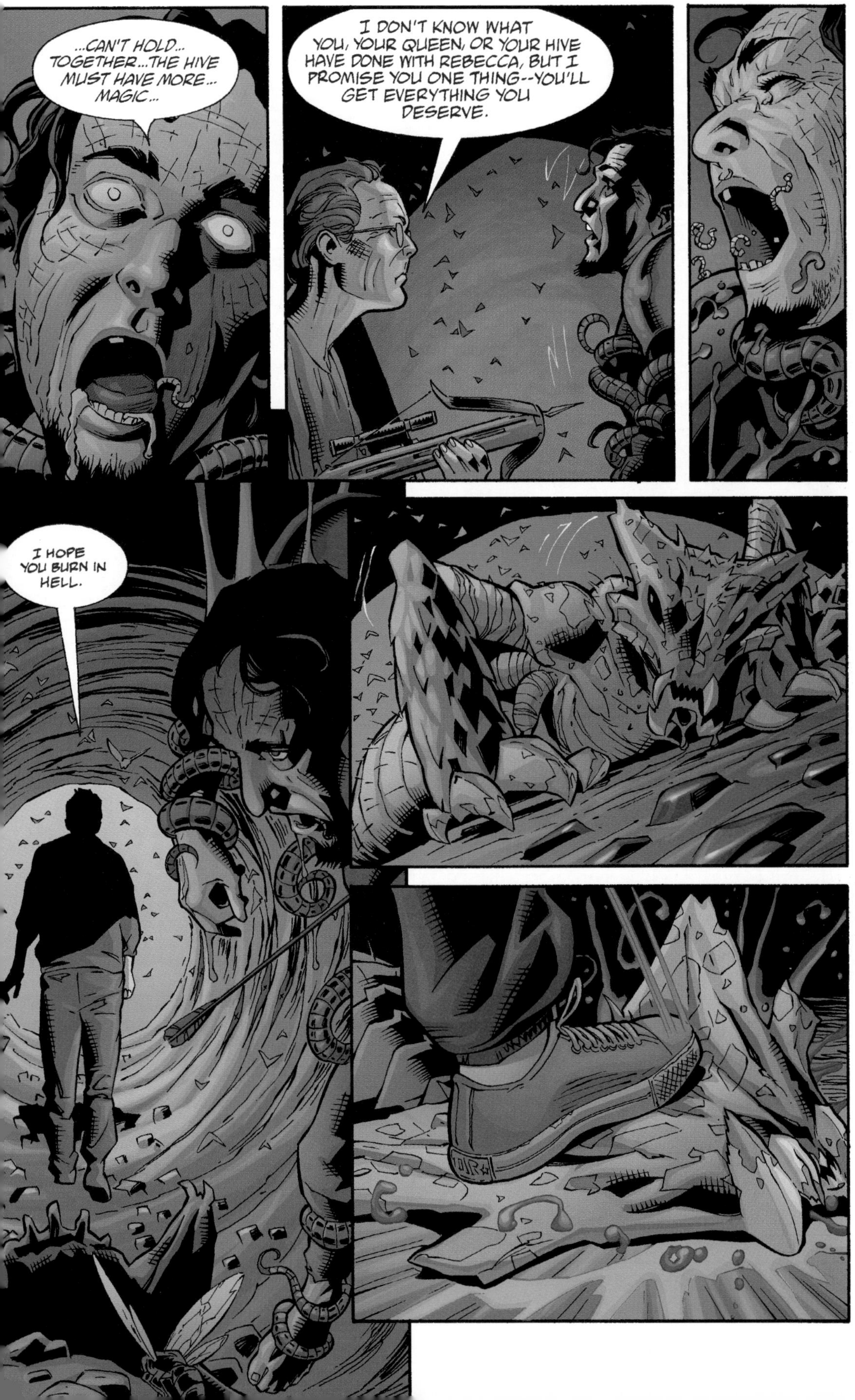
...CAN'T HOLD... TOGETHER...THE HIVE MUST HAVE MORE... MAGIC...
I DON'T KNOW WHAT YOU, YOUR QUEEN, OR YOUR HIVE HAVE DONE WITH REBECCA, BUT I PROMISE YOU ONE THING--YOU'LL GET EVERYTHING YOU DESERVE.
I HOPE YOU BURN IN HELL.

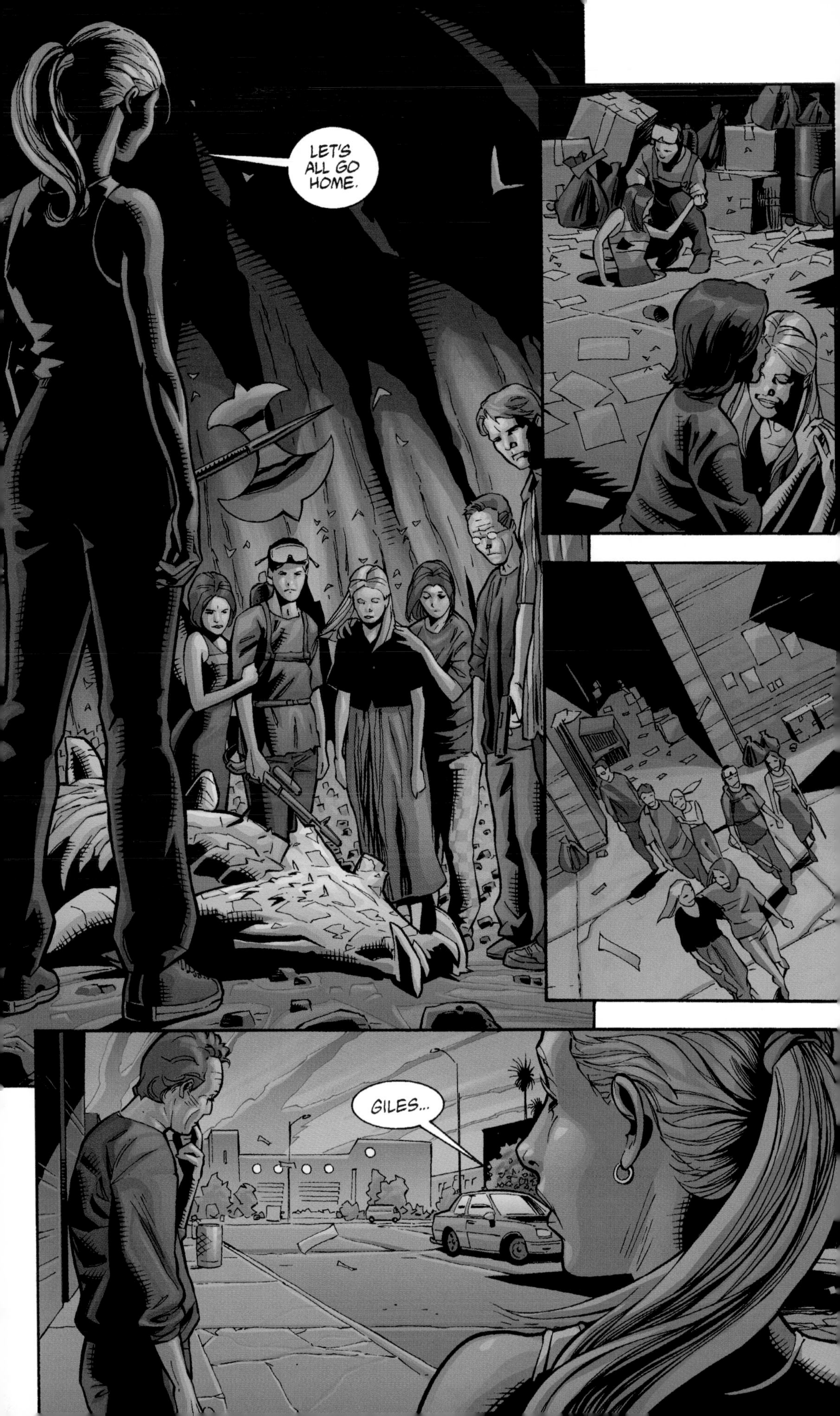
LET'S ALL GO HOME.
GILES...

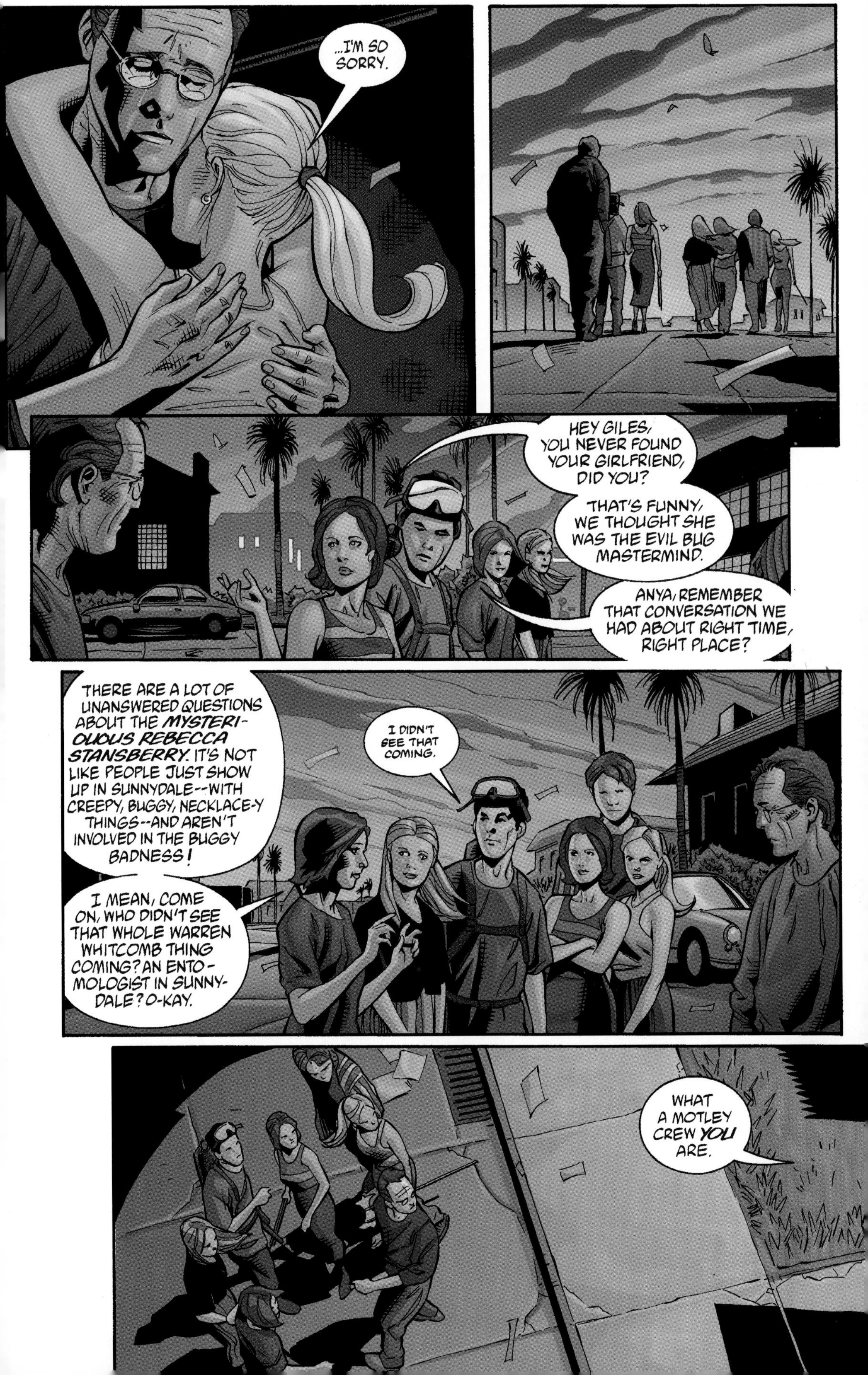
...I'M SO SORRY.
HEY GILES, YOU NEVER FOUND YOUR GIRLFRIEND, DID YOU?
THAT'S FUNNY, WE THOUGHT SHE WAS THE EVIL BUG MASTERMIND.
ANYA, REMEMBER THAT CONVERSATION WE HAD ABOUT RIGHT TIME, RIGHT PLACE?
THERE ARE A LOT OF UNANSWERED QUESTIONS ABOUT THE MYSTERI-OUOUS REBECCA STANSBERRY. IT'S NOT LIKE PEOPLE JUST SHOW UP IN SUNNYDALE--WITH CREEPY, BUGGY, NECKLACE-Y THINGS--AND AREN'T INVOLVED IN THE BUGGY BADNESS!
I DIDN'T SEE THAT COMING.
I MEAN, COME ON, WHO DIDN'T SEE THAT WHOLE WARREN WHITCOMB THING COMING? AN ENTO-MOLOGIST IN SUNNY-DALE? O-KAY.
WHAT A MOTLEY CREW YOU ARE.

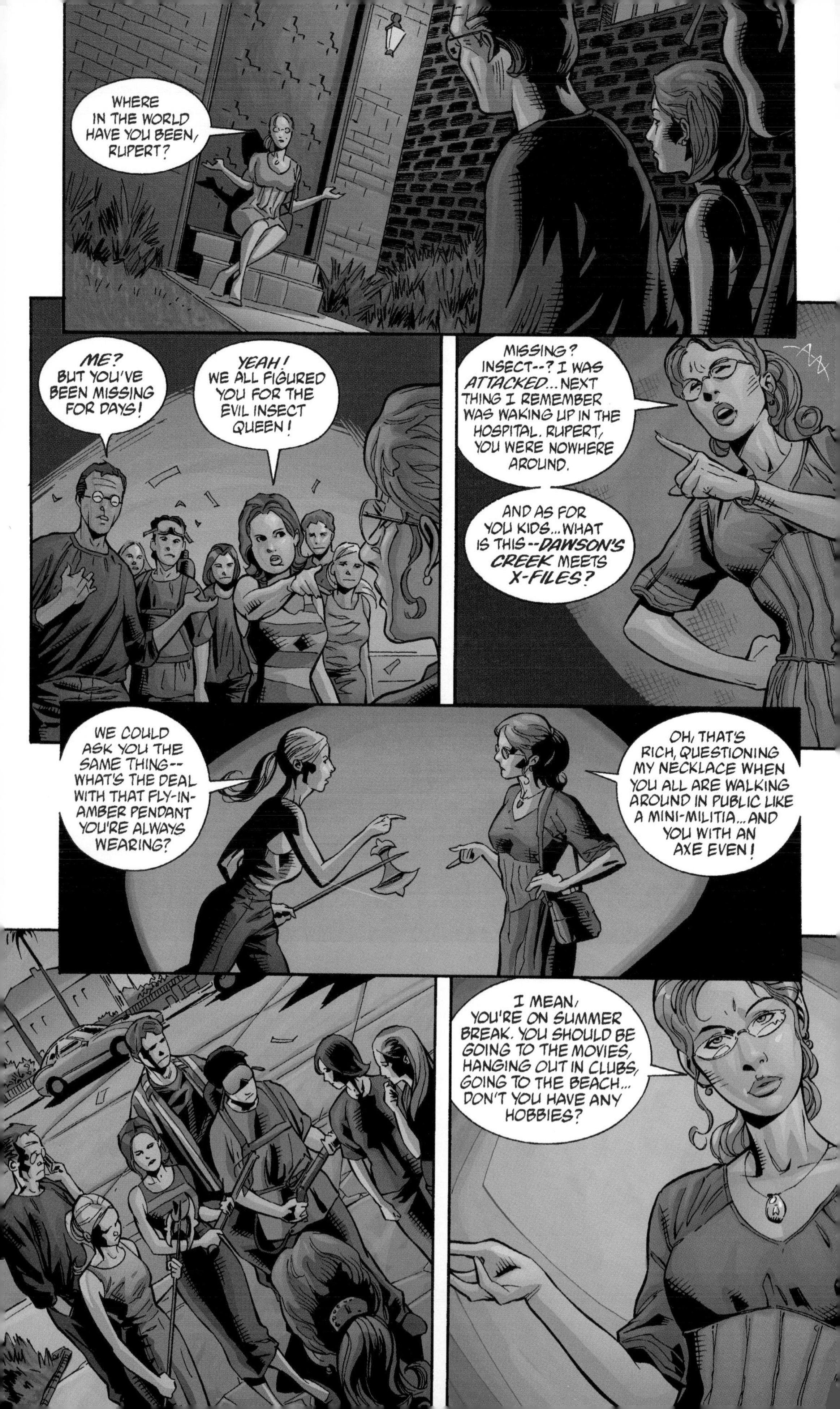
WHERE IN THE WORLD HAVE YOU BEEN, RUPERT?
ME? BUT YOU'VE BEEN MISSING FOR DAYS!
YEAH! WE ALL FIGURED YOU FOR THE EVIL INSECT QUEEN!
MISSING? INSECT--? I WAS ATTACKED... NEXT THING I REMEMBER WAS WAKING UP IN THE HOSPITAL. RUPERT, YOU WERE NOWHERE AROUND.
AND AS FOR YOU KIDS... WHAT IS THIS --DAWSON'S CREEK MEETS X-FILES?
WE COULD ASK YOU THE SAME THING-- WHAT'S THE DEAL WITH THAT FLY-IN-AMBER PENDANT YOU'RE ALWAYS WEARING?
OH, THAT'S RICH, QUESTIONING MY NECKLACE WHEN YOU ALL ARE WALKING AROUND IN PUBLIC LIKE A MINI-MILITIA... AND YOU WITH AN AXE EVEN!
I MEAN, YOU'RE ON SUMMER BREAK. YOU SHOULD BE GOING TO THE MOVIES, HANGING OUT IN CLUBS, GOING TO THE BEACH... DON'T YOU HAVE ANY HOBBIES?

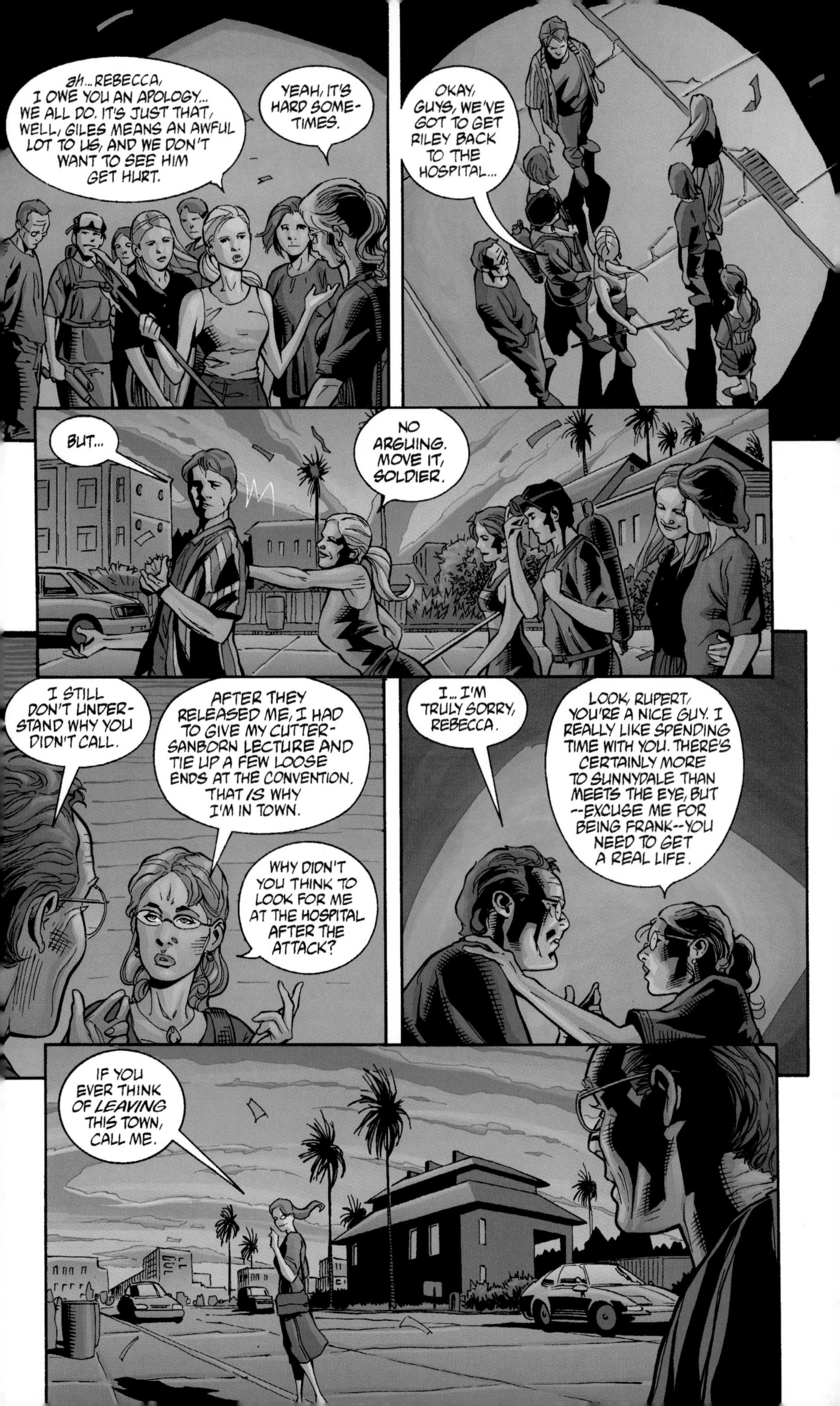
ah... REBECCA, I OWE YOU AN APOLOGY... WE ALL DO. IT'S JUST THAT, WELL, GILES MEANS AN AWFUL LOT TO US, AND WE DON'T WANT TO SEE HIM GET HURT.
YEAH, IT'S HARD SOMETIMES.
OKAY, GUYS, WE'VE GOT TO GET RILEY BACK TO THE HOSPITAL...
BUT...
NO ARGUING. MOVE IT, SOLDIER.
I STILL DON'T UNDERSTAND WHY YOU DIDN'T CALL.
AFTER THEY RELEASED ME, I HAD TO GIVE MY CUTTER-SANBORN LECTURE AND TIE UP A FEW LOOSE ENDS AT THE CONVENTION. THAT *IS* WHY I'M IN TOWN.
WHY DIDN'T YOU THINK TO LOOK FOR ME AT THE HOSPITAL AFTER THE ATTACK?
I... I'M TRULY SORRY, REBECCA.
LOOK, RUPERT, YOU'RE A NICE GUY. I REALLY LIKE SPENDING TIME WITH YOU. THERE'S CERTAINLY MORE TO SUNNYDALE THAN MEETS THE EYE, BUT --EXCUSE ME FOR BEING FRANK--YOU NEED TO GET A REAL LIFE.
IF YOU EVER THINK OF *LEAVING* THIS TOWN, CALL ME.

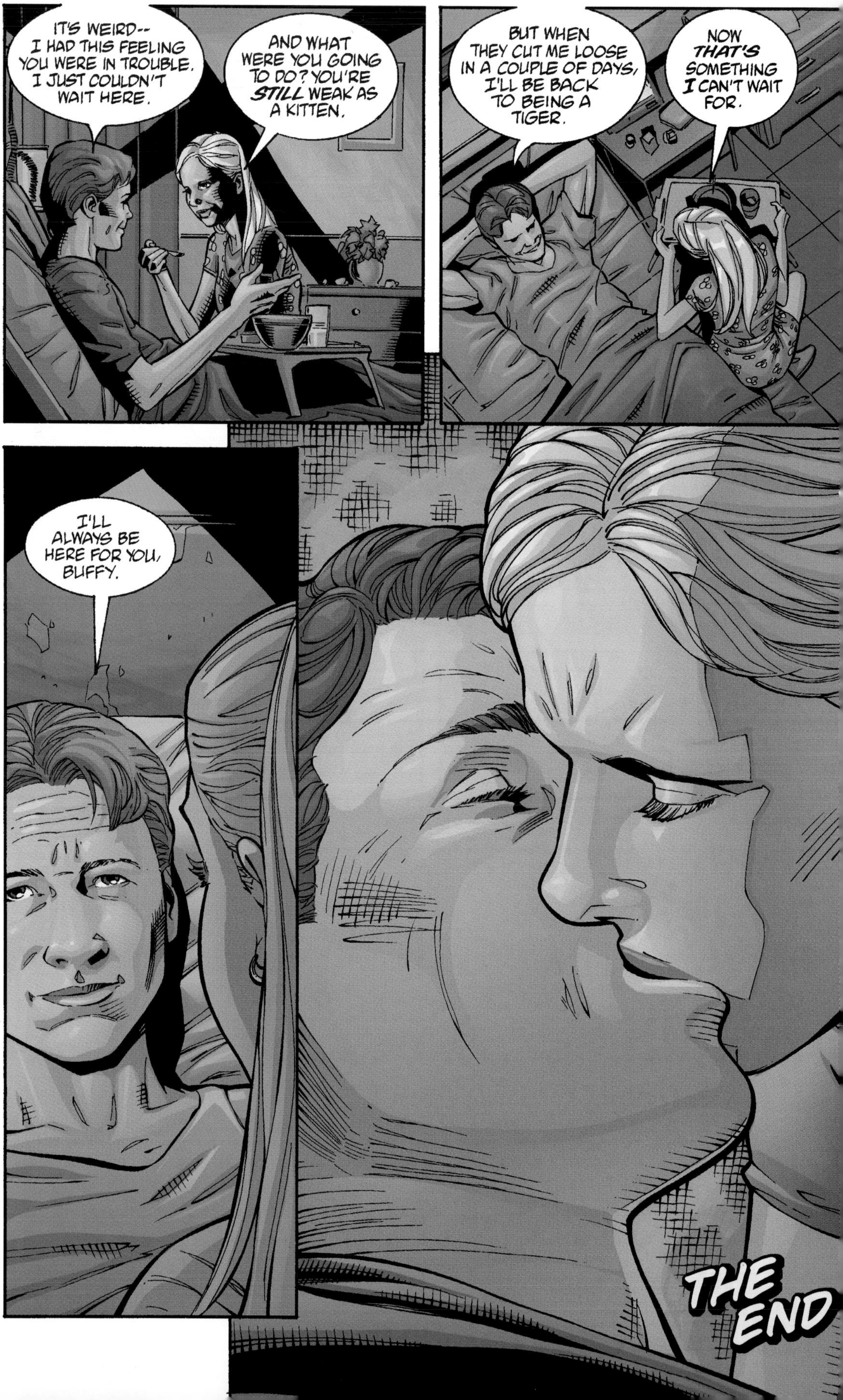
IT'S WEIRD-- I HAD THIS FEELING YOU WERE IN TROUBLE. I JUST COULDN'T WAIT HERE.
AND WHAT WERE YOU GOING TO DO? YOU'RE STILL WEAK AS A KITTEN.
BUT WHEN THEY CUT ME LOOSE IN A COUPLE OF DAYS, I'LL BE BACK TO BEING A TIGER.
NOW THAT'S SOMETHING I CAN'T WAIT FOR.
I'LL ALWAYS BE HERE FOR YOU, BUFFY.
THE END

From *The Field Guide to Occult Entomology* (*La livre des insectes magiques*), by Helene Delambre, with illustrations by Michelle Madsen. (Translated by Deirdre Miller. Samuel Weiser, Publisher, New York, 1971.) Reprinted with permission.

from the anus. This is often accompanied by a shrill chirping sound, which is apparently meant to attract the male of the species, similar to the hornet-like **Felutian Swanback** (see entry above). The noise also attracts nearby predators, which possibly accounts for the **Ubro Dehane**'s scarcity.

Urukhai

Occurrence: Rare. Tropical climes.
Origin: Unknown.

Urukhai are a war-like species of giant, social insects which live in colonies consisting of a Queen and many thousands of workers. Colonies operate as a unified, fiercely territorial, hive mind. Rival **Urukhai** colonies are looked upon as enemies; while the scarcity of the insect makes conflict uncommon, wars between colonies are not unheard of.

Scientists have yet to identify a male of the species, so reproductive habits remain a mystery. Common belief is that, like some natural insects, the males are killed immediately after mating. Additionally, through the use of a special carapace (see entry below), **Urukhai** have the ability to infest individuals of other species, a process through which the victim is rapidly transformed into a member of the colony, usually of the Worker class (see entry below).

Classes

Harvester: The most common, this class closely resembles the honey bee in both size and habit. They exist only to harvest energy from any available source of magic energies, including witches, artifacts, and demons. Experts hypothesize that Harvesters are actually a different species, co-existing with the **Urukhai** in a mutualistic relationship.

Worker: Looking very much like a human-sized version of an ant or termite, this class carries out the labor intensive tasks needed to maintain the hive, from construction and repair to gathering necessities for the hive. Occasionally, Workers serve as vectors for the specialized carapace used to infest other life-forms (see entry below).

Warrior: This giant, heavily armored creature defends the hive. Sometimes confused with the Amazonian **Tank Bug**, these insectoids are roughly twice as large as Workers. The Warrior's role is primarily defensive, though they've been known to appear in what can only be described as war parties.

Fig. 105

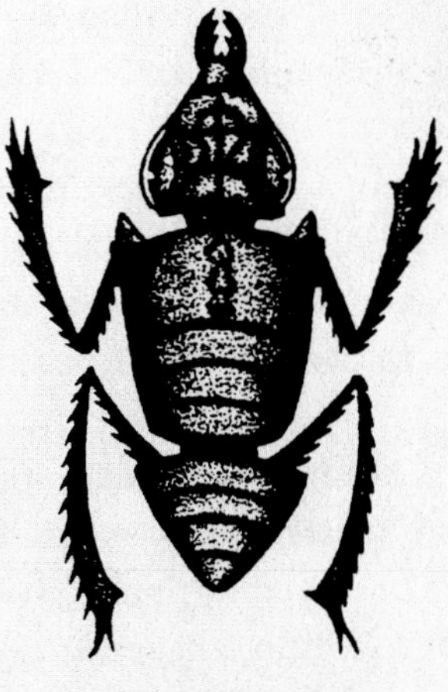

Urukhai worker

The Field Guide to Occult Entomology

Fig. 106

Urukhai warrior

Queen: Like bees and **Repaces**, there is but one Queen per colony, and the hive will protect her at all cost. The Urukhai Queen resembles a Worker with the addition of a large ovule sac, rendering her practically immobile.

Tools

Swarm Stones: There is some contention among scientists as to what role these strange, rune-carved devices play in the life cycle of the **Urukhai**. Most agree that the stones are batteries, receptacles of the magic power that fuels the hive. The Harvester class seems to be drawn especially close to these devices, and it's thought that the energy they gather is somehow transferred into these stones. Some contend that these stones merely control and corral the small Harvesters. Still others believe that the stones act as a catalyst in transforming other life-forms into **Urukhai** Workers.

Carapace: This chitinous shell, when placed upon a host, transforms the hapless creature into a Worker **Urukhai**. The transformation is relatively quick, taking place in two to three days, depending on the metabolism of the host. Each carapace draws its power from a single Swarm Stone, which further supports the belief that the Urukhai are the product of a mystical origin.

Vanik Butterflies

Occurrence: Uncommon. Desert climates.
Origin: Fifth circle of Hell.

Due to its need for extremely high temperatures and dry air, the **Vanik Butterfly** usually dies immediately upon arrival on the earthly plane. In death, it is indistinguishable from the Monarch Butterfly, and generally overlooked by all but the most astute entomologist. When appearing in the high desert, observers generally disregard the insect as a mirage, partly due to the rarity of the Monarch in such climes, and partly because of the trail of flaming methane with which the **Vanik** propels itself in flight.

Arrival of **Vanik Butterflies** on this plane, whether at the bidding of their master (see Beelzebul) or summoned by a local shaman, was considered an omen of doom by the Anasazi primitives of the Sonoran Desert in North America. The Indian word for the winged insect translates roughly into "feces fly," although the gold-rush settlers opted for profanity over alliteration in their translation.

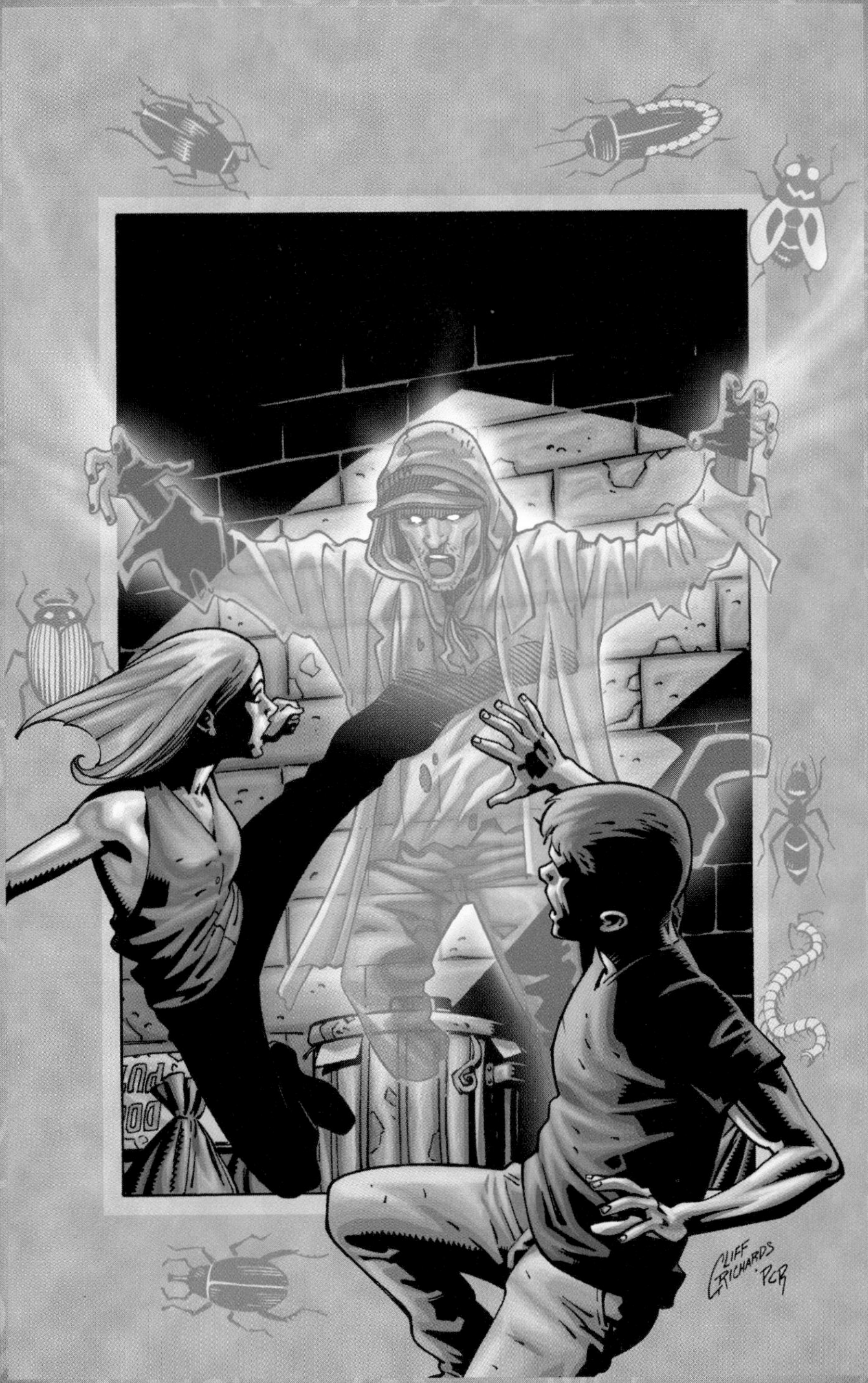
CLIFF RICHARDS
PCR

Art by CLIFF RICHARDS *and* P. CRAIG RUSSELL
Colors by DAVE McCAIG

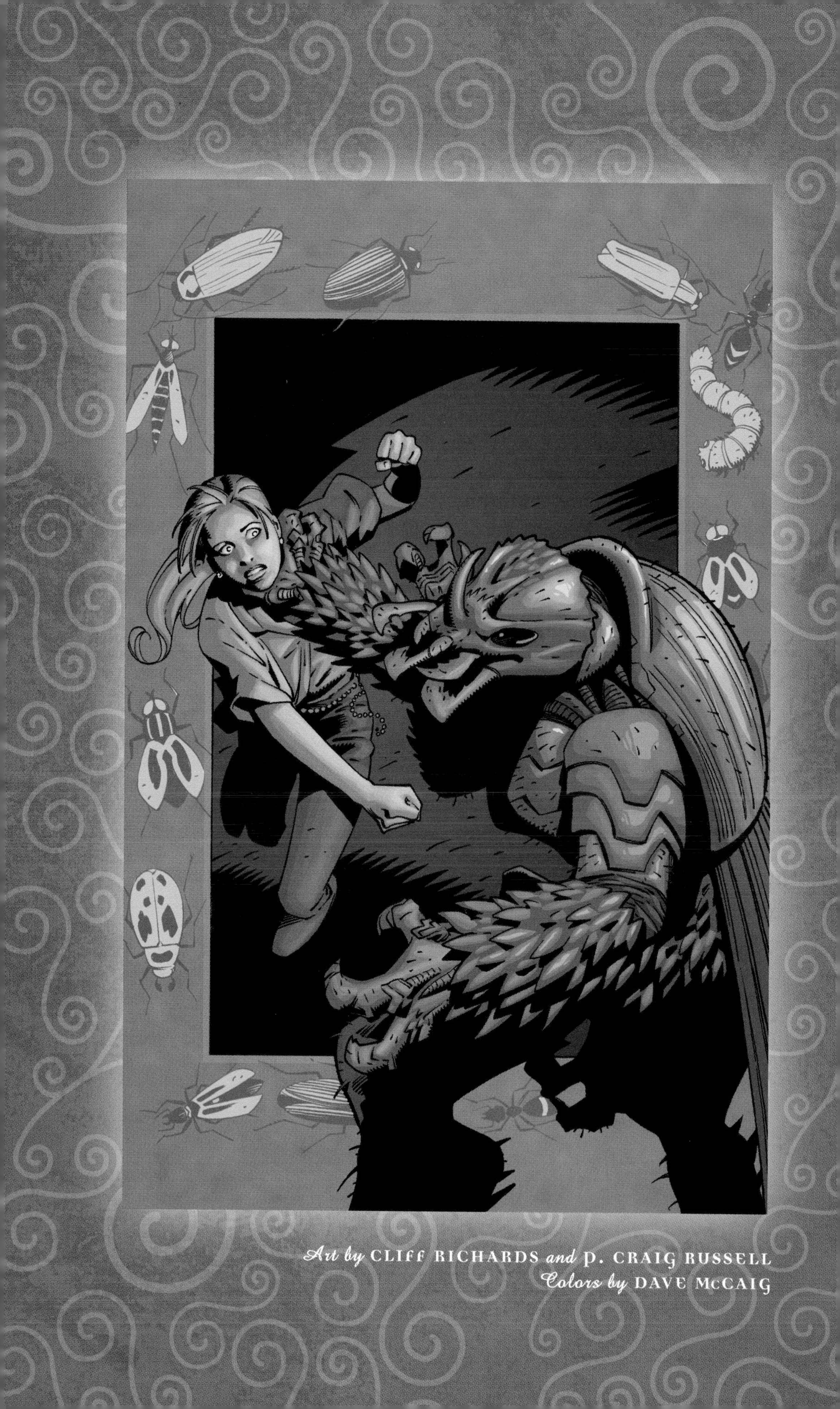

Art by CLIFF RICHARDS *and* P. CRAIG RUSSELL
Colors by DAVE McCAIG

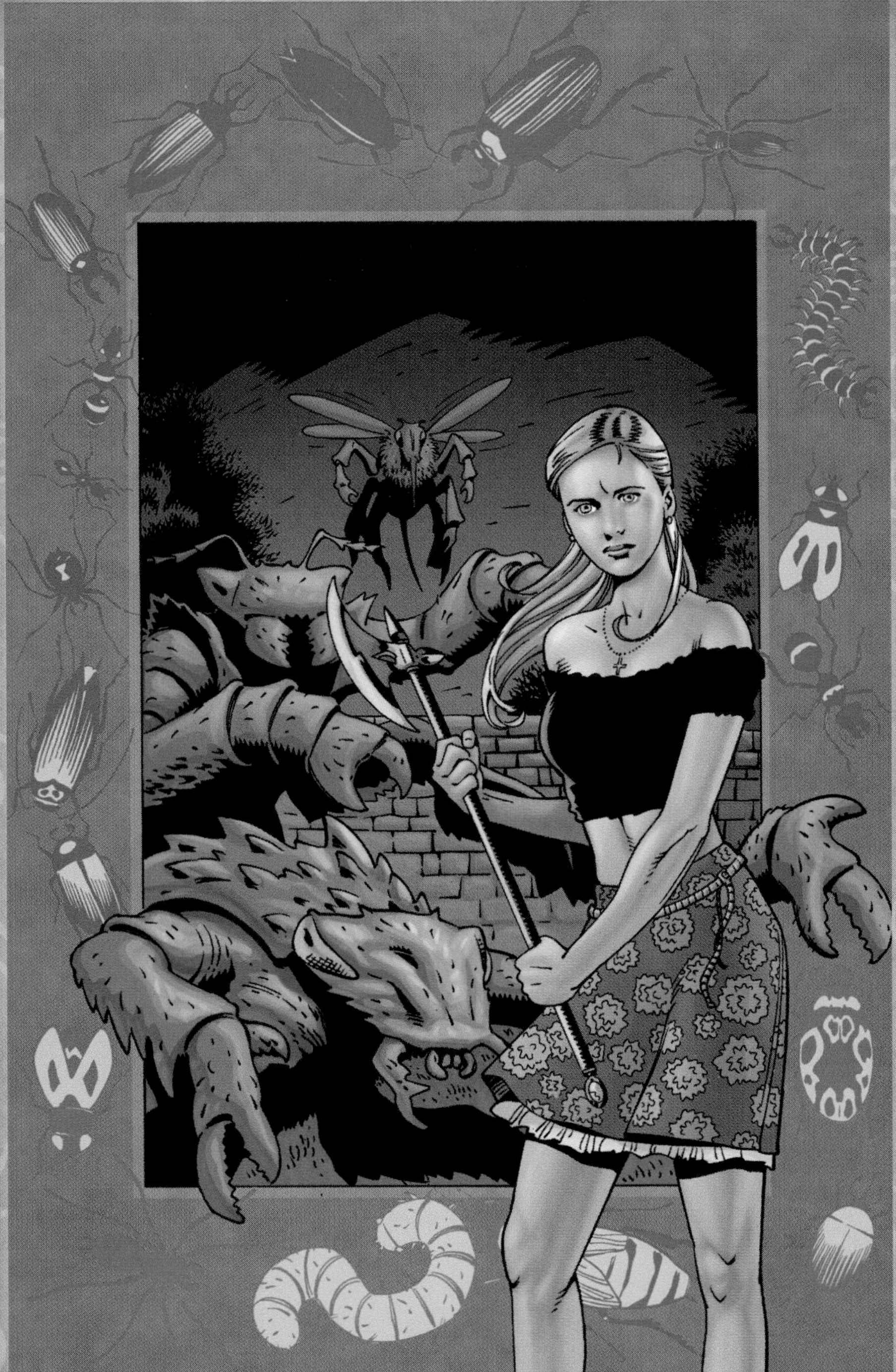

Art by CLIFF RICHARDS *and* P. CRAIG RUSSELL
Colors by DAVE McCAIG

Art by CLIFF RICHARDS and ANDY OWENS
Colors by DAVE McCAIG

STAKE OUT THESE BUFFY THE VAMPIRE SLAYER AND ANGEL TRADE PAPERBACKS

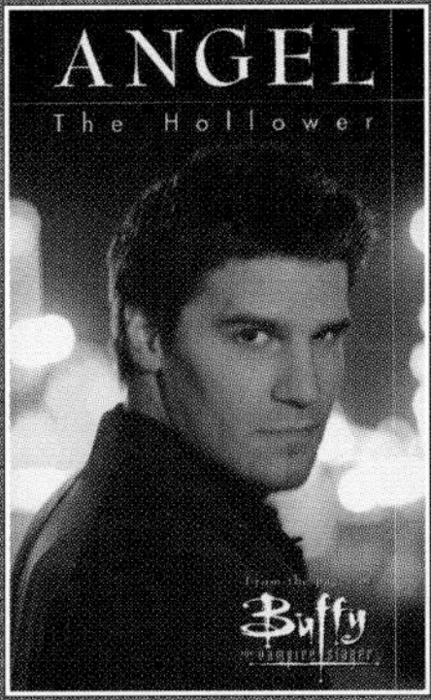
ANGEL
The Hollower
Buffy the Vampire Slayer

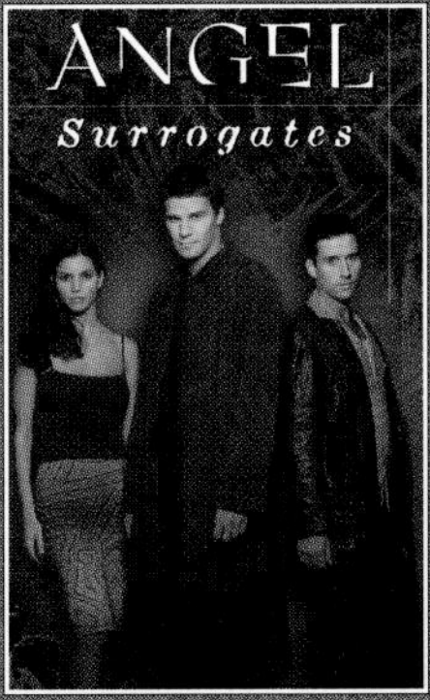
ANGEL
Surrogates

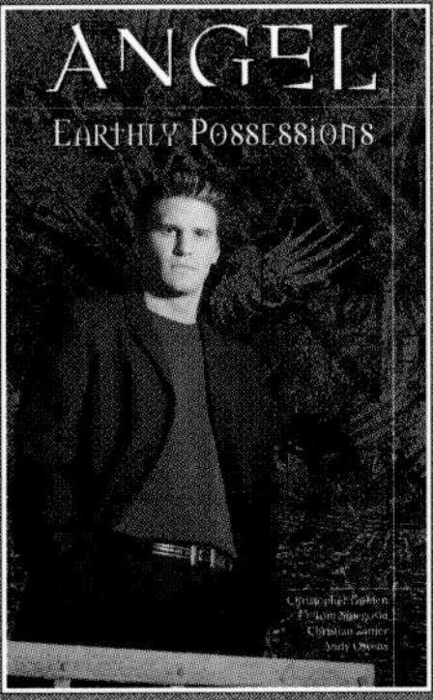
ANGEL
EARTHLY POSSESSIONS

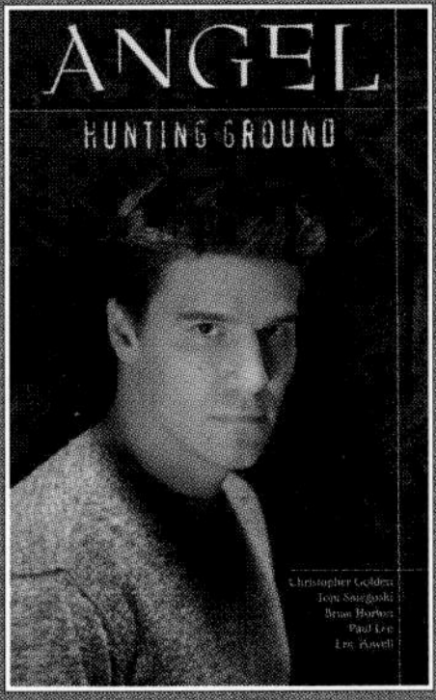
ANGEL
HUNTING GROUND

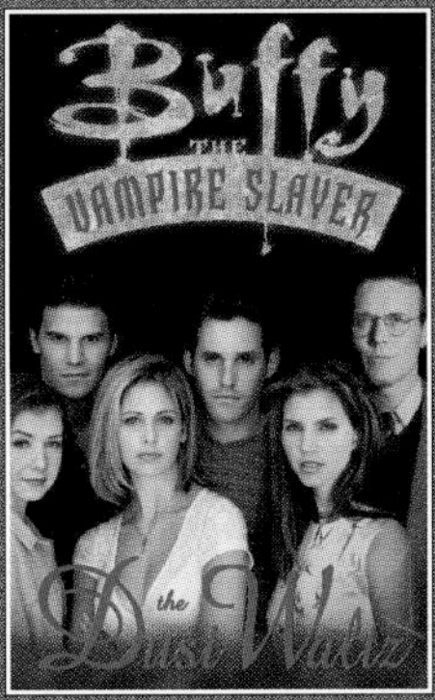
Buffy THE VAMPIRE SLAYER
the Dust Waltz

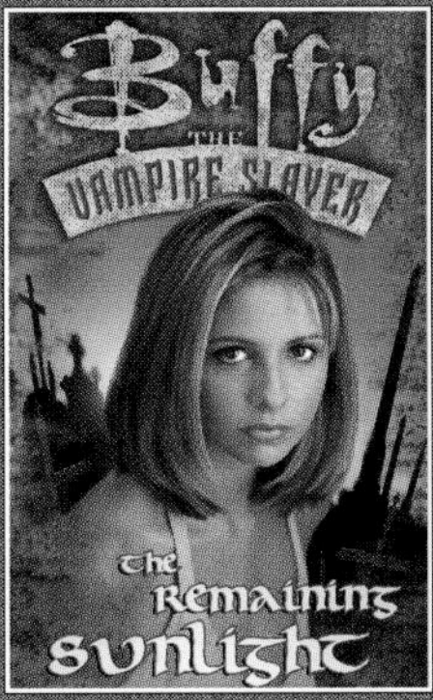
Buffy THE VAMPIRE SLAYER
The Remaining Sunlight

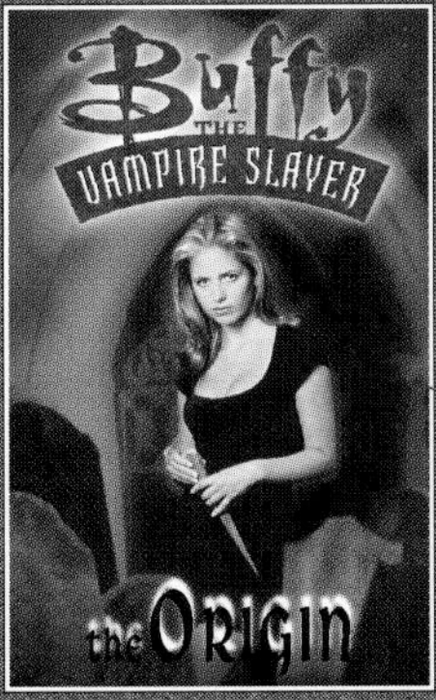
Buffy THE VAMPIRE SLAYER
the ORIGIN

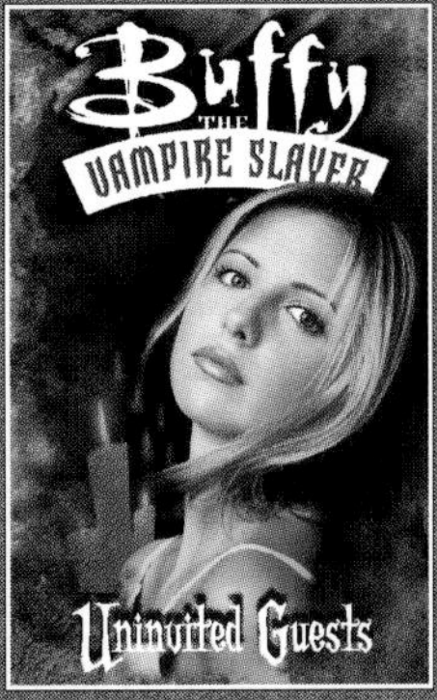
Buffy THE VAMPIRE SLAYER
Uninvited Guests

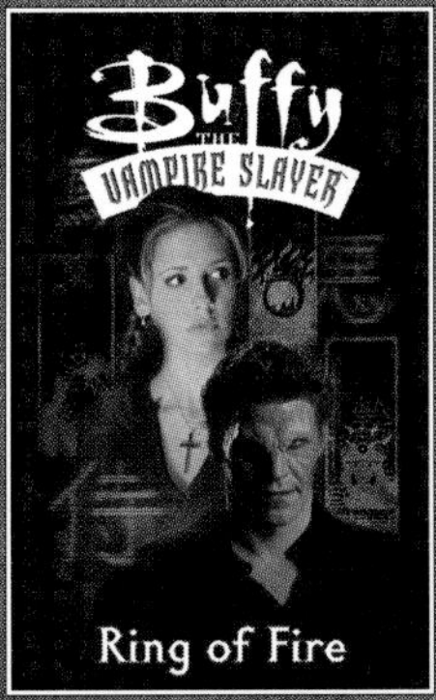
Buffy THE VAMPIRE SLAYER
Ring of Fire

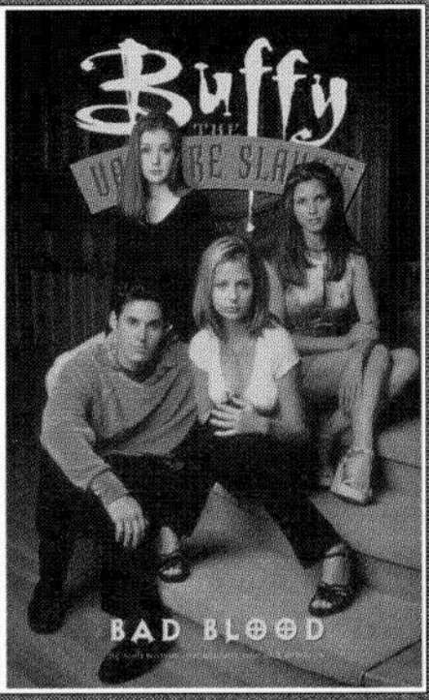
Buffy
BAD BLOOD

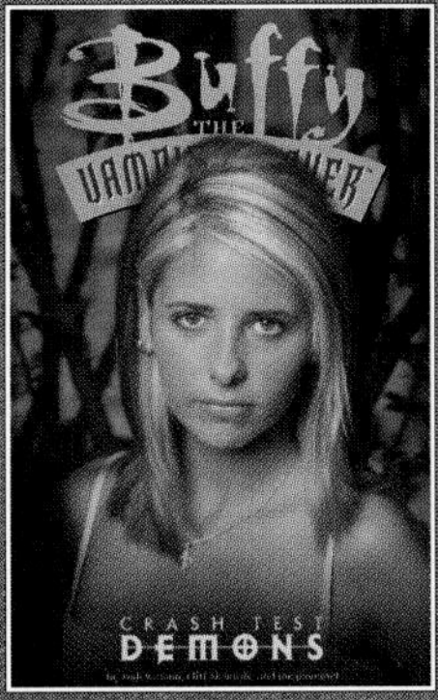
Buffy
CRASH TEST
DEMONS

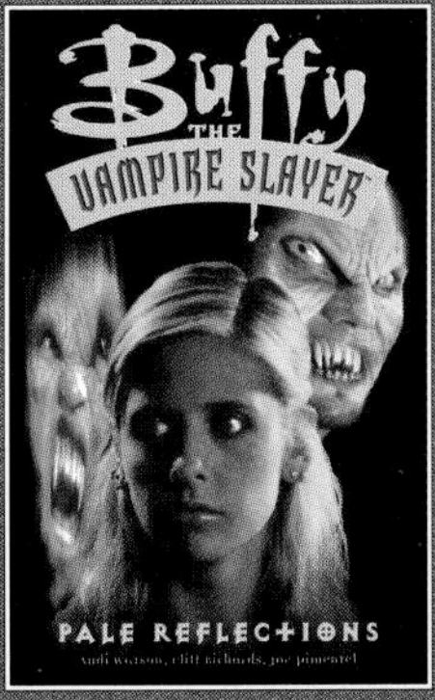
Buffy THE VAMPIRE SLAYER
PALE REFLECTIONS

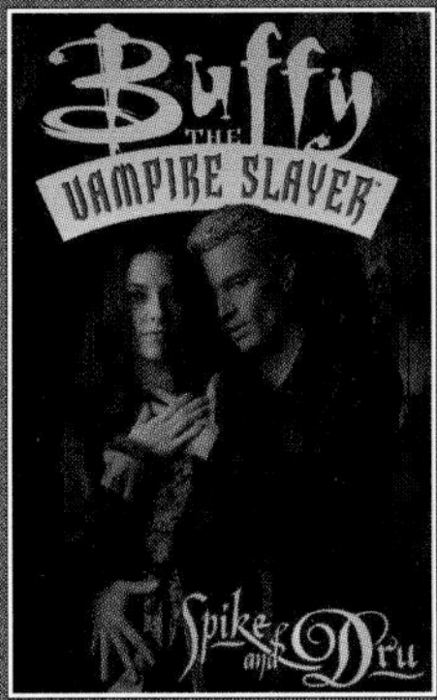
Buffy THE VAMPIRE SLAYER
Spike and Dru

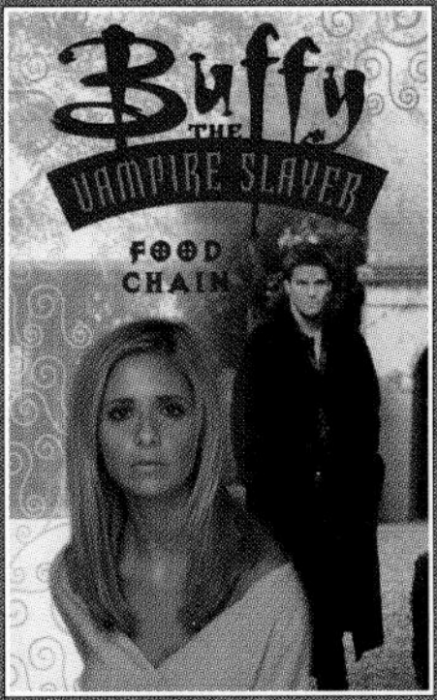
Buffy THE VAMPIRE SLAYER
FOOD
CHAIN

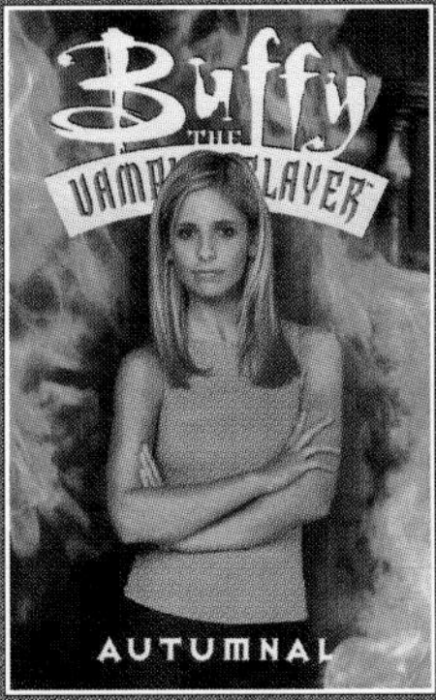
Buffy THE VAMPIRE SLAYER
AUTUMNAL

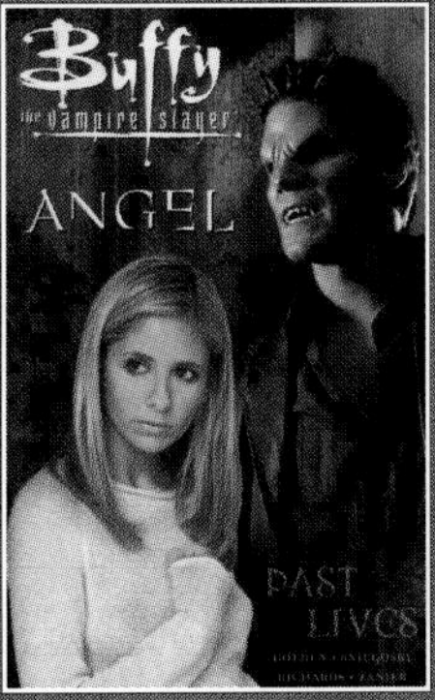
Buffy the vampire slayer
ANGEL
PAST
LIVES

CHECK OUT THESE *BUFFY THE VAMPIRE SLAYER*™ GRAPHIC NOVELS AVAILABLE FROM COMICS SHOPS AND BOOKSTORES!

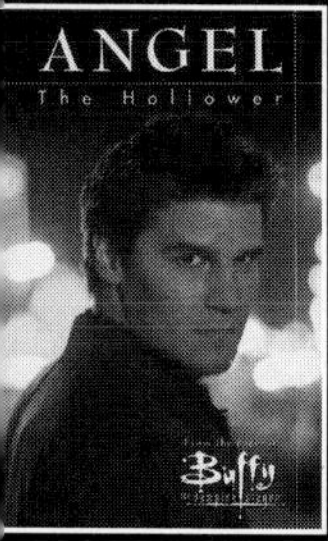
ANGEL
The Hollower
Buffy
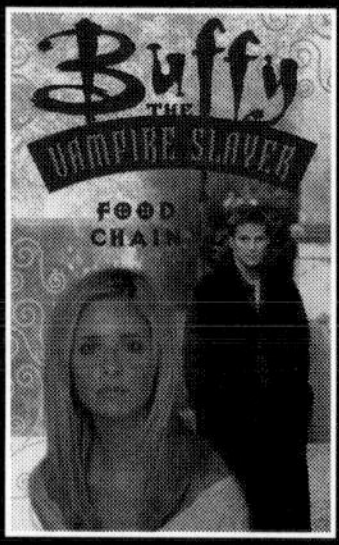
Buffy
the
Vampire Slayer
Food
Chain
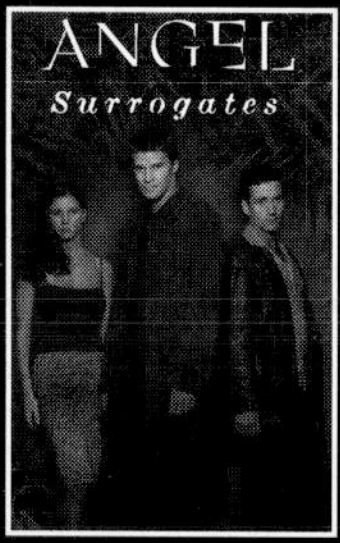
ANGEL
Surrogates
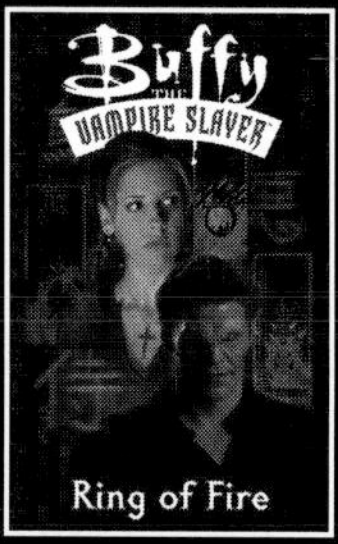
Buffy
the
Vampire Slayer
Ring of Fire
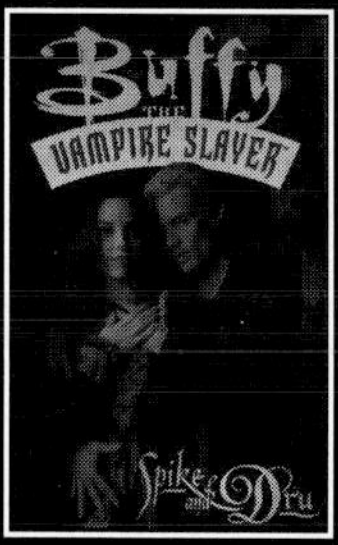
Buffy
the
Vampire Slayer
Spike and Dru

BUFFY THE VAMPIRE SLAYER

THE DUST WALTZ
Brereton • Gomez • Florea
color paperback
ISBN: 1-56971-342-1 $9.95

THE REMAINING SUNLIGHT
Watson • Bennett • Ketcham
color paperback
ISBN: 1-56971-354-5 $9.95

THE ORIGIN
From the original screenplay!
Golden • Brereton • Bennett • Ketcham
color paperback
ISBN: 1-56971-429-0 $9.95

UNINVITED GUESTS
Watson • Gomez • Florea
color paperback
ISBN: 1-56971-436-3 $10.95

SUPERNATURAL DEFENSE KIT
Watson • Richards • Pimentel
color hardcover w/slipcase
comes with golden-colored cross, "claddagh" ring, and vial of "holy water"
ISBN: 1-56971-486-X $19.95

BAD BLOOD
Watson • Bennett • Ketcham
color paperback
ISBN: 1-56971-445-2 $9.95

CRASH TEST DEMONS
Watson • Richards • Pimentel
color paperback
ISBN: 1-56971-461-4 $9.95

Written by *Buffy the Vampire Slayer* TV show writer Doug Petrie!

RING OF FIRE
Petrie • Sook
color paperback
ISBN: 1-56971-482-7 $9.95

PALE REFLECTIONS
Watson • Richards • Pimentel
color paperback
ISBN: 1-56971-475-4 $9.95

THE BLOOD OF CARTHAGE
Golden • Richards • Pimentel
color paperback
ISBN: 1-56971-534-3 $12.95

FOOD CHAIN
Petrie • Golden • Richards • Others
color paperback
ISBN: 1-56971-602-1 $17.95

AUTUMNAL
Boal • Fassbender • Pascoe • Richards
color paperback
ISBN: 1-56971-554-8 $9.95

SPIKE AND DRU
Marsters • Golden • Sook • Powell
color paperback
ISBN: 1-56971-541-6 $11.95

BUFFY/ANGEL: PAST LIVES
Golden • Sniegoski • Richards• Zanier
color paperback
ISBN: 1-56971-552-1 $9.95

TALES OF THE SLAYERS
Whedon • Petrie • Benson • Others
color paperback
Written by *Buffy the Vampire Slayer* creator Joss Whedon, TV show writer Doug Petrie, Buffy's "Tara" Amber Benson, and others!
ISBN: 1-56971-605-6 $14.95

OUT OF THE WOODWORK
Fassbender • Pascoe • Richards • Pimentel
color paperback
ISBN: 1-56971-738-9 $12.95

FALSE MEMORIES
Fassbender • Pascoe • Richards • Pimentel
color paperback
ISBN: 1-56971-736-2 $12.95

CREATURES OF HABIT
Illustrated novel
Fassbender • Pascoe • Horton •
color paperback
ISBN: 1-56971-563-7 $17.95

And don't miss these *Angel* gra novels available at comics sho & bookstores!

ANGEL

THE HOLLOWER
Golden • Gomez • Florea
color paperback
ISBN: 1-56971-450-9 $9.95

SURROGATES
Golden • Zanier • Owens
color paperback
ISBN: 1-56971-491-6 $9.95

HUNTING GROUND
Golden • Sniegoski • Horton • Le
Powell
color paperback
ISBN: 1-56971-547-5 $9.95

AUTUMNAL
Golden • Sniegoski • Zanier • Po
color paperback
ISBN: 1-56971-559-9 $9.95

STRANGE BEDFELLOWS
Golden • Sniegoski • Zanier • Po
color paperback
ISBN: 1-56971-753-2 $12.95

Don't miss the ongoing adventures from *Buffy the Vampire Slayer* and *Angel* comics every month! Available at your local comics shop. To locate a comics shop in your area, call 1-888-266-4226.
www.darkhorse.com • www.buffy.com

Available from your local comics shop or bookstore!

To find a comics shop in your area, call 1-888-266-4226
For more information or to order direct:
•On the web: www.darkhorse.com •E-mail: mailorder@darkhorse.com
•Phone: 1-800-862-0052 or (503) 652-9701 Mon.-Sat. 9 A.M. to 5 P.M. Pacific Time
*Prices and availability subject to change without notice

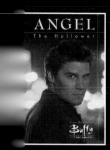